The TYPO3 Guidebook

Understand and Use TYPO3 CMS

Felicity Brand
Heather McNamee
Jeffrey A. McGuire

The TYPO3 Guidebook

Felicity Brand
Melbourne, VIC, Australia

Heather McNamee
Northern Ireland, UK

Jeffrey A. McGuire
Olpe, Germany

ISBN-13 (pbk): 978-1-4842-6524-6
https://doi.org/10.1007/978-1-4842-6525-3

ISBN-13 (electronic): 978-1-4842-6525-3

Managing Director, Apress Media LLC: Welmoed Spahr
Acquisitions Editor: Louise Corrigan
Development Editor: James Markham
Coordinating Editor: Nancy Chen

Cover designed by eStudioCalamar

Cover image designed by Freepik (www.freepik.com)

Distributed to the book trade worldwide by Springer Science+Business Media New York, 1 New York Plaza, New York, NY 10004. Phone 1-800-SPRINGER, fax (201) 348-4505, e-mail orders-ny@springer-sbm.com, or visit www.springeronline.com. Apress Media, LLC is a California LLC and the sole member (owner) is Springer Science + Business Media Finance Inc (SSBM Finance Inc). SSBM Finance Inc is a Delaware corporation.

For information on translations, please e-mail booktranslations@springernature.com; for reprint, paperback, or audio rights, please e-mail bookpermissions@springernature.com.

Apress titles may be purchased in bulk for academic, corporate, or promotional use. eBook versions and licenses are also available for most titles. For more information, reference our Print and eBook Bulk Sales web page at http://www.apress.com/bulk-sales.

Any source code or other supplementary material referenced by the author in this book is available to readers on GitHub via the book's product page, located at www.apress.com/9781484265246. For more detailed information, please visit http://www.apress.com/source-code.

Printed on acid-free paper

Table of Contents

About the Authors

Felicity Brand, Open Strategy Partners. Felicity has more than ten years of experience as a writer and technical communicator. She spent the ten years before that as a business analyst. She has spent much of her career writing a variety of technical content for internal and external consumption—from online help manuals, release notes, and in-house product training webinars, to web content and white papers. Felicity has a special knack for designing visuals and illustrations and a passion for clearly communicating technical concepts.

Heather McNamee, Open Strategy Partners. Heather is a technical communications professional with an M.Sc. in learning and technology. By using her marketing skills for good, she enables the right audiences to find, learn, and get the most out of the products they love. She loves working with subject-matter experts to distill their knowledge so newcomers can be successful. Since 2008, she's developed hundreds of hours of documentation, learning, and certification materials to facilitate open source technology and product adoption.

ABOUT THE AUTHORS

Jeffrey A. "jam" McGuire, keynote speaker, Partner at Open Strategy Partners. Jeffrey helps organizations communicate and grow, finding and telling the stories that connect their technologies with the value they deliver. He builds on more than a dozen years of experience and a strong following at the intersection of open source software, business, and culture. His approach to technology marketing—sharing the human context of complex technology solutions, for example, celebrating their creators' expertise and success—has left its mark in business and open source communities.

About the Technical Reviewers

Kay Strobach started experimenting with TYPO3 around the year 2003. Since then he studied computer science and worked as a TYPO3 professional. He is a TYPO3 certified developer and has spoken at TYPO3 events. His main focus is on the travel industry and the educational sector. He lives in Dresden, Germany, with his wife and his daughter.

Jo Hasenau is an educated graphic designer of the late 1980s, who transformed into a producer of digital media in the 1990s and entered the TYPO3 world in 2002. Today, he is a well-known TypoScript wizard, TYPO3 trainer and coach, external consultant for enterprises and universities, and web accessibility specialist. Together with his wife, Petra, he runs the Cybercraft GmbH in Clausthal-Zellerfeld, Germany. With their project, Coders.Care, they offer service-level agreements (SLAs) for TYPO3 extensions, and they are the official maintainers of popular extensions like Gridelements and the Localization Manager.

Foreword

Having worked on the TYPO3 Association Board for most of the past decade, I've seen the project evolve. When I started in TYPO3, the only way to learn something was by asking questions; even documentation was rare. It was like talking around a campfire in those early days. Today, TYPO3 is still an open, lively conversation where everybody can contribute. It's the differences that have made the voices harmonious; everyone is eager to share their experience. This book is a part of that heritage.

This book captures the warm, welcoming spirit of TYPO3. It's proof of what a great community has gathered around TYPO3 and what we have achieved. The authors, Felicity Brand, Heather McNamee, and Jeffrey A. McGuire of Open Strategy Partners GmbH, have distilled knowledge from the many community members who shared their expertise—and this book wouldn't exist without the community. I heartily thank the many contributors who collaborated on the book.

The TYPO3 Association had a strategic vision to create a different kind of book than we've had for TYPO3 before. We hope it is a catalyst for the reader, an open door into our project. We intend to continue maintaining and updating it over time to keep that door open and the welcome mat out for newcomers.

The decision to work with Apress was part of this strategic vision to extend the project's reach. The chance to work with a renowned publisher can help us bring our favorite open source software to new audiences. We're hoping to see this book translated into other languages—French, Spanish, Chinese, Arabic, and more—so that TYPO3 can continue helping people everywhere and from all backgrounds solve their web publishing needs.

We've long called TYPO3 "the enterprise CMS." Our promise to users is that this is a serious, reliable product, supported by a vibrant professional ecosystem. TYPO3 offers some strongly opinionated ways of putting together a CMS to quickly, economically, and repeatably deliver great client projects—the hierarchical page tree, semantic content elements, robust built-in multisite, and multilingual features, to mention a few. We have a strong focus on backend editor usability, too. TYPO3 is packed with features out of the box compared to many alternatives. Some of TYPO3's feature-USPs include publishing scheduling, image cropping, and form creation without needing additional software or licenses. Simultaneously, TYPO3 offers you the full freedom to expand and extend it to build exactly what you need, based on industry-standard, open source components.

Those are all great technical USPs, but TYPO3's strongest feature is the people in and around it. Few products today, especially in software, can survive without community. Our community leads us, and we go where the users need us to go. And now, dear reader, you're welcome to join us as part of our evolution.

Olivier Dobberkau
President of the Board, TYPO3 Association

Acknowledgments

Thank You!

This book tries to capture one way to find your way into a useful open source software package produced by a wonderful community of individuals and organizations. Like the TYPO3 software itself, many people from the TYPO3 community helped create this book. Help came in many forms: interviews, contributed content, reviews, fact-checking, diagrams, pointers to helpful resources, and general cheerleading. Along the way, we met a lot of people virtually and in-person at community events. With them, we had many inspiring conversations about what we wanted to achieve with this project and how we might best go about it.

We are deeply grateful for all the help and advice we received while working on this book. We did our best to keep notes along the way about who helped us and how, but we fear there may be gaps in the following lists. If we inadvertently left you off, we apologize for the oversight. We couldn't have done it without you. Our thanks also to everyone who has put in the work that has gone into TYPO3 CMS since its creation in the late 1990s.

Thank you:

Alexander Kellner

Anja Leichsenring

Benjamin Kott

Benni Mack

Björn Jacob

Claus-Peter Eberwein

Daniel Goerz

Daniel Homorodean

Daniel Siepmann

David Steeb

Desirée Lochner

Frank Nägler

Frank Schubert

Georg Ringer

Luisa Faßbender

ACKNOWLEDGMENTS

Marcus Schwemer

Martin Huber

Mathias Bolt Lesniak

Mathias Schreiber

Mattias Svensson

Matze Stegmann

Michael Schams

Oliver Hader

Olivier Dobberkau

Robert Lindh

Sanjay Chauhan

Stefan Busemann

Suzanne Moog

Sybille Peters

Tracy Evans

Tymoteusz Motylewski

... and everyone else who helped us on this project

... and everyone who has ever contributed to TYPO3 and open source

And these organizations:

b13

Cybercraft GmbH

Open Strategy Partners GmbH

Pixelant (Resultify AB)

SkillDisplay

Texere Publishing Ltd

Toujou (DFAU GmbH)

TUI UK Ltd

TYPO3 GmbH

TYPO3 Association

University of Vienna

And these events:

T3Con

DrupalCon

TYPO3 DevDays

TYPO3 Camp Vienna

TYPO3 Camp Mitteldeutschland

Acknowledgments

TYPO3 Association

We'd like to acknowledge and thank the TYPO3 Association and all its members. Special thanks to the TYPO3 Association Board, who supported this project from the beginning and provided help and guidance along the way.

TYPO3 GmbH

TYPO3 GmbH supports the TYPO3 ecosystem with products, services, and industry partnerships. They offered their expertise, time, and facilities to support this project. Thank you.

TYPO3 Community Design Team

Thank you to the TYPO3 Community Design Team, who created the book's informative illustrations and diagrams. The assets from these diagrams belong to the TYPO3 community and are freely available for use.

Authors, editors, technical reviewers, and publisher

Although the cover of this book lists three coauthors—Felicity Brand, Heather McNamee, and Jeffrey A. McGuire—it is the product of many individuals' collaborative efforts, contributions, authorship, and editorship. For their essential contributions, our extra-special thanks to Benni Mack, Mathias Bolt Lesniak, Elli Ludwigson, our technical reviewers Kay Strobach and Jo Hasenau, and our fearless project manager Jesi Driessen.

We'd also like to thank our publisher and the team at Apress Media LLC—Louise Corrigan, Nancy Chen, and James Markham—who believed in us from the start and helped keep us on track through it all.

Introduction

As the digitalization of the world continues and accelerates, reliable, powerful, flexible communication and publishing tools are more important than ever. Content management is essential for today's information-rich communication: websites, intranets, applications, mobile apps, web services, digital asset management, web-to-print systems, and so much more.

TYPO3 is made for exactly this. It is an enterprise content management system (CMS) and a powerful communications tool with robust multisite and multilingual support. This book is here to show you the way into this open source CMS and show you some of its potential.

Open source? When assessing new digital tools, open source software should be at the top of your list. With open source, you invest your budget efficiently in features and functionality, rather than license fees to try it. You can make better decisions because you can see, analyze, and understand the source code.

For companies, for developers, for marketers, for students, for you. TYPO3 and its vibrant community offer personal and professional opportunities for you, and solid technical choices for your business. TYPO3 CMS:

- A proven choice, in use for mission-critical applications at every scale

  ◦ Six-year official support for compliance, security, and planning

  ◦ Predictable roadmap, regular release cycles, and a history of stability and incremental improvement

- Standards-based, highly accessible for existing developers, and easy to learn for newcomers

  ◦ Offers great career opportunities

- Supported by comprehensive documentation, training, and certification

- Features clear, functional user experience and structure for editors and admins

  ○ Responsive backend for productivity on any device

  ○ Content staging and previews in workspaces with approval workflows

  ○ Hierarchical content structure for intuitive navigation

This book is divided into two parts:

Part 1: How TYPO3 Works
Part 2: Hands-on Guides

Part 1: Overview

We give you a high-level overview of some essential aspects of TYPO3. If you've never seen TYPO3 before, you'll learn how to make the most of it and understand some of what makes TYPO3 different from other content management systems.

We have divided this part into four chapters:

- TYPO3 Showroom

- Designing and Planning with TYPO3

- Building and Extending TYPO3

- Managing and Maintaining TYPO3

We will introduce you to many of TYPO3's features and capabilities and show you how to make the most of them. Part 1 follows a simplified web development workflow.

In **TYPO3 Showroom,** we'll check out popular features, see what others have done with TYPO3, and build an understanding of TYPO3's strengths.

In **Designing and Planning with TYPO3,** we will explore how to create a visual design and user experience. You'll get an idea of the main concepts of TYPO3 and how to plan a website's layout and functionality.

In **Building and Extending TYPO3,** you'll see how TYPO3 sites are built from the ground up and how design ideas are made into working websites.

And finally, in **Managing and Maintaining TYPO3,** we'll make you familiar with what is involved in maintaining a TYPO3 website and where to find help and support.

Part 2: Hands-on guides

These step-by-step tutorials show you how to work with TYPO3 CMS. Each guide is self-contained, with references to documentation, examples, code samples, and everything you need for the topic at hand:

- Guide 1: Installing TYPO3

- Guide 2: Creating your first TYPO3 site

- Guide 3: Extending TYPO3

- Guide 4: Planning, building, and using content elements

- Guide 5: Creating your first stand-alone extension

- Guide 6: Creating a password-protected members' area

- Guide 7: Translating your site

- Guide 8: Configuring content management workflow

- Guide 9: Creating a business around TYPO3

- Guide 10: Debugging and troubleshooting

After reading this book, you will be able to

- Explain how TYPO3 works in sufficient detail to demonstrate that you understand how it works and how to use it professionally.

- Leverage TYPO3's built-in capabilities.

- Avoid potential pitfalls by understanding its strengths.

- Efficiently configure a secure TYPO3 website.

- Create websites by designing information architecture and adding content.

- Use code samples and tutorials to build custom functionality (if you can already program in PHP).

Who is this book for?

This book is for decision-makers, project managers, developers, marketers, content authors, and editors. It is for anyone who would like to assess or use a CMS like TYPO3. A content management system is a vital tool for every kind of organization in today's digital world. A CMS can run your website or intranet, of course, and a host of other communication channels. Its fundamental purpose, however, is as your information toolset. Everything a CMS does centers on information: storing it, organizing it, publishing it, and making it accessible to those who need it.

For Decision-Makers Who Work with Service Providers

This book will help you understand the capabilities and limitations of TYPO3 and make the most of the CMS using best-practice approaches. You'll learn about the requirements of TYPO3 and its service ecosystem.

We recommend reading *How TYPO3 Works: The TYPO3 Showroom*.

For project managers and TYPO3 consultants

This book will help you manage client expectations and complete TYPO3 projects on time and within budget. You'll learn the possibilities within TYPO3 Core and when and where you could extend it. You'll understand a lot of TYPO3 terminology.

We recommend reading *How TYPO3 Works: Designing and planning with TYPO3*.

For developers: Frontend and backend

Both backend and frontend developers will get an idea of how TYPO3 works from the bottom up. Use the hands-on guides to build and configure best-practice TYPO3 projects. Learn how to build integrations and features using TYPO3's core API.

You'll also learn about skill development and employment opportunities in the TYPO3 professional community.

We recommend reading *How TYPO3 Works: Designing and Planning with TYPO3 and Building and Extending TYPO3*.

For marketers and salespeople

This book is a great starting point for anyone interested in marketing or selling TYPO3-related products and services. While Part 1 gives you an in-depth understanding of TYPO3's strengths and unique selling points, Guide 9 takes you through steps to map the strengths of TYPO3 to your business expertise and providing the best possible value to customers.

Although sections may become more technical than you are used to along the way, they'll make you aware of areas that will be important when talking to customers and making a convincing sales pitch.

We especially recommend reading *How TYPO3 Works: The TYPO3 Showroom* and Guide 9: Making TYPO3 successful for your business.

For content editors

A good editor knows content management is more than just adding text and images to a website. Knowing more about how to plan and build a website is also fundamental in understanding how you can make the most of TYPO3. This book will give you an idea of how to manage a TYPO3 site—and a start to becoming excellent at it.

We recommend reading *Designing and Planning with TYPO3* and *How TYPO3 Works: The TYPO3 Showroom*.

How to read this book

The first part of the book gives a visual overview of how the TYPO3 content management system works, how other people use it, and what you can do with it. It includes diagrams, expert advice, and use cases to provide you useful and memorable learning material.

When you want to start building, use the modular step-by-step tutorials in the second part of the book.

You can browse the book to get ideas and then come back to refer to procedures and view sample code.

There are different ways to read this book.

Read it cover to cover

Absorb the overview material, and then work through the guides step by step. This method will give you a thorough introduction to TYPO3.

Use it as a reference

Dive in anywhere to get a quick and broad understanding of a particular aspect of the CMS, and then use the resource list to find further reading.

A note on versions

This book covers TYPO3 version 10. Software is never static, so by the time you read this book, a new version may have been released and new features added or updated. The TYPO3 Project places great importance on stability and usability. The backend user interface, for example, has not undergone significant changes over many major versions. At the same time, it has been continuously improved, for example, to be compatible with ever-evolving mobile usability requirements on smaller screens, smartphones, and tablets. Consequently, many of the concepts and aspects presented in this book are still relevant for older versions such as version 8 and version 9.

TYPO3 official documentation

The official TYPO3 documentation is comprehensive and actively maintained by the TYPO3 community. This book doesn't replace the documentation; we want to give you a set of great starting points and a path into the CMS. The documentation is a tremendous community resource and the perfect complement (and further reading) for this book.

If you cannot find the answer to a question you have in this book, you might well find the answer in the official documentation. It includes various technical materials, including tutorials and guides, cheat sheets, overviews, and deep dives. All components of TYPO3 Core are covered, as are system extensions, and those third-party extensions that have documentation available. There is a glossary of terms, as well as a number of configuration guides.

You can also contribute to the official documentation—TYPO3 is an open source project, after all! If you want to help improve it, one easy way to dive is to click the "Edit on GitHub" button displayed on every documentation page.

References

This book references the TYPO3 official documentation, interviews with members of the TYPO3 community, and articles written about TYPO3 published in various places.

This book is published both in soft and hard copy formats. Links to online content might change.

The References section at the back of this book is organized by chapter. It lists the references and sources for information used in the content.

Stay informed

Follow the official Twitter account @typo3 and the TYPO3 Slack #Announcements channel.

Security

Subscribe to the "TYPO3 Announce" mailing list to receive notification about security updates for TYPO3 and extensions. The TYPO3 Security Team publishes more detailed information on its dedicated team page on typo3.org. You can also subscribe to the official TYPO3 Security Twitter account @typo3_security.

New releases

You can keep up-to-date on new releases of TYPO3 by subscribing to the "TYPO3 Announce" mailing list.

Each release includes a published news article outlining the benefits and features, technical release notes, announcement emails, and social media posts.

To familiarize yourself with the features and changes included in a new version, read the

- "What's New" on the TYPO3 website

- Release Notes published at get.typo3.org

- Change log in the TYPO3 documentation

Extensions

All extensions mentioned in this book are available at the time of printing. Some extensions may not be current when you view them. They may have become unsupported, outdated, or deprecated, or their functionality has been brought into TYPO3 Core in the meantime.

Whenever an extension is mentioned, it is presented by name in double quotation marks, and its URL is provided in a footnote.

Conventions

Tips and **Notes** are used for the following:

- Helpful suggestions and pertinent anecdotes.

- Some sections in the content in Part 1 are pointers for readers to go out and discover more about a particular subject.

- The content in Part 1 will sometimes refer the reader to a relevant guide in Part 2.

PART I

Overview

CHAPTER 1

TYPO3 Showroom

In this chapter, we'll start by "unboxing" TYPO3 and examining some of its main features. There will be the usual things you expect to see in a CMS and some that might delight you. Next, we'll look at cases and examples of what others have done with this system, so you can see what you can do with it next. To help readers who might be familiar with other CMSs, we've tried to address potential confusion around terminology and differences in approach.

When we say "The TYPO3 Project," we mean the open source project, the community, and ecosystem around it. If you are working with TYPO3 as a client or service provider, it is vitally important that you know about its vibrant professional community, clear governance structures, reliable roadmaps and release schedules, commercial support, and the service offerings around it.

The project not only has a nonprofit entity, the TYPO3 Association, supporting it. The association also founded a company, TYPO3 GmbH, to act as the official vendor on behalf of the project. The company offers value-added services to improve the CMS and its commercial sustainability and ensure success for the whole project ecosystem.

There's a vetted network to lean on, and a growing and enthusiastic community to share knowledge. We'll show you around the community and how to make the most of participating in it. We think all this demonstrates TYPO3's suitability as a solid technology or career choice.

The 90-90 rule and using content management systems

The "90-90 rule," though ironic, is a good guideline for considering how to work with CMSs. At the start of a web development project, you scope out how you'll meet a project's requirements with the capabilities of the system you're using. You can get

© Felicity Brand, Heather McNamee, and Jeffrey A. McGuire 2021
F. Brand et al., *The TYPO3 Guidebook*, https://doi.org/10.1007/978-1-4842-6525-3_1

reasonably far with the built-in functionality, and at some point you have to customize. A classic problem with scoping these projects is that the last 10% of requirements can end up taking 90% of the time (Figure 1-1).

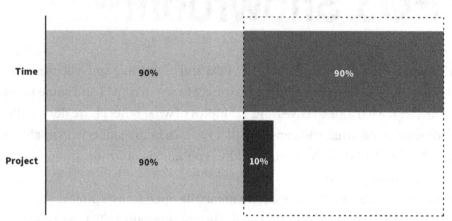

Figure 1-1. *The 90-90 rule*

> *The first 90 percent of the code accounts for the first 90 percent of the development time. The remaining 10 percent of the code accounts for the other 90 percent of the development time.*

> —Tom Cargill, Bell Labs[1]

Every content management system makes assumptions—based on its history, users, and creators—about the essential requirements most projects built with it need. These features make up the core functionality of a CMS and should ideally be 90% of what you want it to do for you out of the box. This is why you choose a system that is a good match to start with.

---

[1]https://www.techopedia.com/definition/21014/ninety-ninety-rule

After that, CMSs have some way to add functionality by enabling or adding extensions, plugins, or modules. At some point, you will come up against a project requirement that isn't met by the core system or an existing extension. This is a very good reason why you should choose an open source solution like TYPO3. It is extensible and flexible enough to be fully customized to meet most or all of your requirements in the end. You or developers working with you can leverage TYPO3's APIs and standards-based architecture to add the unique functionality you need with custom code. This is why the "final" 10% of a project that didn't come bundled with Core or proven community-contributed code needs careful consideration and planning with this in mind.

Think of it this way, though: when you install the TYPO3 CMS to begin a project, you get a solid foundation—best practices and improvements—that world-class experts have invested in the TYPO3 Core for thousands upon thousands of projects over the last 20+ years, not to mention all the work that has been put into its component technologies like PHP, JavaScript, and more. What would the price tag be on all of that if you started from scratch?

This book will help you save time, money, and a great deal of stress while building your web projects and, later, when you are maintaining and upgrading them. The following chapters will introduce you to how TYPO3 works and how to get the most out of it. An important part of that is understanding what it can do for you out of the box and when you should consider adding functionality with custom extensions, and how to extend it properly when you do. "Properly" in this case means creating code that does its job securely and is sustainably maintainable over the life of your project.

Unboxing TYPO3

Now, we'll explore features and functionality that come with TYPO3 CMS. We'll talk about what is available as part of the TYPO3 Core, and the extensions that can augment that functionality.

Find out how to get your site set up in the Guide 2: Creating your first TYPO3 site.

You can see a basic TYPO3 installation with the Module menu on the left in Figure 1-2.

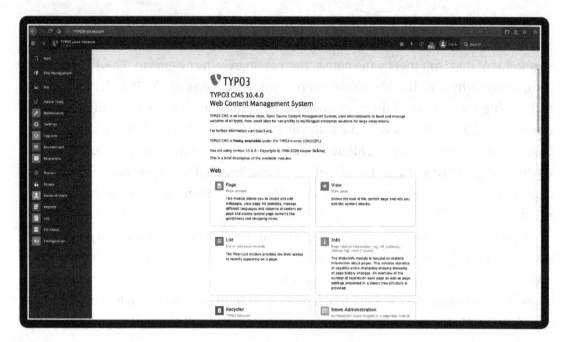

Figure 1-2. *TYPO3 backend, Module menu on the left*

Great projects using core only

Over the last few years, the TYPO3 Core Development Team has been following a policy of adding functionality to the Core through system extensions that meet the project's rigorous testing and quality standards. For many simpler projects, this eliminates the need for third-party extensions or custom code.

At one point, Anja Leichsenring, TYPO3 contributor and Core developer, noticed the TYPO3 Extension Repository (TER) was overflowing with extensions. "We had 200 slider extensions. Contributors had the mindset that, because it's open-source, they should share everything they make," as a result, "The TER exploded." The TYPO3 Core Team felt this was causing confusion and had the potential to reduce consistency and quality within TYPO3 CMS.

Starting with version 6, the Core Team began to pull commonly used features into the Core. They made it possible for developers to build most common website features without installing more extensions or adding custom code. They continued to add more features through version 9, based on what was installed on most TYPO3 sites. Version 10, in turn, builds on version 9, improving fit and finish.

Other CMSs promote the thousands of contributed extensions, modules, or plugins available as a benefit of choosing them. However, in this case, quantity does not necessarily equal quality and can, in fact, cause problems for developers. It can make it harder to identify which methods are best. The difficulty in identifying and vetting secure and reliable code among thousands of options can cause decision fatigue. More importantly, incompatibilities between different approaches can cause configuration headaches and time-consuming refactoring down the road. In the TYPO3 community, the clear direction is to use fewer contributed extensions and to do as much as possible with the Core.

Oliver Hader, Core developer and TYPO3 Security Team Lead, sees the community moving together in this direction. "At community events, I see a lot of people saying they only use one or two third-party extensions in their projects. They try to do as much as possible using Core functionality."

Compared to the competition in the CMS field today, TYPO3's Core components are robust features targeted to the needs of its professional base in digital agencies while also being flexible enough to extend. This powerful Core functionality includes

- Multilingual and translation support

- Content versioning, previews, and approval workflows in workspaces

- Built-in image manipulation and optimization.

- A File System Abstraction Layer (FAL) that allows the seamless integration of any data source

- Decoupled architecture by default, enabling TYPO3 to power any native app, frontend framework, or web service

TYPO3 extensions

TYPO3 CMS is built around the concept of extensions and extensibility. The Core itself is made up of system extensions; some are enabled by default, while others can be enabled when needed. Even with TYPO3's extensive set of Core features, you might encounter clients and projects that need something more. You or your developers can modify existing functionality and add new features by creating your own extension or installing community-contributed third-party extensions from the TYPO3 Extension Repository[2] (TER).

---

[2]https://extensions.typo3.org/

Extensions generally extend TYPO3 in one or more of these three ways:

- Plugins add frontend, user-facing functionality like commenting or shopping carts.

- Modules add backend functionality like site administration or content and editorial activities.

- Site packages contain reusable assets, configuration, or themes for websites.

Find out more about the TYPO3 Extension Repository in Chapter 3: Building and Extending TYPO3.

What's in the box?

To understand the backend interface, we will look at it from different perspectives:

- **TYPO3 administrators** have full administrator access to install, configure, and maintain the TYPO3 system and server environment. They are typically responsible for user access and permissions, as well as the security of the infrastructure.

- **TYPO3 system maintainers** are essentially a special subset of a site's administrators. They are the only users who can access the Install tool and the extension manager. All administrator users have temporary system maintainer access when development mode is enabled in the Install tool.

- **TYPO3 integrators** have administrator access to TYPO3. They are responsible for maintaining and building the website by selecting, installing, and configuring the site and extensions.

- **TYPO3 developers** need in-depth technical knowledge of the inner workings of TYPO3 code, APIs, and subsystems. Developers' access permissions are typically the same as the administrator and maintainer roles, though not all developers have access to the live environment; and development should generally be carried out on local copies of TYPO3. They need to be able to replicate everything the integrator and administrator can do as part of extending, fixing, and optimizing the installation.

- **TYPO3 editors** can log in to the TYPO3 backend and have access to carry out content and authoring-related activities like adding and editing pages, media, files, text, and translations on one or more pages or sites. They don't need specialist developer knowledge to use TYPO3.

Most users fall into one or more of these roles. We'll look at the administrative interface mostly from the perspective of a TYPO3 integrator, who has complete administrative access.

Note   In TYPO3, these common roles correspond to the official certifications[3] that we cover later in this chapter. Roles don't have to be named in this way, but this default paradigm and the role names reflect access level and typical tasks.

Centralized site maintenance

TYPO3 has an administrative interface, which is referred to as the "backend." From here, administrators can configure TYPO3 and their sites. You access the login screen by appending `/typo3/` to your site's URL, such as www.example.com/typo3/.

The frontend and backend are separated by default in TYPO3. In standard installations, frontend user logins do not (and cannot) give editorial or admin access to the backend system. Administrators and content editors log in to the backend to manage their sites and content (Figure 1-3).

---

[3]https://typo3.org/certification/

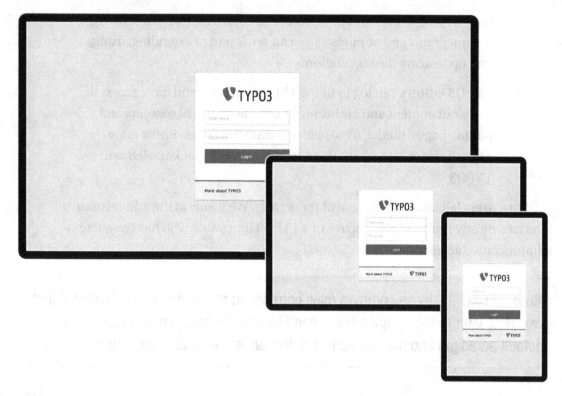

Figure 1-3. *TYPO3 login screen*

Find out more about the site management in Chapter 3: Building and Extending
TYPO3.

Page tree hierarchy

For editors, the hierarchical page tree menu is one of the first concepts for new users to
grasp when learning how to manage content (Figure 1-4). The page tree is an all-in-one
UI used for selecting, adding, and managing pages, available in the several sections of
the Module menu.

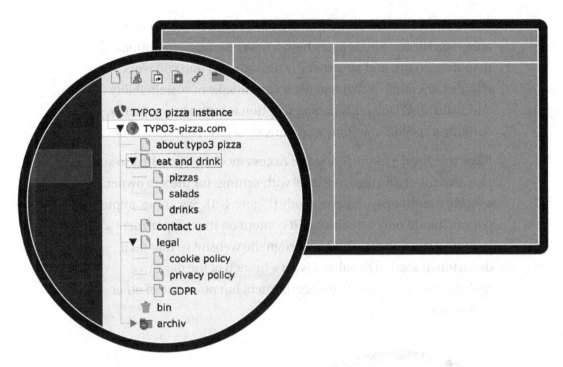

Figure 1-4. *Backend showing the page tree*

Access control: Users, groups, and fine-grained permissions

Only administrative users have complete access to a TYPO3 installation. Most users should only have access to the specific functionality they require to get their job done. Broad permissions are controlled by configuring usergroups, but you can also control access and functionality at the user and page level. The built-in access control system gives administrators lots of options for finer-grained access rules:

Note   TYPO3 differentiates between frontend and backend users. While backend users edit and administrate the websites, frontend users are website visitors who have used a frontend login form on a page to see access-restricted content. Frontend users are not covered here.

> **Usergroups –** You can assign users to one or more usergroups; they receive the access rights given to that group. Permissions are additive and nonexclusive; users assigned to more than one usergroup will have all permissions granted to those usergroups.

11

Users – You can also set permissions to control a single user's access privileges. Single users have a fewer permission options than usergroups, and we generally recommend that you work with groups rather than individual users for the sake of sustainability and scalability. One reasonable exception is limited time access, defining a specific start and stop time, for a given backend user.

Page tree level – In the System ➤ Access module, you can also set permissions at the page tree level with settings for the site owner, specific usergroups, and everybody (Figure 1-5). Say, for example, editors should only be able to edit content on their department's section of the website. You can design the website so that their department section or subsite is on a branch of the page tree and give them edit access to their branch, but not those of other departments.

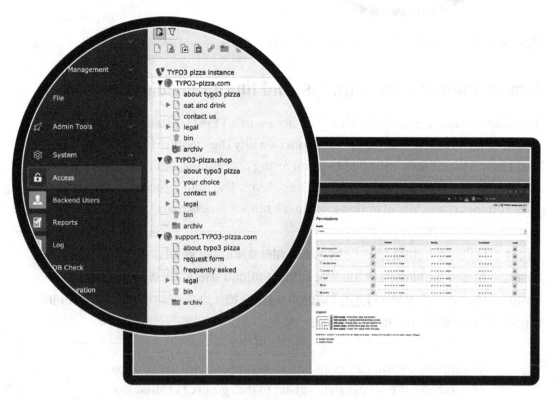

Figure 1-5. *Backend showing System ➤ Access module*

Find out more about user management in Chapter 3: Building and Extending TYPO3.

Multisite management

TYPO3 makes it possible to manage multiple sites with a single instance. Combined with TYPO3's multilingual handling, this powerful functionality makes TYPO3 an ideal choice for many types of large organizations. Universities, with their many departments, professors, social clubs, and so on, all needing their own websites are a perfect example. International companies and NGOs benefit from this built-in functionality:

Centralized maintenance - This centralized model for content and configuration makes updating the software for multiple websites faster, easier, and more secure.

Centralized branding, local flavor - You can have nuanced, centralized control over corporate branding and standards while giving individual teams enough access to tailor their sites to their local or specific needs.

User accounts - TYPO3 integrators can manage users centrally. Website visitors can benefit from a federated identity or single sign-on shared across connected sites within the same installation.

Content - TYPO3 editors can share content between sites, making it easier to distribute content and apply changes globally (Figure 1-6).

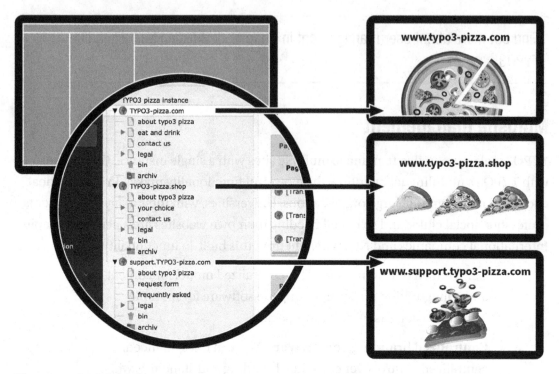

Figure 1-6. *Multisite management*

Multilingual websites

TYPO3 CMS has a powerful multilingual content management built in. You can add and manage hundreds of languages in the frontend and backend while taking advantage of all of TYPO3's centralized control and access management, as shown in Figure 1-7.

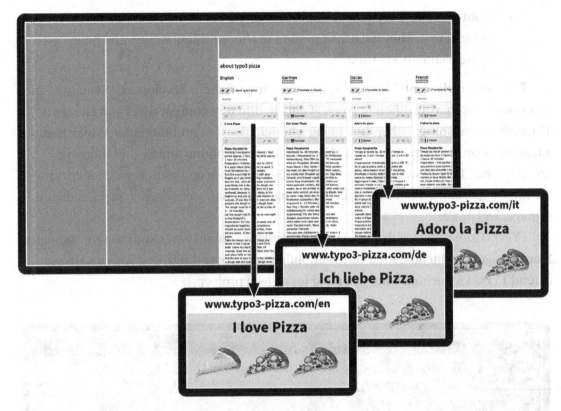

Figure 1-7. TYPO3 multilingual content backend and frontend

Find out more in Guide 7: Translating Your Site.

Content elements

Page content is composed of semantic "content elements," representing different content types, such as headers and images, as well as website UI elements. See Figure 1-8.

By separating text, images, and other data from how it is presented on the website, content elements help designers and content editors strike a balance between editorial control and branding consistency. The compromise benefits both:

- When designers define the look and feel of a project, they style the various content elements in use, ensuring a consistent appearance. They can define the look of a "Text & Media" element, for example.

- Content editors expect to be able to create a page, and then add content to it. They have the freedom to choose when, where, and how those elements are used.

The content elements' "semantic" nature is important to developers. "Semantic" in this case means having different types of data in different content types and elements. The data has meaning: rather than being a bunch of text or undifferentiated information, a map location is a map location, a phone number is a phone number, an image is an image, etc. This allows developers to pull content from any source, process it with business logic, and output the result to any digital format: website, web service, digital signage, and more.

TYPO3 Core comes with a selection of standard content types and content elements. Site packages can include their own, simplified or purpose-built, and you can always extend TYPO3 to include what you need for a given project.

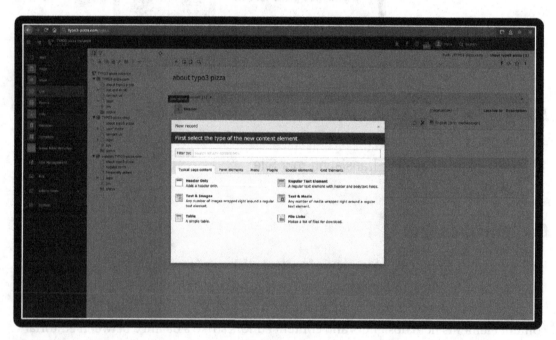

Figure 1-8. *The "Create new content element" window*

Content elements can be content like text and media, but they can also be plugins adding functionality. For example, an event listing or map integration that can be placed on any page.

Find out how in Guide 4: Planning, building, and using content elements.

Workspaces: Versioning, previews, and approval workflows

TYPO3 CMS has a concept called "workspaces" that allow content and editorial teams to work with content in draft mode and send their work and changes through an approval workflow before they are published.

This fixes one of the puzzles in any database-driven content management system: How can you add new content, and then preview it, before making a change on the live production site? Workspaces let you work on upcoming versions of content without affecting the live site.

There are community-contributed content publishing extensions that connect and sync staging and production servers. However, TYPO3's Workspaces provides an elegant solution requiring no additional third-party code, leveraging the underlying database element versioning-management system built into TYPO3 Core.

Find out how in Guide 8: Configuring content management workflow and permissions.

What you can build with TYPO3

TYPO3 CMS works on any modern browser and in any language. It powers digital experiences in any channel: websites, native mobile apps, web-to-print systems, web services, and more. While TYPO3 projects come in all shapes and sizes, TYPO3 excels at enterprise-level content management for global organizations. This is, in part, thanks to its strong multisite and multilingual capabilities. You can build public-facing brand sites, business applications, ecommerce integrations, and user portals. The TYPO3 Project's solid roadmap, consistent release schedule, commercial SLA's, and extended long-term support options help make it a safe bet for mission-critical applications.

Case study 1: Vienna University[4]

The Vienna University Campus website[5] is the main portal for the university, serving more than 93,000 students and over 9,700 employees in 32 languages. Their portal has grown substantially over the last decade and now hosts more than 1,300 domains—all maintained in a single TYPO3 instance (Figure 1-9). The magic behind this project are TYPO3's multisite and multilingual capabilities.

Figure 1-9. *Vienna University main site, student site, and alumni site*

The portal allows TYPO3 integrators to add specific functionality to one or more given domains while leveraging the ease of managing one instance (Table 1-1).

---

[4]https://typo3.com/case-studies/universitaet-wien
[5]https://www.univie.ac.at/en/

Table 1-1. *Comparison of portal growth over the years*

	2006	2019
Domains	12	1,280
News articles	1,400	570,000
Content elements	20,000	420,000
Languages	2	32
TYPO3 instance	1	1

Case study 2: Texere Publishing[6]

Texere Publishing[7] is a successful, venture capital–backed, scientific publishing house founded in 2012 around a single publication. As of 2019, Texere publishes six separate titles online and in print from their TYPO3-based publishing platform. They are thriving and growing at a time when many other publishers are struggling.

Their TYPO3 installation is a single, central publishing hub for all their titles (Figure 1-10). It provides editors content management and web-to-print workflows. In addition, they use it to moderate and publish subscriber content. No third-party systems are required to create landing pages or run marketing campaigns, saving costs, simplifying staff training, and making managing the sites more efficient overall.

---

[6]https://t3con15eu.typo3.org/program-detail/talk/detail/reorganisation-of-the-blsv.html
[7]https://texerepublishing.com/

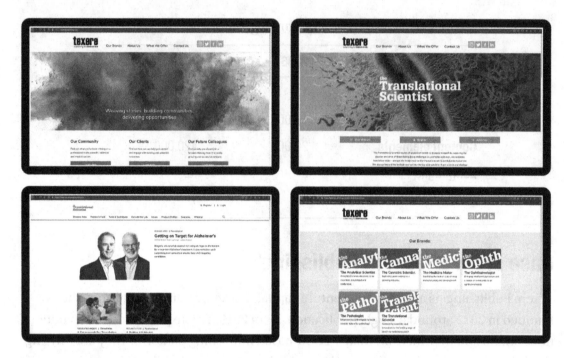

Figure 1-10. *Texere main site and example publication sites*

The unique features of the site include a personalized user experience for subscribers. Logged-in users have access to all publications in one central place. Readers have a personalized newsfeed, and they can bookmark content to a reading list. When they log in, the system returns them to where they left off reading. By making it easier for readers to find and consume great content, the subscription is more compelling. And when readers stick around and enjoy the content, Texere's advertisers are happy, too.

Table 1-2. *Demonstration of scaling up with one TYPO3 instance*

	2012	2019
Domains	1	9
News articles	1	120,000
Content elements	1	60,000
Languages	1	4
TYPO3 instance	1	1

Read more case studies

TYPO3 GmbH keeps a showcase of TYPO3 case studies.[8] Individual agencies also keep case studies on their sites. Look for case studies in sectors that interest you to see what is possible.

The TYPO3 Project and Ecosystem

When you adopt TYPO3, you become part of the community of stakeholders that we often call "The TYPO3 Project." In the open source model, the more you invest—giving feedback, contributing, sponsoring, promoting, and sharing knowledge—the greater the return. You build stronger relationships and a better business network, in addition to improving the software tools you use every day (Figure 1-11).

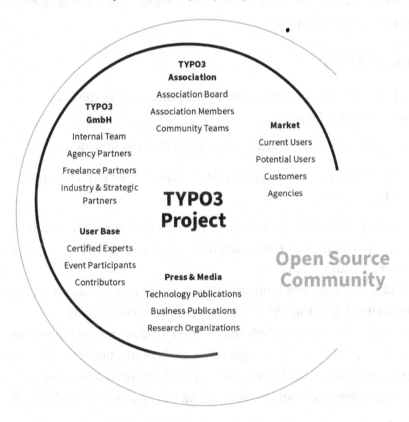

Figure 1-11. *Illustration of the TYPO3 Association, the community, the GmbH, and other stakeholders*

---

[8]https://typo3.com/case-studies

Open source governance

As a member of the Open Source Initiative, the TYPO3 Project is committed to upholding the Open Source Definition through software license review and approval. The term "open source software" was coined in 1998 as a software that provides a set of precise freedoms and benefits, including but not limited to the freedoms to run, study, redistribute, and improve the software on which you rely. These benefits are codified in the Open Source Definition (OSD), which is based on the Debian Free Software Guidelines.

The Open Source Initiative, its members, affiliates, and sponsors promote and protect this fundamental definition through software license review and approval.

"Without this single, standard definition of "open source," software development as we know it would not be possible. There is no trust in a world where anyone can invent their own definition for open source, and without trust there is no community, no collaboration, and no innovation."[9]

Facts about TYPO3

- TYPO3 CMS version 3.x and above is licensed under the GNU General Public License.

- The TYPO3 trademark is owned by the TYPO3 Association.

- TYPO3 CMS was originally created by a Danish developer, Kasper Skårhøj, in 1997.

Kasper Skårhøj supervised the release of TYPO3 under an open source license and created its extension architecture, defining two of its fundamental underpinnings: its ethos and its architectural flexibility.

The TYPO3 Association was founded in 2004, after Kasper had chosen to move on and hand the leadership of the TYPO3 project over to its community.

The open source consultancy OSS Watch[10] defines governance models on a scale depending on how participatory and open to contribution a project is. Having a project founder in place who still has influence on project direction is one of the indicators of less participatory governance, and projects being less open to external contributions.

---

[9]https://typo3.org/project/association/partnerships/open-source-definition/
[10]http://oss-watch.ac.uk/resources/governancemodels

TYPO3 leans more toward participatory governance and collective leadership models. Major decisions about project direction are based on democratic, consensus-driven processes. People who hold positions on the board of the TYPO3 Association are elected by the organization's members. Annual individual membership to the association costs less than €8 per year.

The community is self-organized into teams,[11] like the security team and the documentation team. Core development is organized into initiatives[12] with specialist contributors focused on specific areas like data handling or SEO. Each team or initiative is self-organizing, appointing leaders to manage their activity, and generally operate on a liberal, open contribution policy, welcoming contributions from outside their teams.

Reliable releases

TYPO3 has a regular and dependable release schedule. Predictable releases make it easier to plan for updates and keep sites up-to-date, reliable, and secure. The extended support plans available also increase the expected lifetime of a web application or website.

New major TYPO3 CMS versions come out every 18 months. The TYPO3 Core Team subsequently publishes a sprint release approximately every 6 weeks until the final long-term support (LTS) release. Each LTS version is supported for six years: first, with bug fixes and security updates for 18 months and then with priority bug fixes and security updates for another 18 months. After that three-year time period, TYPO3 GmbH offers a paid extended long-term support (ELTS) service to extend official support for every release, keeping sites secure and compliant with legal requirements like GDPR to run supported software, for a minimum of an additional three years.

The extended project life cycle ensures that TYPO3 installations are more stable and secure for longer (Figure 1-12). The predictability and stability foster longer-term planning and increase lifetime ROI for TYPO3 projects. The TYPO3 CMS Development Roadmap[13] is published on the TYPO3 website.

---

[11]https://typo3.org/community/teams/

[12]https://typo3.org/community/teams/typo3-development/initiatives/

[13]https://typo3.org/cms/roadmap/

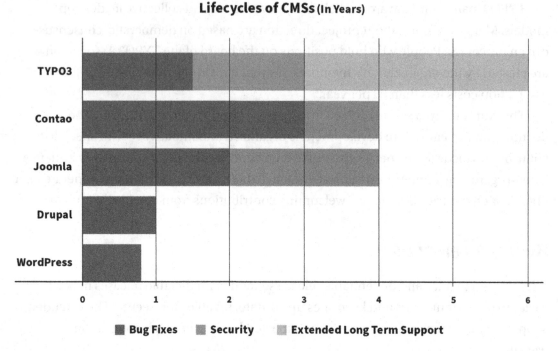

Figure 1-12. *Graphic showing the relatively longer life cycle of TYPO3*

TYPO3 Project community events

At TYPO3 events, you have a chance to meet your peers, share knowledge, make connections, and have a direct impact on the project. Every month, there are local usergroup meetings[14] hosted by agencies and other organizations. And if there isn't a regular meetup in your area, you can always look for kindred spirits in the PHP community, for example, and start your own!

Regional TYPO3 camps and larger conferences take place annually and attract a wider audience.

Community contribution sprints happen on an ad hoc basis, organized by community teams and initiatives.

Local usergroups and regional conferences are often conducted in the local language, so it's usually good to confirm if you plan to travel from afar. Larger annual events are held in English and attract an international audience.

---

[14]https://typo3.org/community/meet/user-groups/

Two official TYPO3 events, organized by the TYPO3 Association and TYPO3 GmbH, are intended to engage participants across the breadth of the professional TYPO3 community:

- The TYPO3 Developer Days are aimed at knowledge sharing and skill building. This is a great opportunity to meet the TYPO3 Core Team and learn about technical innovations and best practices.

- The TYPO3 conference is an event for business leaders, decision-makers, and agency leaders who want to build connections and partnerships inside and outside the TYPO3 community.

Keep an eye on the TYPO3 Project event calendar[15] for up-to-date info.

The TYPO3 community

typo3.org[16] is the project and community home online. The site is a good place to start when looking for all things TYPO3.

The TYPO3 Association[17] is a not-for-profit membership organization based in Baar, Switzerland, responsible for ensuring the sustainable long-term development of the TYPO3 project. It provides funding for community events and initiatives.

TYPO3 GmbH[18] is a commercial company, based in Düsseldorf, Germany, set up by the TYPO3 Association to support TYPO3 CMS. Its mission is to offer commercial products and services to enhance and improve TYPO3 CMS, helping TYPO3 agencies and the TYPO3 Project compete in the global marketplace. Its offerings include 24x7 SLA-based support, independent project reviews, official integrations and industry partnerships, and an official partner program for TYPO3 service providers.

Slack – A lot of real-time interactions in the community happen on Slack. The TYPO3 Project Slack instance[19] includes individual channels for regions, common interests, and community initiatives. There is plenty of peer support offered by volunteers within the community.

---

[15]https://typo3.org/events
[16]https://typo3.org/
[17]https://typo3.org/project/association/
[18]https://typo3.com/services
[19]https://my.typo3.org/about-mytypo3org/slack/

Where to get help

The first place to look for help is in the official documentation and on Stack Overflow. Failing that, feel free to reach out to the community on Slack. You can also reach out to organizations set up to support the community:

Official TYPO3 CMS documentation[20] – This is the first place to look for help on technical topics.

Stack Overflow[21] – This is a popular place to pose and solve TYPO3 problems. You'll find some of the most active members of the community helping out there. It is a comprehensive archive of frequently asked questions with a long shelf life.

TYPO3 GmbH Partners[22] – TYPO3 GmbH manages a network of official vetted TYPO3 GmbH partners.

TYPO3 Extension SLA[23] by Cybercraft GmbH provides support and service for third-party extensions in partnership with the extension maintainers.

Local TYPO3 usergroups[24] – Join the like-minded, the curious, and experienced TYPO3 people at a local usergroup meetup! Some groups hold both online and in-person meetups. Can't find one in your area? Start one yourself!

Contributions welcome!

In open source, contribution is vital to the success of any project. Contribution might include reporting issues, adding improvements, reviewing changes, and helping others, but it can also be by less direct means, such as event sponsorship, contributing to marketing materials or sharing external expertise.

Help others on Stack Overflow and Slack – Even as a newcomer, there will always be things that you know more about than the next person who joins the community. By helping others, you also get a chance to strengthen your knowledge and connections.

---

[20]https://docs.typo3.org/

[21]https://stackoverflow.com/questions/tagged/typo3

[22]https://typo3.com/services/find-a-typo3-partner

[23]https://coders.care/blog/article/service-level-agreements-for-typo3-extensions/

[24]https://typo3.org/community/meet/user-groups

Contribute improvements to TYPO3 documentation[25] – Documentation is managed by a small team with contributors from across the community. If you use TYPO3, you can be a documentation contributor. As a newcomer, your observations and questions are especially important.

The TYPO3 Contribution Guide[26] describes the process of core development.

Report an issue.[27] TYPO3 Forge[28] is the community issue tracker. If you find a technical issue, you can search to see if someone else has already reported it or join Forge and report it so that others in the community can assess and address it appropriately.

Join a TYPO3 Sprint[29] – These are organized on an ad hoc basis—online and in-person—by community teams and initiatives. To keep contribution accessible to all, participant travel and accommodation costs for in-person events can be refunded in many cases. HYPERLINK "https://docs.typo3.org/m/typo3/docs-how-to-document/master/en-us/WritingDocsOfficial/LocalEditing.html#docs-contribute-git-docker"

TYPO3 GmbH Review Friday – Once a month the doors open at the TYPO3 GmbH headquarters in Düsseldorf, Germany, for the community to join a daylong contribution sprint.

Become a TYPO3 Association member[30] – Individual membership is just under €8 for one year. Being a member, you get a say in the project's governance, voting on community budget proposals, and in the general assembly.

Recognizing contributions – Each month TYPO3 GmbH celebrates Developer Appreciation Day (DAD), summarizing the monthly contributions to code and documentation. The TYPO3 Project is also building a TYPO3 karma system for peer-to-peer recognition. This will make it possible to recognize all the different kinds of contributions that keep the community healthy and thriving.

---

[25]https://docs.typo3.org/m/typo3/docs-how-to-document/master/en-us/

[26]https://docs.typo3.org/m/typo3/guide-contributionworkflow/master/en-us/Index.html

[27]https://docs.typo3.org/m/typo3/guide-contributionworkflow/master/en-us/ReportingAnIssue/Index.html

[28]https://forge.typo3.org/

[29]https://typo3.org/community/events/typo3-sprint/all/

[30]https://typo3.org/project/association/

Building TYPO3 skills

So far this chapter has given you an overview of the internals of TYPO3 and the opportunities available for building your website or web applications. You've seen a variety of use cases where TYPO3 provided the right solution for the job, and you've heard about the community and organizations shaping the project.

So, what does it take to build the skills and knowledge to wield TYPO3 as the scalable, multisite, multilingual, multipurpose tool we've promised it can be?

Learning TYPO3

In this section, we're going to give you a tour of the resources available so you're ready to start learning and exploring TYPO3. Depending on what works best for you, you may want to jump right into the TYPO3 documentation to get started, and you may also want to connect directly at community events. On the other hand, you may want to find formal training opportunities for yourself, your developers, or your entire team.

The TYPO3 ecosystem has lots of resources and opportunities to help build the skills you need to make the most of TYPO3. Once you do have experience, you can validate your skills with a series of official certifications.

More TYPO3 resources

There is a list of resources at the back of this book, as well as on the companion website for this book. We'll continue to update our TYPO3 resources list on the book website[31].

TYPO3 documentation

The official TYPO3 documentation[32] is the best resource for problem-solving and learning how to use TYPO3.

Check out the list of tutorials and guides[33], especially the Getting Started tutorial[34] to begin learning how to use TYPO3 step by step.

---

[31]https://typo3book.com/resources
[32]https://docs.typo3.org/
[33]https://docs.typo3.org/typo3cms/GuidesAndTutorials/Index.html
[34]https://docs.typo3.org/typo3cms/GettingStartedTutorial/

Books, videos, and training

TYPO3 offers a range of tutorials, screencasts, and event recordings on the official YouTube channel[35].

Authors Michael Schams and Patrick Lobacher have published certification study guides that are available through Leanpub: TYPO3 CMS Certified Integrator (English)[36] and TYPO3 Extbase (English)[37]. These include mock questions to test your knowledge.

The TYPO3 education committee and training

There is an ever-increasing demand for web development skills. TYPO3 isn't unique in this regard, but the community is in a better position to accommodate new users and provide paths for validating their knowledge through multiple certifications.

The TYPO3 Education Committee designs and manages certifications and runs certification events. They are also developing the TYPO3 Trainer Network.

If you're looking for on-site training for your team, contact TYPO3 GmbH for referral to a trainer.

Certifications

As you build your skills, you may want to validate them in four areas through the official TYPO3 certification program[38] (Figure 1-13).

You can take certification tests online or in person at TYPO3 camps and at the annual CertiFUNcation Day.[39]

You can elect to test your skills and knowledge under any of these four certifications:

- Certified editor

- Certified integrator

- Certified developer

- Certified consultant

---

[35]https://www.youtube.com/user/typo3
[36]https://leanpub.com/typo3certifieddeveloper-en
[37]https://leanpub.com/typo3extbase-en
[38]https://typo3.org/certification/
[39]https://typo3.org/certification/typo3-certifuncation-day/

Figure 1-13. *Showing the icons for the various certifications. Source:* `https://typo3.org/certification`

SkillDisplay

The SkillDisplay[40] service is a tool to allow you to organize learning requirements, study guides, exam preparation materials, and more. You can track your skills, training participation, and certifications on the exam. Rather than a learning platform, it's a skill management platform to guide you in building and validating your knowledge.

The TYPO3 Education Committee has mapped out the skills and prerequisite knowledge needed to pass the TYPO3 certification exams. Even if you're not preparing for an exam right now, the skill paths provide a thorough understanding of what you need to know to make best use of TYPO3.

For example, the skill path for coding standards in TYPO3[41] includes prerequisites like PHP and PSR standards.

---

[40]`https://www.skilldisplay.eu/`

[41]`https://www.skilldisplay.eu/skillpaths/cms-certified-developer-8-lts/skill/coding-standards-in-typo3/`

Summary

TYPO3 CMS's powerful core functionality and its extensibility set it apart from other systems.

As you've seen in this chapter, TYPO3 comes with robust functionality focused on delivering great client websites out of the box. TYPO3 Core comes with capabilities that, in many other CMSs, you would have to add via a third-party code.

These essential features help keep teams building websites happy. TYPO3 CMS provides core functionality meeting a wide range of pragmatic, end client–focused needs, leaving developers free to tackle more interesting problems. TYPO3 also provides the flexibility to extend the functionality of the Core when needed.

When projects do require domain-specific functionality, developers can write custom code leveraging the Core APIs to create new features or add integrations. This extensibility isn't unique to TYPO3 as a content management system. What is different from many others is the extent of the capabilities built in to the software, requiring less customization for most client projects.

TYPO3 community traditions of rewarding and recognizing contribution help motivate community members to give back. The Trainer Network and TYPO3 Certification Program validate the expertise of developers, consultants, integrators, and editors. This helps ensure high standards of project quality in TYPO3 while also helping certified experts find new opportunities.

TYPO3 has an edge over other open source content management systems. It has a long-standing community, stable roadmaps and release cycles, a vibrant professional service ecosystem, and solid independent support options from TYPO3 GmbH. All these help give decision-makers peace of mind when choosing to build mission-critical digital experiences on TYPO3. They also help open the doors of enterprise organizations to TYPO3 digital agencies and service providers.

Next, we'll see how all these parts come together, as we consider how you design and plan a TYPO3 project.

CHAPTER 2

Designing and Planning with TYPO3

This chapter will give a good idea of how to design and plan TYPO3 websites and applications and will explain some fundamental components that make TYPO3 unique.

TYPO3 CMS is a terrific technology for many kinds of projects, especially for dynamic applications set up for clients to manage and edit their own content. Be aware that TYPO3 is not always the answer.

Michael Schams, author of *TYPO3 Extbase*, agrees: "TYPO3 is a great enterprise content management system. It is not a blog system, and sometimes it's overkill for very small sites. TYPO3 is the perfect choice for clients who want to start small and grow."

Different tools and media seem to have a grain, like wood. When you're talking about wood, if you've got "the eye" and the experience, you can quickly spot which way the wood might splinter, parallel to the grain. Software also has a grain, and it also takes "an eye" to see it. Just like with wood, if you work against the grain with software, you can run into perplexing problems. Something that would be relatively easy in one system, taking mere minutes of work, might be monumentally difficult in another, because the software works differently on a fundamental level or has been designed from the ground up to solve a different kind of problem.

The path of least resistance when working with content management systems is to understand a system's

- Core features

- Flexibility and extensibility

- Smallest modular components

- Trends and current best practices promoted among users

- Workflow and approach to implementing a project from idea to launch

© Felicity Brand, Heather McNamee, and Jeffrey A. McGuire 2021
F. Brand et al., *The TYPO3 Guidebook*, https://doi.org/10.1007/978-1-4842-6525-3_2

In this chapter, you'll get to know the "grain" of TYPO3 and how experienced users are making the most of this system around the world. This will help you avoid pitfalls early on in your projects that could cost you an inordinate amount of time and frustration later.

Using TYPO3

To make the most of the opportunities available within any content management system, including TYPO3, you'll first need to understand its fundamental organization.

Here is an overview of some fundamental parts you'll find in TYPO3:

- TYPO3 has a separate backend and frontend, each with distinct user interfaces and independent user management.

- It has a page tree and menu system.

- The smallest components of a TYPO3 web page are content elements.

- It has a centralized site management interface with support for multisite and multilingual installations.

TYPO3 is a powerful enterprise CMS, and in order to make the most of its power, you need to understand the fundamentals and learn some new language and concepts, such as

- TypoScript

- Fluid

- Site package

- Extensions

There is support and documentation[1] available to help you, and there is a very friendly and responsive community of TYPO3 users who want to help you succeed.

---

[1] https://docs.typo3.org/

The relationship between the TYPO3 frontend and backend

By default, TYPO3 has two distinct user interfaces, referred to as the backend and the frontend. If powering a website, the backend is the administrative area of the website, and the frontend is the presentation layer, "the website" itself. Both areas can be accessed through any web browser:

- Website visitors use the frontend to view content or manage their customer account.

- Content creators use the backend to edit text and images.

- Developers and integrators use the backend to configure TYPO3.

Originally, TYPO3 was designed to be a general-purpose framework for managing content. To this day, it delivers a set of principles for content storage, editing, user access, and file management. These principles are delivered with the Core as sensible defaults, flexible configuration options, and open extension points. None of these are set in stone, and you can customize it to meet your projects' or clients' exact needs.

TYPO3 is a decoupled CMS. This means there is a separation between the code and how content is displayed, as shown in Figure 2-1. This gives you the freedom to choose how to build your frontend display layer. It also means that a TYPO3 installation can easily be "headless," and not have a web-facing user interface at all. TYPO3 can just as well power business applications, serve APIs, or be the data engine for native mobile apps.

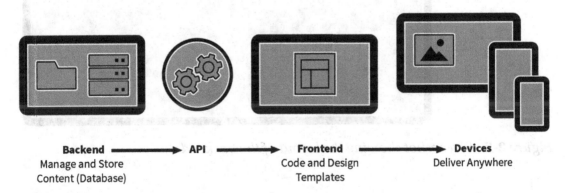

Backend ⟶ API ⟶ Frontend ⟶ Devices
Manage and Store   Code and Design   Deliver Anywhere
Content (Database)   Templates

Figure 2-1. *Typical decoupled CMS. (Source: This work is a derivative of an image from https://www.brightspot.com/blog/decoupled-cms-and-headless-cms-platforms)*

The backend

- Every TYPO3 site of the same version has the same default backend.

- You can configure and customize the backend to fit different user types, skin it for clients, and add and remove functional components, called "modules."

- To access the backend, append `/typo3/` to your site's root URL and then log in. For example, `https://example.com/typo3/`.

- Both administrators and content editors log in to the backend to manage the site.

Figure 2-2 shows an overview of the backend interface and its structure:

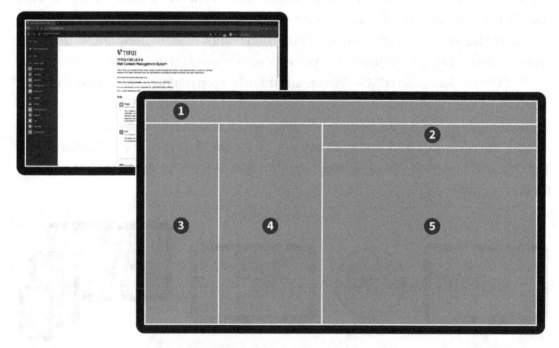

Figure 2-2. *Screenshot showing the layout of the backend*

1. **Top bar** – Access your user settings, logout, search, etc.

2. **Docheader** – Contains contextual buttons depending on what you are doing.

3. **Module menu** – The main menu of the TYPO3 backend. It lists the main modules and their submodules.

4. **Page tree** – The hierarchical structure of your site. Browse through and select pages.

5. **Content area** – Edit pages and content elements.

The frontend

The frontend—your website—could also be called your client application or the presentation layer (Figure 2-3). It may be publicly accessible or an access-restricted intranet.

Content is organized and displayed in the frontend based on how it is configured in templates and in code. See the "Visual Design and Theming" section later in this chapter for information about templates.

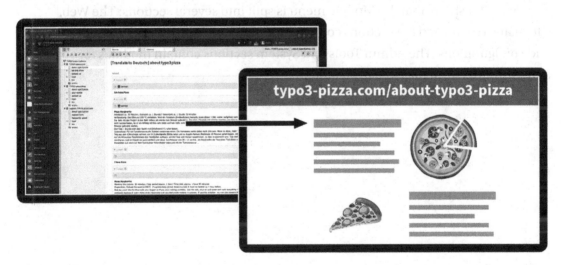

Figure 2-3. *Example of how content elements in the backend relate to content rendered in the frontend*

Figure 2-3 displays the website page tree, the content structure of a page in the backend, and how this can look in the frontend. The website menu structure reflects the page tree's hierarchy of nested pages.

It is important to understand that while some editors use TYPO3 every day, some may only go into the system every two or three months. One idea to make it clearer for editors is to restrict the view so that they only see what they need and nothing else.

Another approach is to organize your site's backend to mirror the frontend information architecture. This can simplify navigating and maintaining site content for editors. If your editors seldom log in to the system, you can also add frontend editing so that they can edit content directly on the public-facing website itself.

Navigation and information architecture

A lot of thought has gone into the design of the backend user interface to make it structured, consistent, and predictable to navigate.

The main navigation in the TYPO3 CMS backend is via the Module menu on the left side of the user interface. You can think of it as an app launcher that opens different areas of functionality within your website.

Figure 2-4 shows that the Module menu is split into several sections: The Web, site management, and file sections contain modules for editors to work on content and configurations. The Admin Tools and System sections contain modules for administrators to manage the installation.

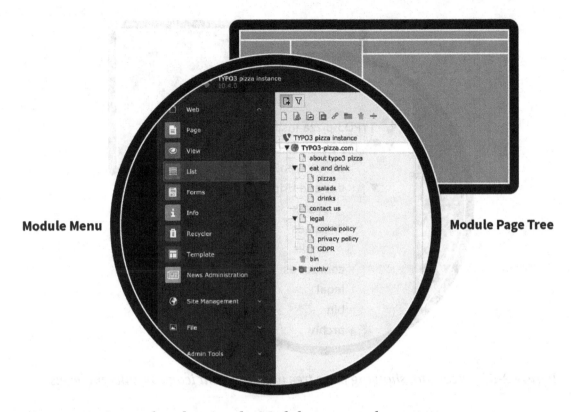

Module Menu   **Module Page Tree**

Figure 2-4. *Screenshot showing the Module menu and page tree*

In the navigation frame, your current selection in the page tree is retained when changing between most modules. Some modules don't require a tree display in the navigation frame.

The page tree and menu system

The Web module always displays the page tree, which represents sites and the hierarchical page structure of your TYPO3 instance.

At the top of the page tree is an entry with the name of your site and the TYPO3 logo. This represents your TYPO3 instance. It is the top node (always ID zero), and it is used to store instance-wide resources such as file mounts and backend user records.

A single installation of TYPO3 can contain multiple websites. The root page of a website has a globe icon (Figure 2-5). Within the root page, you find the page hierarchy of the website.

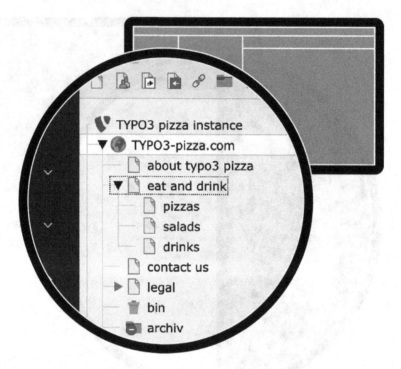

Figure 2-5. *Screenshot showing page tree with different icons at different levels*

A website's page hierarchy typically corresponds to the navigational structure. The first page level is the top-level menu navigation, and nested child pages (or subpages) represent submenus on your site. You can drag and drop pages in the page tree to change their position in the structure.

By default, the page titles you see are also used in the breadcrumb navigation, URL slug, and browser tab (Figure 2-6). This graphic also shows the first-level pages as top-level menu navigation items in the frontend.

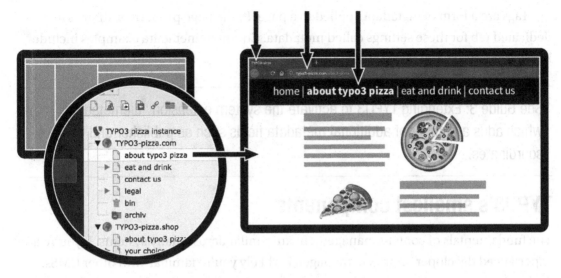

Figure 2-6. *Page title in backend and frontend*

Categories

Like most CMSs, TYPO3 allows you to add metadata and categories to your pages. Augmenting your content this way can improve the user experience and help search engines and potential visitors find you. Categories can also help editors sort through and find specific content, especially on large, information-rich sites.

In TYPO3, categories can be applied to pages and content elements, as well as third-party record types, such as news articles. Categories are powerful; they give you another dimension for organizing content. They can be added and nested to create hierarchies and subcategories. You can slice your data in different ways for different target groups. For example, on a documentation or learning site, you may want to highlight content for experienced and beginner users differently.

Tags and metadata

TYPO3 provides you with the tools to implement your SEO strategy. You can improve search engine ranking by using metadata tags on your pages and images. TYPO3 also generates human-readable and inherently search engine–optimized URLs for your pages.

Tags are a form of metadata applied to a page. In the page properties, there is a dedicated tab for these settings called metadata. Common metadata examples include keywords, author, and description.

See Guide 3: Extending TYPO3 to activate the system extension "filemetadata" which adds a number of additional metadata fields such as publisher and geo coordinates.

TYPO3's smallest components

The fundamentals of content management are similar across many systems. If you're an experienced developer or project manager, it's likely you're familiar with other CMSs. At the same time, even small differences might get in the way of understanding a new system. In this section, we'll make sure you know the fundamentals of TYPO3.

TYPO3 is based around a flexible page concept built up of smaller components, data containers called "content elements." A content element is a specific instance of a "content type." A content type is a data model defining what information goes into a content element of that type, for example, text and an image (Figure 2-7), or a phone number, email, embedded video, header, text, etc.

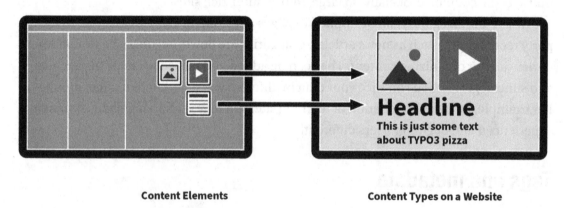

Content Elements   **Content Types on a Website**

Figure 2-7. *Diagram of content element schematic*

Other CMSs use a variety of approaches to content structure. Depending on the structure, you may have to consider the data model very early on in your planning and take into account how data will be displayed in different contexts.

Stefan Busemann, CEO of in2code GmbH, says that "technically, I like the way that the backend is able to abstract data—that you have possibilities to edit every kind of structured data or structured content in the same way, so you don't have to create input forms for different data types. In our development process, we can create flexible solutions for our customers and do not have to worry about any custom input forms. Examples of structured data would be the news, news records, or any kind of products or categories. All record types are edited the same way. I think that's the feature I love most about TYPO3."

This automated form creation and handling is thanks to the TYPO3 Table Configuration Array (TCA). It defines database table fields, if and how they are displayed in the backend, and what kind of restrictions apply to their content.

Find out more about the TCA in Guide 4: Planning, Building, and Using Content Elements.

Visual design and theming

No matter what system or CMS you are using, planning your site is important. It helps you define the information architecture and how to incorporate the design elements and style decisions that make up the framework of your site. You should take time to map out your business processes and goals before you start working with any content management system. Figure out what part you want your digital presence (websites, apps, etc.) to play and what it should deliver. This information should help you document target user groups, their needs, customer journeys, and potential conversions. Begin sketching out some page layouts. There are a lot of decisions to make, but you want to make them before you start work in your CMS because it's much easier to work them out on paper than improvising them while building your site. A designer experienced with the Web and CMSs will be able to help you here.

It is a good idea to organize a workshop to determine your site's structure: the sitemap (Figure 2-8). Plan URL patterns to optimize SEO and involve colleagues and customers to test site navigation and create a meaningful and comprehensible system.

Ultimately, your goal should be to create a result that is flexible and scalable. Choose the most appropriate content elements, extensions, layouts, and templates to facilitate quality content and reusable elements for maximum ease of use.

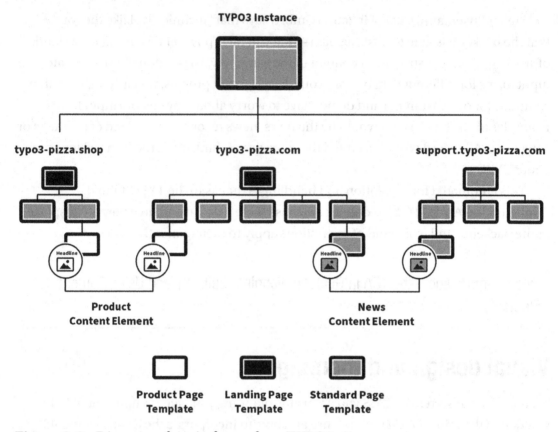

Figure 2-8. *Diagram of a wireframe for a TYPO3 site*

TYPO3 is design- and display-led

Whatever design methodologies you follow, whether you have your own in-house design team or outsource to a third-party design company, TYPO3 lends itself well to many ways of working.

In a traditional design workflow, the designer creates a design using a user interface design tool, such as Adobe XD or Sketch. The frontend developer then creates HTML and CSS files that the integrator brings into TYPO3.

TYPO3 supports style guide–driven development. With this approach, you build a "living" style guide as part of your website. The style guide includes all of your potential design options including interface elements like fonts, buttons, headers, and media. With the style guide built into your website, your design has a single source of truth, and you only need to change an element in one place in the backend to have that change rolled out everywhere across your website.

Living style guides are a powerful way to work because they make your site a fully working prototype, where a paper mock-up or a design tool won't expose every potential problem. For example, if your English-speaking team builds a site from a mock-up for a German client, they might not take into account that German has many longer words than English. If you work with real user data and (German, in this example) content into your working prototype, you'll see the problem or edge case right away. And since you're working in the CMS, you can figure out a solution for it then and there.

TYPO3 fits well with the modular approach of Brad Frost's Atomic Design methodology. It helps you design in a deliberate and hierarchical manner. The five stages of atomic design[2,] from the smallest to the biggest units are

- Atoms

- Molecules

- Organisms

- Templates

- Pages

Atomic design is a mental model that sees a website as both a cohesive whole and a collection of parts at the same time. In TYPO3, the basic building blocks (atoms) are the data fields, and content elements, made up of fields, are the molecules.

Community design resources

Pixelant offers t3kit,[3] a TYPO3-based website package aiming to speed up every part of an agency's site creation process, from kick-starting a TYPO3 installation to launching a site. The package includes a local development environment, accessible templates and content elements, server configuration, deployment strategies, continuous integration tests, and speed optimizations.

---

[2]https://atomicdesign.bradfrost.com/chapter-2/
[3]https://github.com/t3kit

toujou is a TYPO3-as-a-service offering with a range of preconfigured website themes and templates[4] to help you get started quickly. You can view their extensive TYPO3 content element library[5] to visualize different designs and access tutorials and advice on how to implement each element.

The team at jweiland.net has developed a template TYPO3 site[6] with pages demonstrating different layouts and content elements.

Templates

With flexible templates for content elements and pages, you can create websites that provide the custom-tailored customer experiences you need for any given project.

TYPO3 templates were historically built using TypoScript. That is still possible, but the TYPO3 Core and most websites today rely on the Fluid template engine.

When used for website templating, Fluid is effectively an extension to normal HTML code that enables you to add conditional statements, variables, and loops into a normal HTML file. Behind the scenes, the Fluid engine reads your template files and compiles them into lightning-fast cached PHP code.

Templates in TYPO3 are flexible because they can be applied site-wide, to a single page or all of its subpages, even down to content elements. Each template can be applied conditionally, and they can have parent/child relationships to each other.

By convention, a TYPO3 extension's Fluid templates are located within three folders in Resources/Private/:

- **Layouts** – Often just one file defining the parts that are always included, such as the <div> tag wrapper

- **Templates** – One per action, such as list and single data views

- **Partials** – Sections or blocks reused in multiple templates

The Resources/Private/ folder has a sibling folder called "Public" for supporting files like CSS, images, and JavaScript (Figure 2-9). Once you become familiar with this structure and where files are stored, you can embrace the flexibility and focus on creating designs and content elements for your website.

---

[4]https://www.toujou.com/templates/
[5]https://www.toujou.com/service/element-library/
[6]https://typo3muster.de

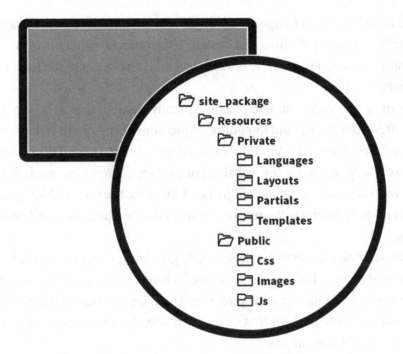

Figure 2-9. *Sitepackage directory structure*

When creating a design for a new website, you can use the TYPO3 Core's Fluid Styled Content Elements extension's default templates and partials. You could make everything yourself, but this leaves you with more work when you upgrade TYPO3. Staying closer to the defaults is the better strategy, where possible.

You can build up a library of finished components so that all you have to do is to change their visual output for a given project. If you need something really new that you haven't implemented in a Fluid template yet, you can use TYPO3's HTML content element to mock it up. Instead of using an external tool to make the design, use TYPO3 during the entire design phase and do everything in one go.

Designing the backend user experience

TYPO3 lets you configure the backend to suit your editors.

Integrators can customize how the backend is displayed to editors when they are working on a page, either creating content or editing page settings. This can be done by defining a backend layout (using TSconfig), which controls the appearance of the page module in the TYPO3 backend. These configurations can be made on the entire installation, a website, and on a page-by-page basis.

47

Backend layouts let you change the columns that are displayed in the page module to more closely represent your frontend design. This removes visual noise for your editors, meaning they can work more efficiently, and it also reduces the learning curve for new editors.

Content and presentation should be conceptually—and practically—separated. The designer, frontend developer, and integrator implement how content is displayed as part of the look and feel of the website. Editors should need only to spend time on the content itself, not how it is displayed on the website. For example, if you have a standard record, such as a news article, the editor should just add the data, the text, and images. The visual output in the frontend is the responsibility of the designer, frontend developer, and integrator.

Anja Leichsenring explains how sites usually give limited formatting options to maintain the design style, but editors often ask for more. "An editor once asked me how she could make horizontally scrolling pink text. The integrator had restricted access to the HTML content elements. I say that's a good choice. You can allow your editors to do anything, but you probably shouldn't."

It's important to give editors freedom while maintaining the integrity of the design. While you generally want to offer them some choices and autonomy, a little goes a long way. Editors should concentrate on content, rather than be overwhelmed with design possibilities—that can also potentially break your carefully planned designs or go against your corporate identity and design guidelines.

See the Guide 4: Planning, building, and using content elements.

Responsive design

Responsiveness is about delivering a fast, user-friendly, and consistent experience for your website visitors, regardless of their device.

With TYPO3, you can create and control your responsive design and breakpoints using HTML5, CSS, and JavaScript. The CMS has features to help you deliver videos, images, and documents in the format, resolution, and bandwidth appropriate for each device. In addition, you can use native interaction widgets on smartphones and tablets (e.g., the number pad and date picker).

Editors can use the built-in page preview function to simulate responsive content displayed on a variety of screen sizes and devices.

The backend is also responsive. It allows your site administrators and editors full access to get their work done from any computer, tablet, or smartphone.

TYPO3 websites can be configured to support Google's AMP (Accelerated Mobile Pages) format, which can help to improve your SEO ranking and load pages faster.

Accessibility

TYPO3 outputs structured data, so you can create an accessible experience for all your visitors. All content elements and frontend functions delivered with TYPO3 Core comply with the 2020 European Accessibility Act, WCAG, and Section 508 in US law.

Accessibility compliance is important, but making a website accessible can take a lot of work. TYPO3's decoupled architecture reduces the effort required. Editors work in the backend to add and manage content. The backend outputs structured data. Integrators can then use frontend templates to create presentation layers that are accessibility-compliant. For example, the templates can contain appropriate markup such as WAI-ARIA, captions, and Alt and title text.

You can configure metadata fields on content and pages to be mandatory, ensuring editors maintain consistency and compliance.

Content management

In this section, we'll look at how you and your team can allocate and tackle content management tasks.

TYPO3 uses a structured content approach and offers scheduled publishing and built-in workflow and approval processes.

Content editors typically carry out the following backend tasks:

- Manage pages and content.

- Create new pages.

- Structure the pages in the page tree.

- Manage content translations.

The TYPO3 Association offers a certification[7] to become a TYPO3 CMS Certified Editor (TCCE). You can take the exam at an event or online.

---

[7]https://typo3.org/certification/editor/

Content management workflow

Content editors often follow a process of drafting, reviewing, and approving content before publishing it to their live website.

Before you use any software to support your work, it is important to map out and understand your business processes. That way, you can set up your software (in this case, TYPO3) to support your workflow.

Whatever your workflow, it is helpful to document it. If your team of editors grows, they'll need something to refer to when maintaining your website. Documentation for editors should not only cover the content management workflow but also include information about SEO principles, writing standards, and how to structure content. This documentation should also define roles and responsibilities among editors.

Workspaces for versioning, preview, and approval workflows

TYPO3 allows you to version your content, so that you can work on unpublished content without affecting your live production site (Figure 2-10). This is managed with the Workspaces feature.

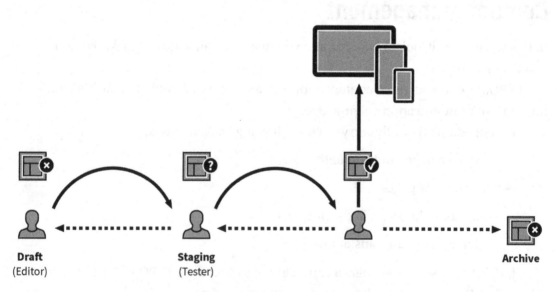

Draft
(Editor)

Staging
(Tester)

Archive

Figure 2-10. *Diagram of content management workflow*

Workspaces use the underlying version management system in TYPO3 Core to control what content belongs to which workspace version of your site. The Workspaces feature is available in TYPO3 Core, but you need to install and enable the system extensions Version and Workspaces to use it and access the management UI.

There are two types of Workspaces:

- **Live –** The default TYPO3 CMS working environment. Any change you make here will be live instantly.

- **Custom –** User-created Workspaces to support workflow processes. You can add, preview, and send changes through an approval workflow before they get published to the live environment.

By default, content in a workspace can go through three stages:

- Draft/edit

- Ready to publish

- Deploy to production

The best content often comes from a collaborative editorial process. You can add additional stages to adapt TYPO3 to suit your workflow (such as internal review or approval from another department) and preview content before publishing (Figure 2-11).

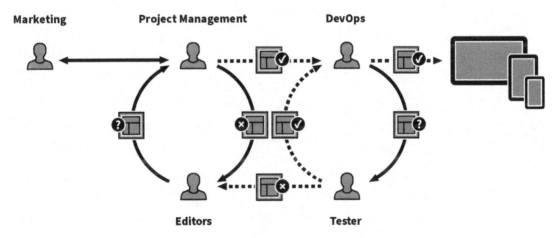

Figure 2-11. *Example workflow*

You can make the review process as simple or complex as you need. Then, you can look at community-contributed extensions to help support your content publishing workflow. For example, the extension "in2publish_core"[8] lets you connect servers to publish from a staging environment to the production environment.

Note   By default, in TYPO3, you can schedule automatic content publishing (and unpublishing) for specific dates and times—and this works without Workspaces or versioning. For example, you can configure Christmas-themed content and images to be visible for the duration of the festive season.

Ease-of-use for content editors

Improving editor's user experience begins with configuring role-based usergroup permissions to reduce visual noise in the backend. TYPO3 is highly configurable, and this flexibility can be overwhelming. Limiting the functions that are visible to editors will simplify the user experience. Show only what they need to do their job efficiently. For example, you can limit which pages and files they have access to and reduce the number of fields they can see and edit (Figure 2-12).

---

[8]https://extensions.typo3.org/extension/in2publish_core/

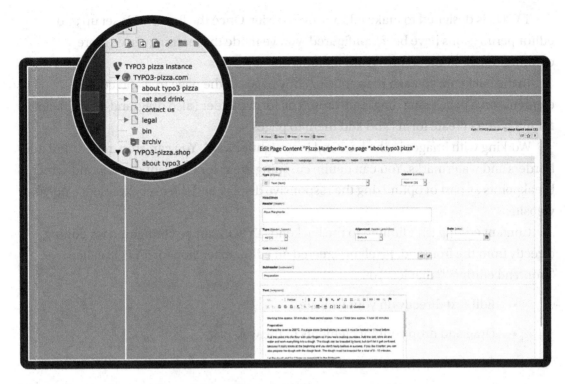

Figure 2-12. *Screenshot of the editing interface*

Sybille Peters, from the University of Oldenburg, explains about the backend user and group permissions: "You can create users, you can create groups, and you can create hierarchies of groups. This means you can configure the backend so that editors don't see all the features. It makes it more intuitive when they only see what they need to in order to do their jobs."

Misguided changes to content can jeopardize your design team's carefully constructed communication strategy. With TYPO3, you can precisely control who can see, modify, or delete content and pages. All editors must log in to the backend. You can define detailed permissions for editing and publishing, and the change log provides an audit trail with a chronological list of changes to the content and who performed them.

Frank Schubert explains: "With TYPO3 you can give experienced editors with deep technical knowledge a lot of flexibility and power to make big changes to the site and its content. Inexperienced editors need a clearer path to getting their job done, with fewer options. This is perfectly realizable with the user group management of TYPO3."

TYPO3 is designed to make editors' lives easier. Once the backend is set up and editor permissions have been configured, you've made the learning curve more comfortable for nontechnical team members.

In the backend, you can rearrange or copy pages in the page tree and content elements on a page using drag-and-drop. The form builder (also drag-and-drop!) helps for integrators create forms and add them to pages.

Working with images in the backend is straightforward. You can crop, resize, and add borders and watermarks. You can define cropping areas for different devices and screen breakpoints as part of optimizing the responsive display and the user experience on your website.

Content editing isn't limited to the backend. TYPO3 can be configured for editing directly from the frontend. Pixelant[9] created an editor extension for TYPO3 called "frontend editing"[10] that lets you

- Edit text directly on your website.

- Drag and drop content elements to the web page.

- Access the page tree.

There are other features that help you work efficiently:

- You can create multiple pages in one action.

- You can edit the same field in multiple content elements at the same time.

- You can perform the same action on multiple pages at once.

Daniel Siepmann, a web developer with Codappix GmbH, talks about some lesser-known features that are extremely helpful for editors working with the backend:

- The multiselect clipboard allows you to select multiple records to copy and paste or move.

- The system extension "Open Documents" adds an icon in the top bar listing all the documents you have open. When you open a record for editing and then click somewhere else, the record is still marked as open for yourself and for other editors. Clicking the icon will display a drop-down menu of records that you recently edited and that are still open.

---

[9]https://www.pixelant.net/

[10]https://www.pixelant.net/typo3-cms/extensions/frontend-editor/

- The bookmark feature lets you bookmark nearly every single view in the backend. If you edit a particular record often, for example, a teaser on your home page, you can create a bookmark to the record. Now, it will be just one click away, in the bookmarks menu in the top bar.

Reusing content

Single-source publishing is important in content management today, and crucial for any website editor. Single sourcing means publishing and reusing the same content in many places or channels while still being able to edit it in one central location.

TYPO3 CMS lets you

- Reuse content elements on different pages

- Reuse content elements and pages across multiple sites

- Reuse images and other file-based assets

- Reuse translations

You can change the appearance of shared content elements and pages through templates and styles. When you use an image in multiple places, you can crop it differently and apply different effects. The source image remains the same, and if you replace the source file, you will see all your image instances change as well.

The "Insert records" content element lets you insert another content element by reference on any page. That means you only need to create content once and reuse it without duplicating it. You edit and maintain the original in one place, but your changes will be visible everywhere.

TYPO3 is constantly evolving. One area receiving emphasis at the time of writing is native support for semantic and hierarchically structured content element types, such as columns, which are not bound to predefined layouts and templates. The TYPO3 Structured Content Initiative[11] was launched in 2019 and its goals are to

- Create a better experience for editors, editing content types in a more intuitive way

- Enable integrators to easily create flexible and reusable content types

---

[11]https://typo3.org/community/teams/typo3-development/initiatives/
structured-content

55

In addition to TYPO3's powerful internal capabilities, the CMS can integrate with external digital asset management (DAM) systems to store, classify, and manage images, videos, and brand identity assets across platforms. This helps editors discover and reuse content, reducing editorial and management overhead.

By default, editors can add media content and assets to TYPO3 by uploading them in the backend (in the File module ➤ Filelist and in certain content elements, such as text and images). This is TYPO3's internal DAM, also known as the File Abstraction Layer (FAL). When you upload a file (e.g., an image), you can add metadata: title, width, height, description, and alternative text. The file is now "single-sourced." Other editors can, for example, use that image in their content without having to repeatedly add copyright information, accessibility metadata, or other legally required information. If the image changes, all references to the image will be automatically updated on all pages and sites where it appears.

You can extend the default TYPO3 FAL by enabling the system extension called advanced file metadata (filemetadata). This adds a number of useful metadata fields to your files, including author name, publisher, copyright notice, and location.

The default storage for media content and assets in TYPO3 is the file system on the server. But you can also configure TYPO3's FAL to use external storage such as an FTP server, Amazon S3 storage, etc. Read more about this in Chapter 3.

TYPO3 multisite

TYPO3 is a true enterprise tool. It supports running and managing very large numbers of independent websites comfortably in a single installation, using a single backend. A TYPO3 CMS installation can scale from one to dozens to hundreds of sites, without compromising on security, performance, or usability in the front- or backend. Users have a single login to manage all websites, and granular user access permissions mean that you can configure editor roles across sites for content sharing and localization.

This centralized configuration model has multiple benefits:

- Upgrade the software for multiple websites at once.

- Share content between sites, making it easy for editors to reach a distributed audience.

- Share overarching configuration options across sites, and tailor more specific ones per site to fulfill a variety of needs within your solution.

- Use a single sign-on (SSO) for users across connected domains.

When to use TYPO3 multisite

TYPO3's powerful multisite features support large website projects, and not just those with multilingual content and translation needs (Figure 2-13).

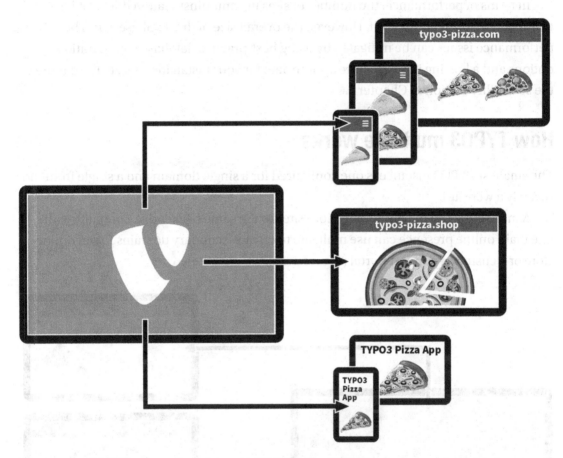

Figure 2-13. *Diagram showing one TYPO3 backend instance and multiple frontends*

You don't need a multilingual use case to benefit from a multisite installation. In addition to localizing for an international audience, a multisite solution suits projects, for example, where product names and legal requirements vary from region to region. It also gives power to your marketing team to manage brand strategy, shared media, color palettes, and more across multiple sites. Marketing can focus on executing great content campaigns without having to ask IT for help or permission with publishing, asset sharing, editing, translating, or content asset distribution across a federated network of sites.

Of course, multisite doesn't suit every use case. The multiclient capability has some factors to consider, including high server loads as the number of clients, and especially the number of pages, grows. In the end, there is no real performance difference serving 1 site with 1,000,000 pages and 100 sites with 10,000 pages each.

In terms of performance, the number of sites in a multiinstallation does not have to impact performance in itself. However, the overall size of the database can. These performance issues can be mitigated by using best-practice database configuration options and a hosting infrastructure appropriate for your installation's size. Read more in the scalability section in Chapter 4.

How TYPO3 multisite works

The smallest TYPO3 instance is one configured for a single domain and a single frontend (usually a website).

A multisite setup means adding more sites to the same backend. A company with one main online presence can use multisite to create secondary domains for an online store or a customer support portal (Figure 2-14).

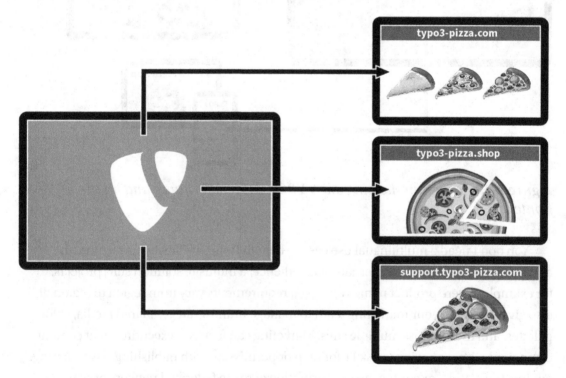

Figure 2-14. *Multisite with shop and support domains*

In this case, the branding remains consistent across the sites, but the purpose and navigation of the sites are different. Text reuse is low, but configuration options can be shared.

An international company can use multisite to create a localized site per region. Not necessarily with translated text but with content that is adapted to the local audience and region-specific legal requirements (Figure 2-15).

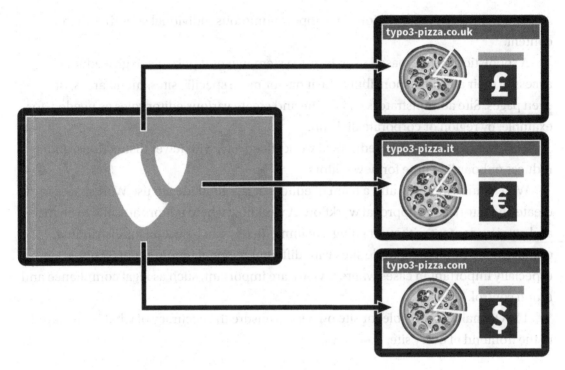

Figure 2-15. *Multisite with regional domains*

In this case, branding is consistent and text reuse is high.

Multisite maintenance

TYPO3 multisite introduces an efficient workflow that can save you considerable time, cost, and effort, if done right:

- Only one installation of the CMS has to be maintained and updated, saving support costs.

- Maintaining one shared configuration can save a lot of time and improve consistency.

- Multitenancy saves space.

- Configure editor roles across multiple websites.

See the section in Chapter 4 about multisite administration and maintenance.

Editors working with multisite

A single TYPO3 CMS installation can support numerous individual sites that share content.

A sophisticated role-based user access system makes it possible to give editors access to their area of responsibility, be it one or more specific sites, menu areas, or even pages. Site administrators can define and create various editor roles as needed, for example, by region or corporate division.

This makes it possible for editors to work effectively, with fewer distractions, and reduces onboarding time for new editors.

With a multisite setup and a team of editors, it is a good idea to use Workspaces to create an editorial and approval workflow. A workflow where editors are able to change and preview content without it going live immediately can be useful for distributed organizations running multiple sites with different regional requirements. This is especially important in cases where reviews are important, such as legal compliance and brand control.

TYPO3 makes it possible for site owners to ensure the accuracy of what is displayed in the frontend of every site.

Multilingual websites with TYPO3

Reaching global audiences is essential for many digital businesses today. Even without global targets, many countries and regions use more than one language in commerce and daily life. TYPO3 was built from the ground up to help you communicate with international audiences in mind. Handling multiple languages and translated content has always been a strength, and TYPO3 enables you to manage multilingual web projects with ease. TYPO3 supports content translation by default, and you can manage any number of languages within a single TYPO3 installation.

TYPO3 offers uncluttered, efficient authoring experiences for content editors, clear translation workflow, and seamless user experiences across websites. You can choose to translate content manually in-house or seamlessly integrate with third-party translation management services.

Approaches to multilingual site configuration

There are two main approaches to setting up your TYPO3 site for localization: multitree and single-tree (Figure 2-16).

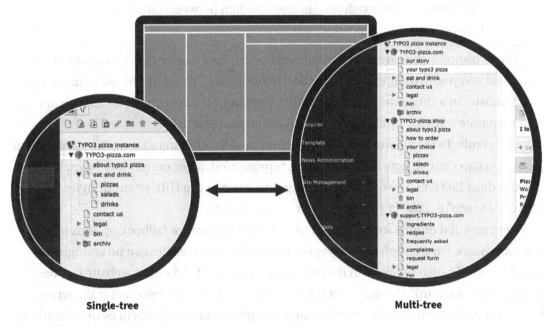

Single-tree   **Multi-tree**

Figure 2-16. *The different page tree approaches*

The multitree approach means that you place languages and regions into separate parts of the page tree:

- **This is good** if your websites are different in scope, navigation, and/or size.

- **This is excellent** if you have a large, comprehensive website in one language and would like to run smaller websites in other languages.

- **It also works well** if your websites need totally different content and navigation for different languages, regions, or cultures.

- **The drawbacks -** The multitree approach, however, requires more maintenance overhead and doesn't leverage the power of TYPO3's localization capabilities.

The single-tree approach means that you have one page tree for all languages:

- The content on each page can be translated to different target languages.

- Content editors can see and work with all translations in a single view.

- By default, website visitors can easily switch between different translations of a page.

The two approaches are not mutually exclusive. They can be combined for a more advanced setup with different domains and subdomains. You may choose to have your main website in a single tree (e.g., in English, German, and French) and then use one or more separate trees for smaller sites (e.g., Russian and Spanish).

By default, TYPO3 generates the URLs for the different language versions of a given page. You can choose how the language is represented, most commonly by including the standard ISO 639-1 two-character language code in the URL or subdomain: `https://example.com/fr` or `https://fr.example.com`.

You can build quite a sophisticated solution with language fallback options on a per-page basis. For example, a Norwegian translation of a website can be configured to fall back to Danish or Swedish if a page is not translated. An entire website can be available in "standard" German, but offer certain pages in versions specifically written for Austrian, German, or Swiss readers, for example, reflecting differences in legislation. TYPO3 takes care of switching languages, as well as setting metainformation for search engines.

Multilingual content and localization

With the single-tree approach, working with multiple languages is straightforward for content editors. The editing interface displays the original and translated versions of your content side by side in a single view, or you can view a single language at a time (Figure 2-17).

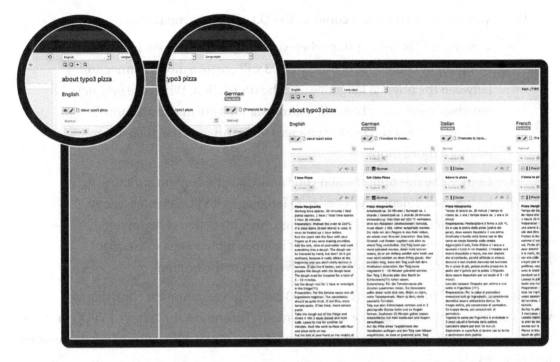

Figure 2-17. *Screenshots of editor user interface showing multiple languages*

Have a look at Guide 7: Translating your site for more information.

TYPO3 defaults to the utf8mb4 character set, which includes non-Latin character sets like Arabic, Chinese, and many others—even four-byte Unicode characters—think emojis! It also supports varied writing directions. When writing and editing, you can even quote right-to-left text (e.g., Hebrew) within a left-to-right block of text.

Reaching an international audience is not just about translating text. TYPO3 supports true localization, which means tailoring your website to fit your different audiences. This could mean "translating" media items to suit the market. Through the Filelist module, you can localize your media assets, providing translated metadata for each language. For example, you could have an image with caption, title, and text alternative in localized versions.

Translation workflow

Whether you are translating content manually or using a service, it is important to have a solid workflow. If you use Workspaces, you can implement a stage called "translation" in your publishing workflow.

When you choose to translate content, TYPO3 offers two methods:

- **Translate** – Use this option when you have a strict translation workflow or content structure. TYPO3 will create a direct connection between the original language and the translation. When the original language content is changed, the translations are marked as out-of-date, and you can see the changes in the original language when editing a translation.

- **Copy** – Use this option when you would like the content structure to be free and independent between languages. TYPO3 creates a copy of the content in the target language. No connection is maintained between the original and the translation, which means subsequent versions of the translations can diverge from the original.

The "translate" mode means that TYPO3 can help you maintain consistency when you have separate teams localizing content. This mode also allows TYPO3 to automatically mark translated content for review and notify translators when the original text changes.

When it comes to the effort of translation, many website projects choose to translate all content before launch. Subsequent updates are then handled differently depending on the workflow. If you have access to multilingual editors, they can translate content on an ongoing basis. Alternatively, you can "save up" content updates for a while and then use a service to translate everything at once.

Translation in the TYPO3 backend is a manual process. It requires translators to have access to your TYPO3 backend, and to have knowledge about how to navigate and use the editing interface. This method also means they cannot use tools like translation history and terminology databases.

The localization manager (l10nmgr)[12] extension for TYPO3 lets you access the power of translation services and, when used in conjunction with the localizer[13] extension, automates your workflow. These extensions mean you can export content in a standardized XML format for provision to a translation service provider. External translators can work outside TYPO3, relying on their own tools, and then give you files containing translated content, which you import back into your website. These extensions work together to give you a fully automated workflow with a helpful graphical user interface.

---

[12]https://extensions.typo3.org/extension/l10nmgr/

[13]https://extensions.typo3.org/extension/localizer/

You can also fully automate and customize your workflow with the l10nmgr and localizer extensions. For example, you might create an automated job to export sections of your website to be sent to your language service provider. You can also configure an import service to automatically import translated XML files into your TYPO3 site. See Figure 2-18.

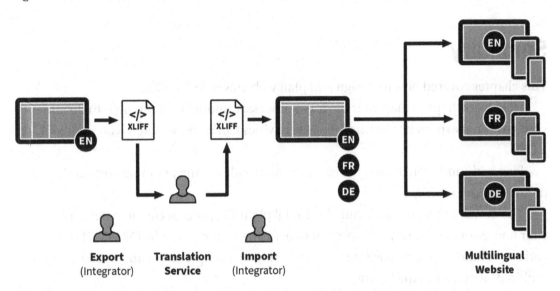

Figure 2-18. *Showing the content editing workflow for translation*

TYPO3 also integrates with a variety of translation services, such as LanguageWire,[14] DeepL,[15] and Virtaal.[16] This allows you to streamline your workflow even further, because the services are tightly integrated with TYPO3. Editors can send content for translation directly from within the backend.

Localize your backend

TYPO3 is a truly multilingual CMS. The backend, available by default in English, is translated into many languages. This means that you can provide editors with a localized backend user interface. Different users can choose to display the backend in the language of their choice. Working with a user interface in their preferred language can increase editors' confidence and effectiveness within the CMS.

---

[14]https://www.languagewire.com/
[15]https://www.deepl.com/en/translator
[16]http://virtaal.translatehouse.org/index.html

There is a dedicated TYPO3 special interest group[17] organizing the translation effort.

TYPO3 translations are hosted on Crowdin[18], a cloud-based content localization solution. Contributed extensions can also be translated. If your language is missing, please add it and start the translation in Crowdin, so that others can participate in the translation and also use it.

Summary

This chapter covered how to design and plan websites with TYPO3.

Hold workshops to map your business process. Conduct user research to document your customer experience journey. These activities can be done before you even look at a CMS.

Plan early and then iterate. Revisit decisions made during planning and validate them with user testing.

The decisions you make during this initial planning process can help determine your framework and how you approach structuring your content in TYPO3. These early structural decisions position you for scaling to multiple sites and translation into multiple languages in the future.

Once you start to implement your website structure and design in TYPO3, you can use any one of a variety of different design approaches and methodologies. An array of extensions and community-developed resources are available to help you.

Your plan should also cover the structure of your editorial team. This will help you map out user groups and permissions and help you design your backend to suit your editors' needs.

Don't just design your frontend. Put some work into designing your backend so that editors can concentrate on content and be productive within your design framework.

---

[17]https://typo3.org/community/teams/typo3-development/initiatives/
  localization-with-crowdin/

[18]https://crowdin.com/project/typo3-cms

CHAPTER 3

Building and Extending TYPO3

In this chapter, we'll look at the underlying architecture of TYPO3, what is built in as Core features, and how you can extend it with custom code.

As we discussed in the previous chapter, "Designing and Planning," you can save yourself a lot of extra work by understanding the tools you use. This translates into knowing when to configure what is there, when to find third-party extensions, and when to write your own.

The birds-eye view: What am I getting myself into?

In the "Designing and Planning" chapter, we took you on a tour of the backend user interface. We also looked at the relationship between the backend and the frontend and how to think about your users' needs.

In this chapter, we'll take a closer look at *how* this all works together, what the pieces of TYPO3 are, and how a request is fulfilled when you visit a website page.

In this section, we'll talk about how to start using TYPO3 and a few best practices for how to structure your project from the beginning. Key components we'll review include TYPO3 CMS itself; a local development environment, including Composer; and Git. In other words, you need the CMS, a place for it to run, and ways to track and manage your work.

These components and tools must be set up at the start of your project, so that you can start to share your work, recover from mistakes, and avoid extra unnecessary work later on.

Another component to consider early on is a hosting provider. Before you know it, you'll be ready to take your project live online and show it to the world. We'll cover what to look for in a web hosting provider in detail in Chapter 4; here, we will discuss it only in general terms, and where it belongs in the workflow.

© Felicity Brand, Heather McNamee, and Jeffrey A. McGuire 2021
F. Brand et al., *The TYPO3 Guidebook*, https://doi.org/10.1007/978-1-4842-6525-3_3

TYPO3 system layers

Like most CMSs, the TYPO3 system architecture is multilayered (Figure 3-1). The backend and frontend user interfaces sit on top of the application layer, which in turn sits on the infrastructure layer. The web server, database, and PHP in the infrastructure layer are prerequisites for running TYPO3.

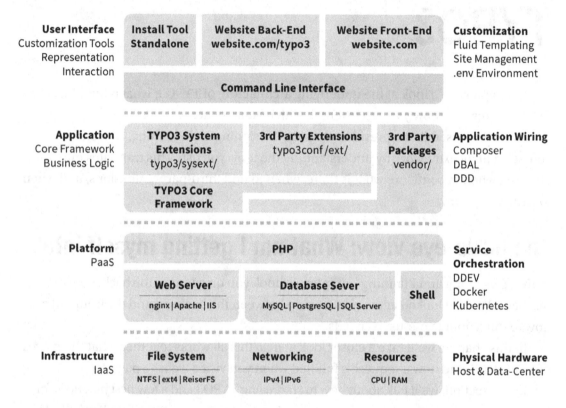

Figure 3-1. *Layers of the TYPO3 system*

This figure shows the TYPO3 technology stack, with the different layers labeled on the left side and potential tools and libraries labeled on the right side.

Table 3-1 describes the different layers in more detail.

Table 3-1. *TYPO3 system layers defined*

Infrastructure and platform layers	To run TYPO3, you need the physical hardware infrastructure. TYPO3 requires a web server with PHP and a database.
Application layer	The TYPO3 Core framework interacts with system and third-party extensions via the TYPO3 extension API. Extensions are clearly confined code additions, such as plugins, backend modules, application logic, skins, and third-party apps. The Core and extensions interact with each other seamlessly and operate as a single, unified system.
User interface layer	The two user-facing aspects of TYPO3 are the TYPO3 backend and the TYPO3 frontend. The backend is the administrative area where you manage content and configuration based on what extensions have been installed. It is the **content-creation** side. The frontend is the **content-delivery** side. Most commonly in a website, the frontend is where templates, CSS, content, and logic from extensions meet to deliver your project to the world. The frontend doesn't have to be a website, it could be a native mobile application, a web application built in a frontend framework, or an API to interface with other systems.

Before you install TYPO3, we recommend that you prepare a local development environment, so that you can install and test functionality locally before publishing to a live system. The TYPO3 community has widely adopted DDEV-Local as the preferred local development environment for TYPO3. DDEV-Local, based on Docker container technology, makes it possible to wrap up and share your entire project with someone else. A developer, designer, Windows, macOS, or Linux user can start it up and see what you've been doing straight from their browser. DDEV has TYPO3 project initialization and configuration helpers built-in, making it very simple to get started. It's also highly customizable, so as you discover more specific needs, you can modify the configuration to suit your project.

Next, you'll need to think about tracking your project in a version control system, for example, Git. Using a version control system will allow you to track changes over time, recover from mistakes, and collaborate with colleagues and clients.

Dependency management is something else to consider. Composer is the recommended method for managing the TYPO3 install and extensions.

Daniel Goerz recommends some useful approaches to getting started with TYPO3 in his article "Good practices in TYPO3 projects"[1] including

- Use Composer.

- Use Git.

- Use a configuration switch mechanism.

- Keep everything clean and maintainable.

- Use an automated deployment process.

Installing TYPO3

A great place to start is the official TYPO3 documentation. The Getting Started tutorial[2] walks you through the required steps for installing TYPO3. It's best to start with a simple project and follow that from beginning to end, rather than to make your first project a complex giant.

Alternatively, you can use this book and follow the steps in Guide 2: Creating your first TYPO3 site, which steps you through installing TYPO3 and the Introduction Package. A distribution is an extension enriched with design templates and precreated demo content to create a website ready for use. The Introduction Package[3] provides some templates and theming to display the content you create in the backend. It is lightweight, providing best-practice examples, demoing a lot of TYPO3 functionality, and using a subset of the available Core extensions.

Other ways to install TYPO3

There are various ways to install TYPO3, depending on your environment, server setup, and infrastructure.

---

[1]https://usetypo3.com/good-practices-in-projects.html

[2]https://docs.typo3.org/m/typo3/tutorial-getting-started/master/en-us/Introduction/Index.html

[3]https://extensions.typo3.org/extension/introduction/

The TYPO3 community generally recommends that you install TYPO3 using Composer[4], a dependency manager for PHP. However, it is also possible to download the source code in other ways, such as compressed packages or by using Git directly. Check out the Download section at get.typo3.org.

When you install TYPO3 using Composer, all extensions and distributions must also be installed using it as well. You can read more in the "Installing Extensions" section later in this chapter.

We asked a few people from the TYPO3 community how they go about setting up a new TYPO3 project.

Michael Schams says "It depends on the project, but I usually use a custom-made Docker container for TYPO3 development. In bigger projects—or if changes by multiple developers are required at the same time—we use shared 'dev' instances. The tools, packages and extensions I use depend on the project, too. My standard tool set is:

- Debian GNU/Linux and Docker as the underlying infrastructure.

- Atom, a simple code editor, or PhpStorm as an IDE (integrated development environment).

- GitKraken and GitLab/GitHub for version control.

- PSR-2 and phpDocumentor to ensure my code follows coding standards.

When I launch a TYPO3 website, I leverage the benefits of modern cloud solutions and set up an enterprise environment on Amazon Web Services (AWS)."

What am I working with?

Once you have installed TYPO3, you'll see some standard files and folders shown in Figure 3-2 and described in Table 3-2.

---

[4]https://getcomposer.org/

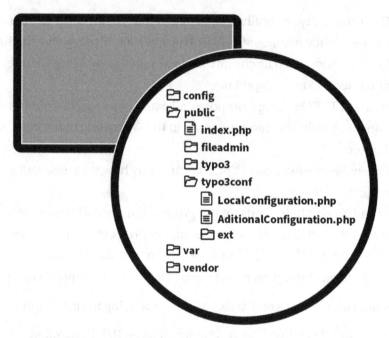

Figure 3-2. *Image listing TYPO3 files and folders*

Table 3-2. *TYPO3 standard files and folders*

config/	Holds information relevant for your website, primarily the site configuration.
public/	This is the main entry point for URLs and the web server's public-facing directory.
public/index.php	The index.php file is used for rendering all TYPO3 websites. It is the starting point for request handling by TYPO3, and you shouldn't touch it.
public/fileadmin/	The folder where all assets, images, PDFs, etc., from the editors will be uploaded and made available.
public/typo3/	The TYPO3 Core source code. This is (like public/index.php and vendor/) automatically updated when TYPO3 is updated, and managed 100% by TYPO3.

(continued)

Table 3-2. (*continued*)

public/typo3temp/	Files like compressed CSS files, dynamic images generated via TYPO3's image generation for scaling or cropping images. The files in this folder are temporary and may be deleted. They are regenerated on the fly when they're needed again.
public/typo3conf/	Holds LocalConfiguration.php, a system-wide configuration file, as well as AdditionalConfiguration.php, which is loaded right afterward. There's also PackageStates.php, which tracks enabled extensions.
public/typo3conf/ext/	All community extensions that are loaded via Composer or the extension manager or created specifically for this TYPO3 website.
var/	Contains system files, like caches, temporary files, logs and sessions, and language labels.
vendor/	The Composer vendor directory contains third-party packages and libraries.

The official TYPO3 documentation[5] provides a detailed list of the contents of the TYPO3 CMS package installed via Composer.

TYPO3 Core primarily consists of the API (application programming interface), which defines a framework for managing project content. The base features of the API include content storage, user permissions and access, content editing, and file management. These features are delivered via system extensions that use the API. All the content is stored in a database that TYPO3 then accesses via the API.

TYPO3 also uses Extbase and Fluid. Extbase is an object-oriented framework written in PHP, developed especially for TYPO3 CMS. To generate the frontend, TYPO3 uses the web templating engine Fluid to combine content stored in the database with static HTML templates.

---

[5]https://docs.typo3.org/m/typo3/guide-installation/master/en-us/In-depth/
ThePackageInDetail/Index.html

TYPO3 Coding Guidelines

TYPO3 Core developers strictly adhere to the TYPO3 CMS coding guidelines. Developers who create extensions are strongly encouraged to follow these guidelines, too. The coding guidelines are documented in the TYPO3 official documentation[6]; most of the guidelines follow industry standards.

Coding guidelines make the code easier to read, speeding up code reviews and making it easier to learn by example. It can also improve consistency, prevent many errors, and facilitate automated testing.

The official guidelines cover these languages and use cases:

- PHP

- JavaScript

- TypeScript

- TypoScript

- TSconfig

- Xliff

- YAML

- reStructruedTest (reST)

The guidelines specify how TYPO3 code, files, and directories should be organized and formatted. With Extbase and Fluid, many tasks work automatically when you respect the naming conventions for classes, files, and methods. TYPO3 uses the "convention over configuration" approach, combined with a logical naming scheme to make the source code as readable as possible.

TYPO3, standards, and PHP-FIG

You're encouraged to use common libraries and standards when you're developing custom software for TYPO3. The TYPO3 community is constantly striving not only to improve the CMS's features and functionality but also to lower the barriers for new developers. To this end, there is an ongoing effort to adopt industry standards.

---

[6]https://docs.typo3.org/m/typo3/reference-coreapi/master/en-us/CodingGuidelines/
Index.html

TYPO3 follows most of the PHP Framework Interoperability Group's[7] (PHP-FIG) PHP Standards Recommendations (PSRs). PHP-FIG is a "group of established PHP projects whose goal is to talk about commonalities between our projects and find ways we can work better together." To this end, PHP-FIG collaboratively develops and maintains the PSRs, which are technical definitions of best practices. In line with open source traditions, implementing PSRs makes it easier to adopt, adapt, share, and improve code between projects.

TYPO3 uses PSR-7[8] for HTTP request messages and the PSR-15[9] "middleware" standard for handling incoming requests and return responses. It also uses some standard Symfony libraries, including Symfony's Mailer API, dependency injection (following PSR-11[10]: container interface), and the standardized event dispatcher (implementing PSR-14[11]).

Approaches to developing with TYPO3

When working with TYPO3, the best practice is to do as much as possible using Core APIs and configuration. If they meet your needs, you get the benefit of Core reliability, security, scalability, compatibility, and ease of maintenance.

Next, look to popular, well-maintained, extensions (see Guide 3: Extending TYPO3). Finally, if you can't find the functionality you're looking for, you can build it. Rather than distributing code in a proprietary way, consider contributing your extension to the TER (TYPO3 Extension Repository). This makes your work available to TYPO3 community members who might return the favor by contributing improvements (Figure 3-3). And if it makes sense, the TYPO3 Core Team is always on the outlook for functionality that can be incorporated into the Core.

[7]https://www.php-fig.org/
[8]https://www.php-fig.org/psr/psr-7/
[9]https://www.php-fig.org/psr/psr-15/
[10]https://www.php-fig.org/psr/psr-11/
[11]https://www.php-fig.org/psr/psr-14/

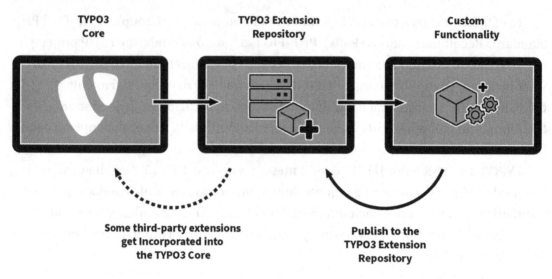

TYPO3   TYPO3 Extension   Custom
Core   Repository   Functionality

Some third-party extensions   Publish to the
get Incorporated into   TYPO3 Extension
the TYPO3 Core   Repository

Figure 3-3. *Simplified customization workflow*

Any time you customize code for your TYPO3 project, you increase the effort required to maintain and upgrade your TYPO3 instance. It is a good idea to document where you customize something or implement proprietary code. You need to be aware of breaking changes and code you need to look at when planning an upgrade—or should security issues arise.

Think of custom code as a liability. Kay Strobach sagely points out that "The best extension you can have is the extension that never got written." He is extending Robert Galanakis's wisdom that "The code easiest to maintain is the code that was never written." Jeff Atwood's goes a little further, explaining why "The best code is no code at all. Every new line of code you willingly bring into the world is code that has to be debugged, code that has to be read and understood, code that has to be supported. Every time you write new code, you should do so reluctantly, under duress, because you completely exhausted all your other options."[12]

Use Core functionality wherever possible. Avoid adding custom code wherever possible. The community, companies and organizations and all the developers behind TYPO3 since the late 1990s have given you a lot to work with.

---

[12]https://news.ycombinator.com/item?id=10979240

TYPO3 and the command line

You can use the command-line interface (CLI) to execute tasks in TYPO3 such as clearing the cache, adding database fields, and importing data.

TYPO3 comes with a dedicated entry point for CLI requests. When you install TYPO3 using Composer, the binary file (which contains a list of available commands) is stored in the "vendor/bin" folder by default.

The extension "TYPO3-Console" provides a way to register and call commands through a command-line tool called "typo3cms." It can execute many TYPO3 actions, making it useful for automation, deployment, upgrades, and continuous integration workflows.

Tip   The more you can automate, the less you leave to chance of human error. Set up cron jobs (on macOS and Linux, "scheduled tasks" on Windows) in the CLI to trigger recurring tasks in the Core scheduler.[13]

Configuring and customizing

Here, we will cover what goes into setting up TYPO3 and configuring it for your specific needs—from business logic to design and usability. Going from a generic TYPO3 installation to something truly yours: your website, your project. We recommend getting started by making a version-controllable TYPO3 sitepackage. Then, we'll look at some key configuration systems.

Start with a TYPO3 sitepackage

Once you have installed TYPO3 and started to build and design your website, we recommended that you create a sitepackage.

A sitepackage is a way to bundle everything your site needs—including the theme and configuration—into an extension.

---

[13]https://docs.typo3.org/c/typo3/cms-scheduler/master/en-us//Installation/CronJob/
 Index.html

Sybille Peters, from the University of Oldenburg, describes what a sitepackage might include

- Backend layouts

- TypoScript for site and included extensions

- Rich text editor configuration

- TypoScript and Fluid for the template

- All template assets (JavaScript, CSS, images, etc.)

There are two approaches. You can download a sitepackage that someone else has created. It will contain everything that is required for building the foundation (in particular the visual appearance) of a website. Not all sitepackages provide demo database content, potentially leaving the creation of a home page and special pages, such as a 404 page, up to you.

Alternatively, you can create your own sitepackage. The sitepackage (whether you download one or create your own) gives you a storage location for your site's static files and configurations that you can put under Git version control and include as a composer dependency. It will be included both on your live site and in your local development environment.

There are potential downsides to leaving design, configuration, and other files you upload to TYPO3 in the default fileadmin folder on your web server. These downsides include security risks, lack of version control, and problems when upgrading. The answer is to use a sitepackage. You benefit from a standard and consistent file structure, just like any other TYPO3 extension (Figure 3-4). Sitepackages make deployments and upgrading smoother, helping manage your dependencies to other extensions and the TYPO3 version. Changes and dependencies in your website design template—HTML, CSS, JavaScript files, etc.–can be easily tracked when they are bundled in a sitepackage.

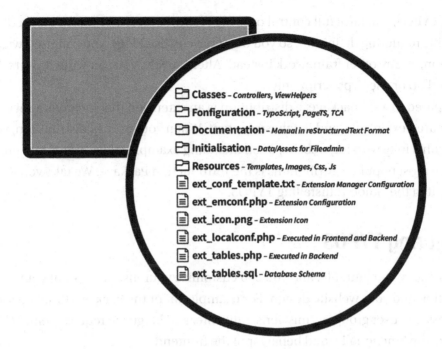

Figure 3-4. *Components of a sitepackage*

When you have a sitepackage that makes setting up projects—perhaps for a
particular use case—quicker, easier, and more reliable, you can reuse it when setting up
new sites. Even better, you can share it with the wider community through the TYPO3
Extension Repository.

The official TYPO3 documentation contains a comprehensive sitepackage tutorial[14]
describing the steps for creating a sitepackage extension without requiring programming
skills. Another helpful resource is the sitepackage builder,[15] which is a tool to help you
build a sitepackage.

TYPO3 uses the Fluid templating engine by default, and Fluid suggests a specific
directory structure to store design template files. Creating a sitepackage manually means
creating the appropriate folder structure and adding files in the places Fluid expects
them to be.

---

[14]https://docs.typo3.org/m/typo3/tutorial-sitepackage/10.4/en-us/
[15]https://www.sitepackagebuilder.com/

With TYPO3, you have full control over the HTML source. TYPO3 isn't locked in to a specific rendering definition, so you don't have to use Fluid. You can use Twig, Foundation, or any other framework instead. Alternatively, you can write it yourself from the ground up or use TypoScript only.

Compared to a sitepackage, a distribution is an extension that includes a set of preconfigured extensions and database content. When you install a distribution, you end up with a fully working website, often including example pages, users, and groups. One of the most popular distributions is the Introduction Package. We take you through installing it in the Guide 1: Installing TYPO3.

Configuring TYPO3

TYPO3 is highly configurable, and you can customize your instance to suit your organization and your website design. For example, tailor the backend to set up your user access and user group permissions, multisite, and language requirements. Then, customize the functionality and behavior of the frontend.

There are several approaches to configuration. TYPO3 can be configured manually in the backend, by installing extensions, or by loading configuration files. We recommend storing as much configuration as you can in files within your version-controlled repository as a best practice.

Configurations can be applied broadly or more specifically. Here are some examples of that configuration granularity and some TYPO3-specific terms for you to become familiar with.

Installation-wide configurations

- Global variables are used for system-wide configuration.

- The Table Configuration Array (TCA) is used to configure how database fields behave in the backend.

- User settings can be configured globally for backend users.

At a more granular level

- TSconfig is used to make backend-related configurations for specific pages and user groups (Page TSconfig and User TSconfig).

- TypoScript is a configuration method mostly used for configuring frontend rendering.

- Flexforms are used to configure frontend plugins and content elements.

- Feature Toggles are used to switch a specific TYPO3 function on or off.

- YAML is used for configuration by some system extensions, like site handling and forms.

You'll find a comprehensive configuration guide in the official TYPO3 documentation[16] that dives deeper into each of these methods.

Table Configuration Array (TCA)

The TCA is a global array in TYPO3 and a central element of the TYPO3 architecture. It defines how fields are displayed and validated in the backend and how fields are used in the frontend by Extbase.

It extends the definition of database tables beyond what can be done with SQL, and it defines which tables and fields are visible and editable and how.

The TCA Reference guide[17] is the complete reference for developers using the Table Configuration Array.

TSconfig

TSconfig allows you to configure the backend without the need to write PHP code. It uses the same syntax as TypoScript.

TSconfig has two variants: configuration for pages (Page TSconfig) and configuration for users and groups (User TSconfig). Its power lies in its hierarchical structure.

User TSconfig can be set for each backend user and group. Group configurations are inherited by any member of those groups. Typically, you use User TSconfig to configure any settings found in the User Settings, enable or disable certain views, change the editing interface, or otherwise change users' editing options. User configuration overrides any configuration set for modules in Page TSconfig.

---

[16]https://docs.typo3.org/m/typo3/reference-coreapi/master/en-us/ApiOverview/
Configuration/ConfigurationMethods.html

[17]https://docs.typo3.org/m/typo3/reference-tca/master/en-us/Index.html

Page TSconfig can be set for each page in the page tree. Pages inherit configuration from their parent pages. Typically, you would use Page TSconfig to make different pages in the page tree behave differently. It is very useful for single-tree, multisite projects.

The TSconfig Reference guide[18] gives a full list of properties and guidance about using and setting TSconfig.

TypoScript

TypoScript is a declarative configuration language. It is used in TypoScript templates to configure plugins and frontend rendering, often in combination with the Fluid templating engine. TypoScript can be looked at like the "glue" between your content in the database and your output rendering. It defines how your data is shown in the frontend, and it can be anything: HTML, JSON, plain text, or RSS feeds.

TypoScript is used to build a PHP array, so it is a language for configuration, rather than a programming language.

There are various frontend templating methods you can use with TYPO3, and you use TypoScript to specify which method to use. (TypoScript can even act as its own templating engine.) However, the accepted best practice is using Fluid templates.

The TypoScript Template Reference[19] lists all the object types and properties of TypoScript used in frontend TypoScript templates. "TypoScript in 45 Minutes" is a useful tutorial in the official TYPO3 documentation, aimed at teaching you the fundamentals of TypoScript.[20]

Fluid

The Fluid template engine is a secure and extensible way to customize the HTML-based output for any PHP project. If you are familiar with HTML markup, Fluid's syntax is very similar. It is encapsulated—no PHP code is ever mixed with HTML code—making it secure even in the hands of a less-experienced developer or designer. The Fluid template engine evolved over time together with Extbase, as a part of the TYPO3 universe. It is now published as an open source stand-alone PHP library and is also used in other CMSs.

---

[18]https://docs.typo3.org/m/typo3/reference-tsconfig/master/en-us/Index.html
[19]https://docs.typo3.org/m/typo3/reference-typoscript/master/en-us/Index.html
[20]https://docs.typo3.org/m/typo3/tutorial-typoscript-in-45-minutes/master/en-us/

Using a templating engine allows you to separate content and presentation. The engine reads content (text, images, etc.) from the database, which is the product of your application's business logic, and renders it using the presentation logic in your template file. Presentation logic can include delivering different representations of the same content, based on context (when, where, or how it is being published).

On a practical level, the separation of concerns means that designers can work on the visual appearance and usability of the website at any time, while the editors get on with their work, focusing on content creation, maintenance, and publishing.

File storage

All files stored in TYPO3 CMS are managed through the File Abstraction Layer (FAL). Files are stored in a location you specify. Information about those files is stored in the database. The FAL creates a link between a given file, the record representing that file, and its metadata in the database.

By default, TYPO3 CMS stores files in the local fileadmin/ directory, which is created during installation. This can be customized and configured. For example, TYPO3 can be configured so that all files uploaded by a particular user are automatically added to a specified directory.

FAL lets you connect your TYPO3 instance to remote storage and data sources like SFTP, Amazon S3 cloud storage, and more, with third-party extensions. Regardless of which file storage you use, users are able to browse all available files from within the TYPO3 backend.

The database record for a given file stores information and relevant metadata like file name, file size, file type, width, and height. Whenever a file is used in TYPO3, for example, attaching an image to a content element, a database reference is created between the file record and the content element. A central reference table (sys_file_reference) tracks where files are used within the TYPO3 CMS installation. The FAL also keeps these references intact when files are moved or replaced.

The FAL is also behind TYPO3's "recycler" functionality, which allows you to restore deleted files or delete them permanently.

Access control options

Who can access what? In Chapter 1, we introduced the concepts of user groups, users, and the different levels of user permissions.

The official TYPO3 documentation has a comprehensive section on user management, covering users, groups, permissions, and privileges.[21]

Configure user permissions

Take time to design backend user groups before you start building your website. Work with your clients or editorial staff to understand their needs and workflow.

TYPO3 supports fine-level permission granularity. You can grant access rights on a per-page and per-user basis, but be mindful that many minute differences or individual permission sets can create administrative overhead and are difficult to maintain.

Best practice is to organize users in groups—"usergroups" in TYPO3 parlance—and to only make changes at the group level. This is far more sustainable and scalable, as users' needs shift and change. Groups can also inherit access rights from each other. Always design user group permissions from general to specific.

Desirée Lochner explains this point in her article "Creating TYPO3 Backend Usergroups Your Clients Will Love,"[22] using a house metaphor (Figure 3-5) to illustrate the different levels.

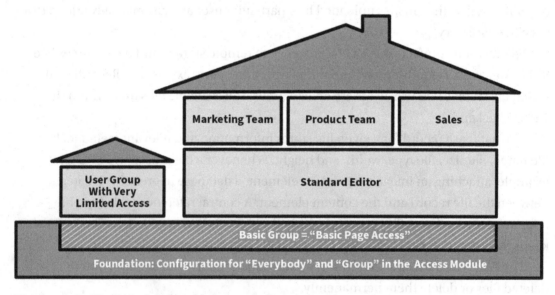

Figure 3-5. *Permission level house analogy*

---

[21]https://docs.typo3.org/typo3cms/GettingStartedTutorial/UserManagement/Index.html
[22]https://b13.com/blog/creating-typo3-backend-usergroups-your-clients-will-love

The "Basic Page Access" level (the preceding "foundation" level) is the most general, and each subsequent usergroup inherits access rights from this group while getting more and more specific. For example, you can configure user groups for editors from different departments, like marketing, product management, and sales. These user groups might need access to different pages and content elements.

Sybille Peters, from the University of Oldenburg, echoes this approach. "You can have a group called 'Basic,' with some fundamental editing rights, and various groups for sections of the website. The number of groups and their relationships depend on your site's needs. At my university, we use hierarchical groups that reflect the organization and the various parts of the website."

If you have translated content, you can restrict editors' access to one or more specific languages.

In the frontend, you can limit access to certain sections or content by requiring a frontend user login, for example, for a members-only part of a website. Frontend logins are strictly separated from the backend logins used by your editors and administrators.

System extensions

TYPO3 comes with some system extensions (as opposed to third-party, community-contributed extensions, discussed later in this chapter) that provide functionality you can choose to enable.

Manage extensions from the Admin Tools ➤ Extensions module in the TYPO3 backend (Figure 3-6). Here, you can enable or disable extensions and access per-extension configuration options.

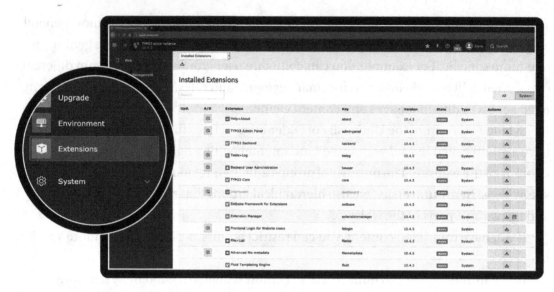

Figure 3-6. *Screenshot of the Extensions module*

There is a range of system extensions, covering a variety of features, such as workspaces, scheduling, and reports.

Daniel Homorodean suggests that the first system extension most users might start with is the form framework, which adds the Forms module to the backend. You can use it to create forms for your website, for example, a contact form. The official form framework documentation[23] gets you started with this extension.

Enhancing TYPO3 with extensions

Some open source CMSs boast about the sheer number of contributed extensions or modules available from their community. In contrast, the TYPO3 Core Team works hard to bring essential functionality into Core, so that websites can be built with less third-party code.

Through the TYPO3 Extension API, all extensions connect themselves to the TYPO3 Core (Figure 3-7).

---

[23]https://docs.typo3.org/c/typo3/cms-form/master/en-us/Introduction/Index.html

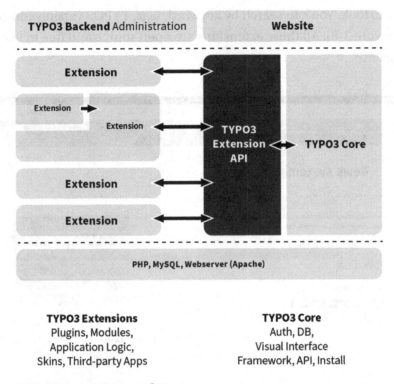

Figure 3-7. *TYPO3 extension architecture*

Even though extensions are provided by various authors in the community, the Extension API[24] and Coding Guidelines[25] ensure that extensions can connect to TYPO3 Core and function well with other extensions and custom code. These guidelines also ensure that TYPO3 maintains a unified appearance and provides a consistent user experience.

TYPO3 Extension Repository

The official catalog of community-contributed extensions is called the TYPO3 Extension Repository (TER)[26]. If you are looking to add common functionality such as a calendar or contact form, or something for a more-specialized use case, the TER is

---

[24]https://docs.typo3.org/m/typo3/reference-coreapi/master/en-us/ExtensionArchitecture/
  Index.html

[25]https://docs.typo3.org/m/typo3/reference-coreapi/master/en-us/CodingGuidelines/
  Index.html

[26]https://extensions.typo3.org/

the first place to look. You can search by keyword, tags, TYPO3 version compatibility, and author (Figure 3-8). All these extensions are open source and free to use under the GNU GPL[27] license.

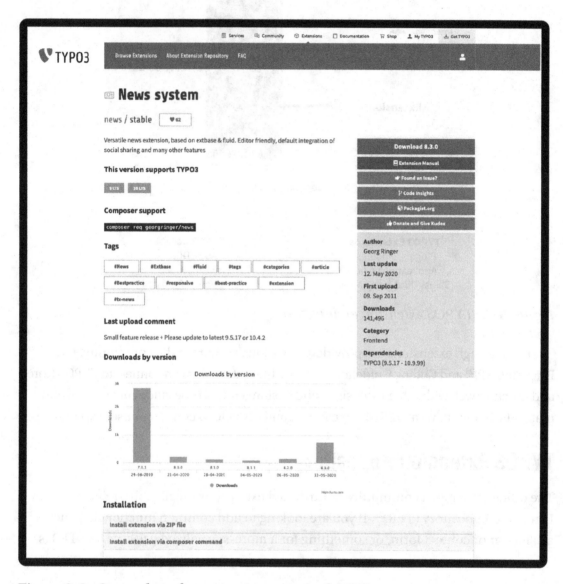

Figure 3-8.   *Screenshot of an extension page in the TER*

The page for each extension lists standard information about it, for example:

- Name and unique extension key

- Status (beta or stable) and supported TYPO3 versions

- A short description

- Author name

- Link to documentation

- Issue queue for bug reports

- Download instructions for the zip file and Composer

The TER allows the community to share functionality in a standardized, collaborative way. Individuals and agencies can extend their capabilities by using other people's extensions, while also contributing extensions, based on their own strengths and needs. We'll talk more about how to contribute your own extension to the TER later in this chapter.

Not all community-contributed extensions are housed in the TER. Developers can also upload their extensions to a Git repository (e.g.) and let the community download the code from there. We recommend that you register your extension on Packagist,[28] the default Composer package repository.

Check out Guide 3: Extending TYPO3

Installing extensions

The TYPO3 documentation includes instructions for importing, installing, and configuring extensions.[29]

Community-contributed extensions are managed in the same way as system extensions, using the Admin Tools ➤ Extensions module (shown in Figure 3-7).

---

[28]https://packagist.org/explore/?type=typo3-cms-extension
[29]https://docs.typo3.org/m/typo3/reference-coreapi/8.7/en-us/ExtensionArchitecture/
   Installation/Index.html

Depending on how you are hosting TYPO3 and whether you are using package management (like Composer) will determine how you install and update extensions. If you are new to web hosting or not familiar with Composer, then using the TER and the Extension Manager module in TYPO3 is an acceptable method. However, if you installed TYPO3 via Composer, you must also use it to install and update extensions, rather than the TER.

The Composer Helper page[30] lists the composer packages for TYPO3 system extensions. You can filter by version and select a default, minimal, or full setup. The page builds commands you can run in the terminal to install the resulting packages.

Adding common functionality

There are robust, proven extensions available for common functionality seen on websites and in web applications today. The TER includes extensions, such as the news and blog extensions, TYPO3 Console, search, and calendar.

Daniel Homorodean mentions news as the first community-contributed extension most people start with. It is a very popular extension you can use to publish news or blog articles, but it provides much more than that. For many, it has become their extension of choice for highly customizable presentation of chronologically organized content.

The mail system extension supports sending template-based emails. TYPO3 comes with a default layout for emails, and the email content is built using the Fluid templating engine. The official documentation[31] contains a guide showing how to configure the extension and how to create and send emails. If you are building a larger, mail-heavy TYPO3 project, you might benefit from a testing tool such as MailHog[32] (which is also shipped with the DDEV-Local development environment) and a relay service such as SendGrid or Mandrill for managing email.

Between TYPO3 Core and community-contributed extensions, there is a lot of functionality available.

We asked a few members of the community what extensions they use. Stefan Busemann, CEO of in2code GmbH, says "I think the extensions which we use mostly are News, Gridlements, Powermail, Caretaker, and typo3_console."

---

[30]https://get.typo3.org/misc/composer/helper
[31]https://docs.typo3.org/typo3cms/CoreApiReference/latest/ApiOverview/Mail/Index.html
[32]https://github.com/mailhog/MailHog

Sybille Peters says that TYPO3 has a "vast supply of extensions for embedding content in a page and extending functionality, for example: News, Open Street Map, as well as extensions for single sign-on (CAS, Shibboleth), and integration with Varnish."

Daniel Siepmann, a web developer with Codappix GmbH, says: "We always use Composer. I wouldn't do any software project without using a dependency manager. Nowadays, you have the concept of the sitepackage, which is considered best practice throughout the community. Use Composer and use a sitepackage."

He adds, "Don't code a new TYPO3 extension for every project. With Composer, you can use any Composer package out there, so you don't have to implement most of the features yourself, because nearly every problem has already been solved."

However, there will come a time when you have a unique need or find a functionality gap and have to build your own custom extension.

Building custom extensions

If you can't find what you need in community-contributed extensions, it's time to build it yourself or engage an agency to help you.

Michael Schams, author of the *TYPO3 Extbase* book, offers some examples of what you can create by writing code on top of the TYPO3 Core: "A site that allows users to configure and order a customized wheelchair, or a site to manage sales contracts and bookings of agricultural products to ship tons of fertilizer."

To customize TYPO3 with your own code, you build your own extension. See Figure 3-1 in this chapter for an illustration of the application layer in TYPO3.

Writing extensions can take a bit of practice. Benjamin Kott, responsible for the UX design of the TYPO3 backend, talks about his experience developing extensions: "I tried and constantly got better and more efficient. I started to question the solutions I found on the internet, which drove me to create new ones. TYPO3 barcamps really helped me. I could present my developed solutions, which were quickly accepted by the community, and somehow I ended up on the Core Team."

Why build a custom extension

There are various reasons why you might consider building your own extension:

- **Functionality** – After searching the TER and Git repositories, you may be unable to find a community-contributed extension that meets your project's or your client's requirements.

- **Deprecation** – You may need functionality from an older LTS version. Over time, some features have been removed from Core, and you may have business requirements that still rely on one or more of them.

- **Community contribution** – You might create an extension that is better than existing ones for a particular task. Contributing to the community like this makes the system better for everyone, and you may reap the benefits of someone else improving your code, too.

- **Incompatibility (maybe)** – After upgrading to the latest TYPO3 LTS, you may find that an extension you're using is not yet compatible with the latest release. Open source developers are people, too. Life gets in the way sometimes. In this case, we recommend that you reach out to the maintainer to offer them help with the upgrade, or even take over as the extension maintainer if the original author isn't able to keep it up-to-date.

Approaches to building a custom extension

When writing an extension, you are strongly encouraged to follow the TYPO3 Coding Guidelines,[33] which the TYPO3 Core developers strictly adhere to. See the TYPO3 Coding Guidelines sections earlier in this chapter for more information. You will need to become familiar with the architecture and style of the framework.

---

[33]https://docs.typo3.org/m/typo3/reference-coreapi/master/en-us/CodingGuidelines/ Index.html

There are many cases where building your extensions from scratch makes the most sense. Writing pure PHP code and calling Core API methods to get data for your Fluid templates combine the full power of TYPO3 with the flexibility of custom code.

Many developers use Extbase, the Model-Controller-View framework developed especially for TYPO3. Extbase ensures a clear separation between different concerns. Using it in combination with the Fluid templating engine, you get a holistic solution.

Extbase ensures modular design, so the development time and associated costs are reduced for both initial development and ongoing maintenance. Extbase also lessens the burden on the developer when it comes to security-relevant and repetitive tasks: for example, the validation of arguments and the persistence of data. Using Extbase means the extension source code becomes a lot more readable, more flexible, and more extensible.

Knowledge in object-oriented programming, domain-driven design, and the model-view-controller paradigm is essential for working with Extbase. Familiarity with test-driven development will also be helpful.

In the article "The TYPO3 Extbase Book—Interview with the Author,"[34] Michael Schams explains that "Extbase follows the paradigm 'convention over configuration'. Once a developer knows the conventions, they automatically know class and method names, properties, where to find files and directories, etc. Following the convention makes an extension logical and easy to understand for other developers."

Watch out: With the ease of use comes another layer of abstraction. Designing ineffective object relations can lead to a slow extension with many unnecessary database queries.

Basic workflow for creating extensions

If you are taking the Extbase/MVC route, you can use the extension builder to create a TYPO3 extension (Figure 3-9). The extension builder is itself an extension available from the TER.[35]

---

[34]https://typo3.org/article/the-typo3-extbase-book-interview-with-the-author/
[35]https://extensions.typo3.org/extension/extension_builder

Basic Workflow

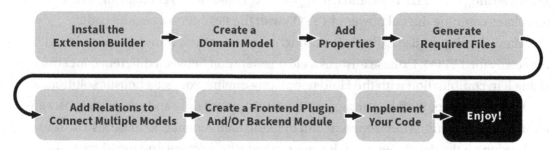

Figure 3-9. Workflow for creating extensions

For the simpler extension we mentioned earlier, the sitepackage builder[36] can set you up with a clean structure to build on, with less overhead.

The extension builder builds and manages your TYPO3 extensions based on Extbase and Fluid. It provides a graphical editor to build your domain model and generates most of the boilerplate code necessary, including the TCA, models, repositories, and language files. It generates the necessary files for you to populate with code.

Both Extbase and Fluid rely on a specific directory structure[37] to work (see Figure 2-9 for an illustration of the structure). The Resources/Private folder contains the Layout and Templates folders. These are mandatory and contain a plugin or module's templates. It also contains the optional Partials folder, which is for reusable template snippets. The extension builder will always create the correct directory structure for you.

If you find that you need to write code to implement several different features, don't put it all into a single extension. Try to limit the feature set and avoid writing one huge extension that does everything. Daniel Siepmann, a web developer with Codappix GmbH, says "It's better to have one hundred extensions with one feature each than one extension which delivers one hundred features. We build smaller packages that can be put together to create bigger things. Compare it to the UNIX philosophy, where you let one program do one job, and do it well. That way, if we don't need it, we don't have to include it. It's not bad to have a hundred TYPO3 extensions if everything just does one thing. You can see exactly which features meet your needs."

---

[36]https://sitepackagebuilder.com/

[37]https://docs.typo3.org/m/typo3/reference-coreapi/master/en-us/
ExtensionArchitecture/FilesAndLocations/Index.html

Fluid templating

Knowledge of Fluid templating is important for building good extensions with Extbase. The Fluid template engine is used to customize HTML-based output for PHP-based projects. It reads template files, processes them, and replaces the tags and variables with dynamic content.

Fluid templating is built on top of XML and is quite similar to HTML. It is extensible and secure by default: it prevents common cross-site scripting (XSS) attacks. You can add custom logic with ViewHelpers, PHP classes that allow you to add complex functionality to your application, such as conditional statements, variables, and loops.

More than 80 ViewHelpers are included with TYPO3, allowing you to generate forms, resize images, embed HTML files, and much more. See the ViewHelper Reference guide for more information.[38]

You can use Fluid-powered TYPO3 extensions for every design methodology and every single layout of your site. Extensions using Fluid are easy to integrate.

Daniel Siepmann, a web developer with Codappix GmbH, explains that some people may consider it a drawback that TYPO3 does not come with standard frontend themes, but he says "I think the power of TYPO3 is that you have to think and implement everything yourself. It's easy with Fluid, because you can copy and paste your static HTML and replace the dynamic parts with variables. This means that you can optimize for your use case and for your customer and have a clear distinction between content, data preparation, and data output. You can attach other output formats, such as PDF, RSS, CSV, and XML."

For more information, see Guide 5: Creating your first stand-alone extension.

Sharing your extension

Now that you have built an extension, you may consider sharing it with the TYPO3 community.

---

[38]https://docs.typo3.org/other/typo3/view-helper-reference/master/en-us/Index.html

While some extensions are easy to share, others are not. This is often the case when agencies develop very specific, custom functions for a client and the code is very use case–specific or proprietary.

However, if your code is open, you can simply share it by uploading your extension to a version-control system such as GitHub[39] or Bitbucket,[40] and letting the community download the code from there.

According to Michael Schams' book *TYPO3 Extbase*,[41] the best practice is to publish to the TYPO3 Extension Repository. This has several benefits:

- It is the central and official catalog of all TYPO3 extensions.

- The Extension Manager module lists all available extensions in the TER and allows you to download and install them in non-Composer installations.

  - **Tip:** Those who install TYPO3 via Composer can't use TER-only extensions. Make your extension available to these integrators and developers by registering your extension on Packagist, the default Composer package repository.

- Your documentation is automatically rendered and accessible at `https://docs.typo3.org`.

When you publish code extending TYPO3, you must license it under GNU GPL[6] version 2 or higher. This means that anyone can take your work and use it, as well as develop it further and republish it.

Anyone with a valid TYPO3 account can log in at `https://extensions.typo3.org`, register an extension key, and publish their extension.

---

[39]`https://github.com/`

[40]`https://bitbucket.org/`

[41]TYPO3 Extbase, third edition (English) Modern Extension Development for TYPO3 CMS with Extbase

Summary

In this chapter, we focused on how TYPO3 works.

It's important to specify the functionality you need before you start your project and how you want your website to behave. This will help you choose the extensions you need to install, define the right configurations, and understand whether you need to write custom code for your project.

You're going to save yourself time if you understand what's available in TYPO3 Core before you add community-contributed extensions or consider writing custom code.

Next, you might like to jump to the Guides section of this book to see how you can get started building a project, step by step. Start with the guide "Installing TYPO3" to set up TYPO3 locally and try it out.

To hone your skills, see the official TYPO3 documentation[42] and the Resources section of this book and dive deeper. There are also lots of presentations and tutorials in the TYPO3 YouTube channel.[43] If you prefer face-to-face learning, consider participating in user group meetups, TYPO3 camps,[44] and contribution sprints.

If you'd really like to look under the hood, you can look at TYPO3 from the inside by browsing the API[45] or look at the extension code published by the community.

In the next chapter, we'll look at launching and maintaining TYPO3. We'll cover hosting, updates, security, and performance, to make sure your website runs smoothly.

---

[42]https://docs.typo3.org/m/typo3/tutorial-getting-started/master/en-us/
  Introduction/Index.html

[43]https://www.youtube.com/user/typo3/

[44]https://typo3.org/community/events/official-typo3-event/all

[45]https://api.typo3.org/

CHAPTER 4

Managing and Maintaining TYPO3

In this chapter, we'll look at how to keep your TYPO3 website or application running reliably and securely.

The TYPO3 Project offers a dependable roadmap and release process. For decision-makers particularly concerned about the long-term cost of maintenance, TYPO3 CMS offers excellent opportunities to maximize ROI, with a six-year official support window for the LTS (long-term support) version of every major release. The community supports major versions with updates and patches for three years. Official extended long-term support[1] (ELTS) is available as a paid service from the TYPO3 official vendor company, TYPO3 GmbH,[2] for a further three years. You get six years of security and regulatory compliance with regimes like the EU's GDPR that require companies to run up-to-date, officially supported software. The TYPO3 platform further offers regular, backward compatible "point releases" for security and other small improvements, and regular major version releases every 18 months, enabling reliable cost, resource, and update planning.

If you're responsible for the ongoing maintenance of a content management system, this chapter will give you an idea of what to expect when upgrading TYPO3 CMS for security patches, maintenance updates, and major upgrades.

Performance is important. We'll cover default settings as well as configurations to optimize speed. We'll also talk about the scalable nature of TYPO3's system architecture.

---

[1] https://typo3.com/products/extended-support

[2] TYPO3 GmbH acts as the official vendor for the open source TYPO3 CMS. TYPO3 GmbH is fully owned by the TYPO3 Association, the nonprofit representing the TYPO3 Project and community.

TYPO3 CMS is designed for security and privacy compliance by default. The TYPO3 Project includes an official security team and industry-standard issue reporting processes.

TYPO3's centralized site management model makes it ideally suited for multisite and multilingual setups and federated cross-publishing. Whether you're hosting international magazine subscriptions or publishing in countless languages, TYPO3 is an ideal choice.

A vibrant service provider ecosystem means you don't have to do it all yourself. You can employ professionals to help you at any stage of your project, from design and implementation to operation and maintenance, and there are excellent hosting options available.

The TYPO3 release cycle

TYPO3 follows a structured development workflow, resulting in a clear and consistent release cycle. Like for many other large and complex open source projects, moving to a process with time-based semantic releases has delivered many advantages. This method makes it easier to communicate and plan, and the pace of development and innovation picks up.

TYPO3's modular structure makes it possible for extension maintainers to plan upgrades in sync with the CMS's release calendar. At the point of delivery, where agencies and organizations are building websites, the regular and reliable schedule makes it easy to plan investments in new development and legacy project overhauls.

Before development begins on a major version, the TYPO3 Product Team schedules estimated release dates for each point-release version—the Development Roadmap.

The TYPO3 Development Roadmap[3] is published on the TYPO3 website. The roadmap

- Outlines the overall goals of each major version

- Details the primary focus for each release

- Includes release numbers and estimated release dates

---

[3]https://typo3.org/cms/roadmap/

- Displays the support schedule

- Provides a PHP compatibility chart

The Development Roadmap outlines the goals for the next major version. These are intentionally kept at a high level because they apply to TYPO3 CMS as a whole, rather than just the version itself.

Per-version support

When compared to other open source content management systems, TYPO3 CMS offers the longest support cycle, as illustrated in Chapter 1, Figure 1-1.

With TYPO3, users can enjoy up to six years of support for each major version:

- **Long-term support (LTS)** - Three years of free support and security fixes by the TYPO3 Core Team and the community for the current and preceding LTS versions

- **Extended long-term support (ELTS)** - Three additional years of paid support provided by TYPO3 GmbH and security and compliance support for older LTS versions.

Types of releases

There are different types of TYPO3 releases during the life cycle of the product. TYPO3 follows semantic version numbering. This means that there are three numbers that make up the version number using the format: "major.minor.patch". Releases of TYPO3 versions are announced on the "TYPO3 Announce" read-only mailing list.[4]

A long-term support (LTS) release comes out every 18 months, but there are numerous releases before and after (Figure 4-1). During the development phase, the TYPO3 Core Team publishes regular, scheduled "sprint" releases building up to the final LTS version. Once an LTS version is released, it is supported with regular maintenance releases containing bug fixes and security patches for 18 months, and security patches only for 18 months more. After this, support releases are continued for at least three years longer under the extended long-term support (ELTS) program.

---

[4]http://lists.typo3.org/cgi-bin/mailman/listinfo/typo3-announce

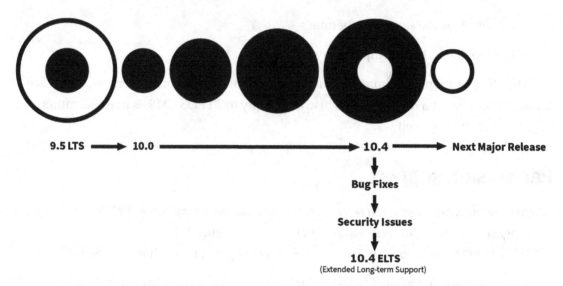

Figure 4-1. *Diagram showing the workflow of the types of TYPO3 releases*

Sprint release

The path toward an LTS release follows the steady cadence of sprint releases. Development during this time is open and transparent; it includes active contribution and feedback from the community. Everyone is encouraged to test sprint releases, with the caveat that they are not suited for business-critical live production sites. A sprint release is only supported until the next sprint release is published, and there is no guarantee of backward compatibility between them.

LTS: Long-term support release

The TYPO3 Project Lead[5] defines when a new version has met the criteria to become an LTS release. The launch of the LTS version is often celebrated with release parties in the community to highlight features, talk with contributors, and help promote adoption.

---

[5]https://typo3.org/community/teams/typo3-development#c7483

Maintenance release

After the LTS is released, that version goes into its maintenance phase. The TYPO3 maintenance release schedule[6] contains estimated release dates for maintenance releases. During this phase, there are also unplanned releases, such as critical bug fixes and security releases.

End-of-life release

The End-of-Life (EOL) release is the final release before the community retires a TYPO3 CMS version. This marks the end of official, guaranteed support for maintenance and security issues from the Core Team.

ELTS: Extended long-term support

After a version is declared EOL, it becomes a part of the extended long-term support (ELTS) program, a paid service managed by TYPO3 GmbH. ELTS can extend your return on investment and prolong the lifespan of your website or web application for up to three additional years.

Note   that you should consider your needs and options and make plans for upgrading your websites well before the end of this additional three-year period.

Updating TYPO3: Minor release

Like any software, TYPO3 needs regular attention.

It is important to keep up-to-date with the latest releases to maintain the health and security of your TYPO3 installation. Security updates and maintenance releases ensure that security threats are neutralized and system stability is optimal. Legal and regulatory frameworks like the EU General Data Protection Regulations (GDPR) require running officially supported versions of software for compliance.

---

[6]https://typo3.org/cms/roadmap/maintenance-releases/

An update describes when you apply a minor or "point" release, for example, maintenance releases, security updates, and bug fix releases. They typically include less significant, nonbreaking changes to code. A point release is a change within a version (e.g., changing from release x.x.0 to x.x.1).

In these releases, the database structure and backend UI typically do not change, because point release versions are supposed to be backward compatible. End-user training would only be required following a version update if there is an explicit change to a user-facing feature or workflow.

When to update

If an update is available, the best practice is to apply it as soon as practical. In the case of security updates, the severity will help you assess how to prioritize the update. You may need to act immediately. If the security update affects an extension you don't use, it may not be necessary for you to take any action. It is advisable and the best practice to react swiftly to every security release unless you can be 100% certain it does not affect your installation.

Sybille Peters, from the University of Oldenburg, explains how she decides when to update:

- **Security updates** – We update ASAP!

- **Point-release updates** – We usually do not update right away because sometimes there are regressions. We test the update first, wait a couple of days, and then update.

- **Major updates** – These require long-term planning. We also use a test system to try out the various steps of the update.

When planning your maintenance schedule, factor in several updates throughout the year. Identify how much downtime they may inflict on the system so you can manage client expectations.

TYPO3 code follows strict best practices, making updates generally quick and efficient to apply. The compartmentalized structure of the TYPO3 Core and extensions makes it easy to quickly apply updates to sections of code as required. The developer community understands that doing it right makes it easier for everyone.

Stay informed

See the "Stay Informed" section of the Introduction for channels and links to keep in touch with information about TYPO3 releases.

Planning an update

Preparing to update requires checking your system for compatibility by comparing your current version to the new one. This will help you understand the minimum system requirements (e.g., PHP versions), deprecations, and any changes to files, paths, and commands.

See the "Stay Informed" section of the Introduction for links to resources to familiarize yourself with the features and changes included in a new version including release notes and the changelog.

Having this knowledge beforehand will give you a sense of scope: how long the update might take and how much effort is required on your part. In addition, it will help you prepare appropriate test cases. It will also help you plan communication with clients, editors, or end users who need to be aware of updates to the site.

Update workflow

Following the all-important planning phase, the workflow to update your TYPO3 CMS is straightforward (Figure 4-2).

Figure 4-2. *Simplified update workflow*

The TYPO3 documentation[7] outlines the workflow in detail. In simple terms

- Prepare your development or testing environment.

- Make a backup of your current site and verify that it is complete and can be restored successfully.

---

[7]https://docs.typo3.org/m/typo3/guide-installation/master/en-us/Upgrade/Index.html

- Download[8] and install the source code for the target version.

- Flush the cache.

- Deploy the updated site.

After the update, follow deployment steps to publish the new site according to your hosting solution. This phase may involve quality assurance and acceptance testing, as well as communicating about the successful deployment to relevant stakeholders.

Upgrading TYPO3: Major upgrade

Typically, a major upgrade involves migrating from one stable long-term support version to a newer one (e.g., upgrading from release 9.5 LTS to 10.4 LTS). An upgrade can also be considered major if there are significant new features, deprecations, or breaking changes in the new version compared to your current version. TYPO3 aims for reliable backward compatibility between versions. Most breaking changes are introduced in the first sprint release of a release cycle. See the section about types of releases earlier in this chapter for more information.

A major upgrade can introduce changes to

- System requirements (e.g., PHP or MySQL versions)

- Database structure

- Visual appearance (user interface)

- User experience, including

  ◦ New features

  ◦ Backend admin workflows

  ◦ Editor experience and workflows

- Content rendering (which, in turn, can affect your templates and styles)

---

[8]http://typo3.org/download/

Due to the potential significance of these changes, major upgrades carry a higher risk and require more time and effort to allow for preparation and backups, quality assurance testing, and potential user training.

Upgrading any custom code in your installation can cost you more time and effort than TYPO3 Core. The good news is that TYPO3 contains some helpful tools that make upgrades smoother and easier:

- **The extension scanner**[9] scans your code for API deprecations and gives you pointers on upgrading your code.

- **The upgrade wizard**[10] automatically prepares a series of wizards to run following a major version upgrade. They will either take care of updating database records and extensions to meet the new version requirements or present you with clear instructions on how to carry out a given task or step in the process manually.

The TYPO3 Project's official vendor company, TYPO3 GmbH, offers paid support options; help is available if things go unexpectedly wrong. You can purchase an ongoing service-level agreement (SLA),[11] or you can have independent experts carry out a project review[12] to check your site before an upgrade. A project review will give you an estimate of the complexity of an upgrade to help you avoid pitfalls and plan where extra time might be needed.

Why upgrade?

Keeping pace with major versions will ensure optimum performance and security of your site and give you the latest user-friendly editing and administrative experiences (Figure 4-3).

---

[9]https://docs.typo3.org/m/typo3/reference-coreapi/master/en-us/ApiOverview/ExtensionScanner/Index.html

[10]https://docs.typo3.org/m/typo3/guide-installation/master/en-us/Upgrade/UseTheUpgradeWizard/Index.html

[11]https://typo3.com/services/service-level-agreements

[12]https://typo3.com/services/project-reviews

Minor Update
TYPO3 Version x.x.2 > x.x.3

- Security
- Bug Fix
- Compatibility

Major Upgrade
TYPO3 Version 7.x.x > 10.x.x

- Security
- Performance
- Backend Features
- Usability Improvements

Site Rebuild
TYPO3 Version 10 LTS

- New Functionality
- Industry Standards
- Optimization

Figure 4-3. *Benefits of upgrading*

Benefits and good reasons to upgrade

- New, useful features

- Faster performance

- Improved editor and admin experience (UI, UX, and workflow)

- **Security** – Stay compatible with future security updates

- Fixed bugs

- Regulatory and legal compliance (e.g., GDPR)

Many TYPO3 agencies upgrade their clients' sites from one LTS release to the next, following the release schedule, every 18 months.

When to do a major upgrade

When a new major LTS version is released (roughly every 18 months), you should consider a major upgrade. See the section earlier in this chapter about TYPO3's regular release cycle.

When planning your maintenance schedule, look at your calendar and identify the best time to do major upgrades in terms of usage, clients, and events. Use TYPO3's development roadmap and release schedule to plan ahead and manage both your clients' expectations and your team's workload.

Read about how to stay informed about changes and release dates in the TYPO3's release cycle section earlier in this chapter.

Planning a major upgrade

Preparing to carry out a major upgrade involves comparing your current version to the target version, to check your system for compatibility with a newer TYPO3 version.

See the "Stay Informed" section of the Introduction for links to resources to familiarize yourself with the features and changes included in a new version including release notes and the changelog. This will help you understand the minimum system requirements, deprecations, and any changes to files, paths, or commands. Unlike a point-release upgrade, a major upgrade will require an in-depth technical analysis for

- Any breaking changes and deprecations in TYPO3 Core

- Third-party extension compatibility

- Deprecations affecting any custom code

- Your technical implementation of the site, for example, how you handle templates

- PHP compatibility with your server architecture

- Third-party services, integrations, CDNs, hosting requirements, infrastructure, etc.

Having this knowledge beforehand will help you get a sense of scope—how long the upgrade might take you and how much effort is required on your part. In addition, it will help you prepare test cases suited to the new functionality and changed behavior. It will also help you prepare communication and training for clients, editors, or end users who will need to be aware of updates to the site.

Alex Kellner, comanaging director at in2code GmbH, has completed many major TYPO3 upgrades and TYPO3 migration projects for their customers. Some of his key findings are

- Communicate.

- Show migration status frequently.

- Report problems early.

- Include your content editors in communication about the schedule, problems, and successes along the way.

Workflow for a major upgrade

Major upgrades require more steps, more checks, more time, and more risk management. The upgrade itself has more steps and will take more time (Figure 4-4). The preparation phase and postdeployment work can be more involved. Quality assurance can be both human and automated, using test plans to verify the upgrade to an agreed "definition of done." You will need to communicate with internal and external stakeholders and make time for staff and user training—and don't forget to update your documentation!

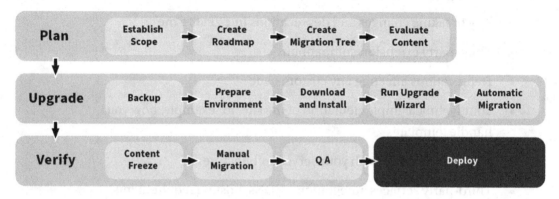

Figure 4-4. *Major upgrade workflow*

Alex Kellner, comanaging director at in2code GmbH, says that for a successful upgrade, the majority of the work is up front, in the planning phase. These are his 13 steps to a successful migration of a large TYPO3 installation:

1. **Establish scope –** Assess the existing site's extensions. How many are there and what is the quality of the code? Do new TYPO3 Core features make any of them obsolete? Consider if these extensions will be updated, replaced, migrated, or deleted. Look at the interfaces and configuration (TypoScript, TSconfig, PHP, YAML, etc.). Is refactoring required?

2. **Create a roadmap –** Work with your client and stakeholders to schedule updates, migration, content freeze, and rollout.

3. **Take a snapshot of the page tree –** Make note of all the current live environment's page types, content elements, plugins, headings and text formatting, image positions, and languages.

4. **Evaluate content –** Work with your client to determine which elements need to be migrated. Are there any new elements? Can any elements be omitted? This analysis is always worthwhile. The "additional_reports" extension shows plugin usage and helps you spot features you might be able to do without.

5. **Start from scratch –** Create an empty instance on a new development server with all required functions and upgraded extensions. Create a new page tree based on your snapshot with all the functions, content elements, layouts, plugins, etc.

6. **Update –** Import the old database and files. Run the upgrade wizard and the database compare function.

7. **Automatic migration –** Perform individual migrations of content from old systems to the new ones. These migrations are executed in the command line.

8. **Manual migration work –** Attend to problems resulting from the automatic migration or changes in content layout (e.g., images or tables embedded in the rich text editor, grids within grids, text spans, image sizes, editor hacks, etc.). You may have to restructure the page tree as part of this refactoring.

9. **Content freeze –** This is the transition time between final migration and launch. No one should add or change any content during this phase. The duration varies depending on the work required and the size of your team.

10. **Final migration –** Step-by-step migration protocol completed.

11. **Manual changes –** Page-by-page checks, for example, to adapt content or add images.

12. **Relaunch –** Take the new TYPO3 instance live (DNS updates, virtual host entries, etc.), enable backend access, and notify editors.

13. **Postmigration review –** Transfer experiences to the next project. Document steps in the migration log. Monitor site performance. Communicate with stakeholders about the success of the process and to show the value of your work.

The TYPO3 documentation outlines the upgrade workflow in detail.[13] Sybille Peters, from the University of Oldenburg, has a lot of experience upgrading TYPO3 sites and shares some of her tips:

- Make the updated copy available to some key users during a test phase and provide a direct feedback mechanism (on our site, logged in members of our organization see a button that takes them to a feedback form).

- Use a tool like "dpxdt"[14] to do a before-and-after screenshot comparison test.

- Run a test that crawls the site and counts errors (HTTP status codes, not including 200 "OK").

- Block backend access for editors during the update. Make the backend accessible for system maintainers only.

Establish scope with an upgrade plan

Upgrading software, especially when it's your mission-critical web infrastructure, can have an impact on many groups of people. These stakeholders can include your client and your client's customers, or your sales and marketing teams. The impact can be massive when it goes wrong—downtime can even mean loss of revenue. Major upgrades need careful planning and preparation. You'll need a plan and a schedule to manage the upgrade and keep everyone informed along the way.

Before you upgrade, enable the deprecation log on your current website so that it can track any calls to deprecated or outdated methods in TYPO3. This will help you prepare a to-do list to use during the upgrade. Depending on the size, complexity, and activity levels on your site, anything from one to four weeks might be needed to fill the logs with a comprehensive picture of the state of your installation.

---

[13]https://docs.typo3.org/m/typo3/guide-installation/master/en-us/Upgrade/Index.html
[14]https://github.com/bslatkin/dpxdt

In the article "Master Challenging TYPO3 Upgrade Projects,"[15] Marcus Schwemer suggests that a good task to include in this phase is to "create a section in the page tree where every available feature and view is visible." This is where the customer can sign off on the features that will be available after the upgrade. From a testing perspective, it shows the part of the page tree you must test. If a feature works here, it can be considered to work elsewhere, too.

Sanjay Chauhan of NITSAN Technologies developed an extension called "ns_ext_compatibility"[16] to help with upgrades. It compares your current version to any target version and prepares a compatibility report (Figure 4-5). You can download a report of all the changes to send to stakeholders to give them an idea of scope of work for an upgrade.

Compatibility Extension

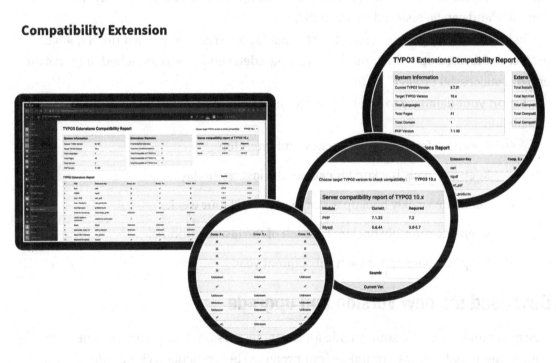

Figure 4-5. *Screenshots from ns_ext_compatiblity extension*

[15]https://typo3worx.eu/2018/12/master-challenging-typo3-upgrade-projects/
[16]https://extensions.typo3.org/extension/ns_ext_compatibility/

Prepare your local development environment

Prepare your local development environment so that you can test the upgrade. Export your database and files from your live site to ensure it correctly represents your live site.

In his article "Upgrading Projects,"[17] Daniel Goerz says "Use the target system requirements. The new TYPO3 Core may need a specific version of PHP and MySQL. Use it as early as possible in the upgrade process to identify issues you have overlooked."

Backup

Make a backup of your current site before you start the upgrade process, so that you can safely revert to your existing site. Once a backup has been created, verify that it is complete and can be restored successfully.

In his article "Upgrading Projects,"[18] Daniel Goerz says "You can get rid of the old project as the last step, some time after the upgraded version was launched. It marks the end of a successful project."

Export your database to an SQL file and make copies of all the files in your TYPO3 installation.

A good practice for backup frequency and retention

- Keep one daily backup for each of the last seven days.

- Keep one weekly backup for each of the last four weeks.

- Keep one monthly backup for each of the last six months.

- Keep one backup for each subsequent year.

Download the new version and upgrade

Download and install the source code for the target version. You can use a dependency management tool such as Composer (our preferred best practice), clone using Git, or manually download[19] and install the source code.

---

[17]https://usetypo3.com/upgrading-projects.html
[18]https://usetypo3.com/upgrading-projects.html
[19]http://typo3.org/download/

If you are not using Composer, which will install dependencies like extensions as well as TYPO3 Core, install extensions that are included with the new TYPO3 version.

Use the upgrade wizard to walk through the steps required to upgrade your database records.

You can build your own upgrade wizard and customize it for your needs. Core developer Jigal van Hemert explains how in his TYPO3 Developer Days session from 2019.[20]

Cleanup

Run the database analyzer to remove obsolete tables, field definitions, and columns from the database. Clear backend user preferences, and flush caches. Check that everything is running and displayed as expected.

After the upgrade, follow deployment steps to publish the new site according to your hosting solution. This may involve scheduling postdeployment quality assurance and acceptance testing, as well as announcing the successful deployment and new features to your client or stakeholders. A major upgrade will most likely also require training for editors and updates to documentation and user guides.

Alex Kellner, comanaging director at in2code GmbH, wrote a possible roadmap for major update projects (e.g., migrating from version 6.2 to 9.5) using his "migration"[21] extension.

- Update:

  - Start with an empty database and the new target TYPO3 version. Create test pages and build your new functions there.

  - Add other required features to this small test instance (e.g., news, powermail, content elements, etc.).

  - Store the complete configuration (TypoScript, TSconfig, etc.) in a sitepackage.

---

[20]https://t3dd19.typo3.com/program/sessions/build-your-own-upgrade-wizard-27
[21]https://github.com/einpraegsam/migration

- Prepare:

  - Import your old database into the new instance.

  - Complete the steps in the update wizard.

  - Compare the database using the Install tool.

- Migrate:

  - Export your new database to an SQL file.

  - Add an extension (e.g., key migration_extend) with a composer.json and require in2code GmbH/migration there.

  - Install the migration extension (e.g., in require_dev section).

  - Start with adding your own migrators and importers to your extension. (Remember to add a configuration file to your extension.)

  - Enjoy migrating, rolling back the database, updating your scripts, migrating again, and so on.

Upgrading custom code and third-party extensions

Extending TYPO3 with community-contributed extensions and writing your own custom code are what deliver bespoke features to your clients and users.

While upgrading TYPO3 Core is usually straightforward, upgrading extensions and custom code will require more effort. For some installations, the bulk of a TYPO3 upgrade may involve updating custom code or finding alternatives to nonupdated extensions.

Custom code

The best practice is to write custom code only when necessary—and keeping it close to TYPO3 Core APIs when you do. This way you can avoid or minimize the risk of code that is hard to upgrade.

Before you upgrade, enable the deprecation log on your current website to identify calls to deprecated methods and arguments. This will help you prepare a to-do list of code to investigate and update as part of the upgrade.

Your ultimate goal is to have no entries in the deprecation log triggered by your own code.

Extensions

Community-contributed extensions don't necessarily keep pace with each release of TYPO3. Frank Nägler writes about typical issues you may encounter when upgrading TYPO3 with third-party extensions. In the article "Issues You Might Run into When Upgrading TYPO3 Extensions,"[22] he explains that extensions can change or lose functionality, be abandoned, or just lag behind the latest version. His article goes on to explain ways to address these problems.

While it is easy to say that you should use as few extensions as possible, Daniel Goerz explains that "You most likely won't be able to run your TYPO3 system without the help of extensions." In his article, "Updating TYPO3 Projects,"[23] he talks about how to minimize problems with upgrading extensions. Prior to upgrading, you should clean up the code base, double-check all installed extensions, and reevaluate the requirements for the system.

Find unused and uninstalled extensions and remove them. As Daniel says, "Every removed extension eases your upgrade."

Daniel recommends asking yourself these questions:

- Is the functionality provided by the extension still needed?

- If you need the functionality, ascertain whether the functionality is provided by the new version of TYPO3 Core.

- Does the TYPO3 Extension Repository[24] have modern alternatives for the functionality?

- Can you implement the functionality on your own?

- Are there alternatives to the extensions that you doubt will work after the upgrade? Don't hesitate to ask the TYPO3 community about this. Somebody might have just the right solution for you.

- How will the PHP version required by the new TYPO3 Core affect your extensions?

---

[22]https://typo3.com/blog/issues-you-might-run-into-when-upgrading-typo3-extensions/
[23]https://usetypo3.com/upgrading-projects.html
[24]https://extensions.typo3.org/

For each extension, decide whether you want to remove it right away, remove it during the upgrade, replace it, or just keep it and update it. After this review, you should have a list and a migration strategy for every extension.

The extension scanner[25] feature is one of the TYPO3 community-built tools that can help you upgrade your extensions. The extension scanner

- Helps you analyze your site to plan and estimate the scope of your upgrade.

- Outlines what has changed between your current version and the target version.

- For each required fix, it includes the issue number and gives an idea of how to address it.

- Provides a status check on custom code by identifying outdated or deprecated API calls.

After working through the upgrade wizard, rather than checking deprecation and error logs, adjusting source code, and executing manual test suites, the extension scanner helps you identify what most likely needs to be fixed by using a traffic light system:

- **Red** - Breaking or removed code

- **Orange** - Deprecated code

- **Green** - No faults found

The results of the scan will help you plan the scope of the upgrade and factor in rewriting code that references legacy or deprecated APIs.

If you are using an extension that is marked as deprecated, it will be removed in the next major release. You have time now to make the necessary changes and update your code to use its replacement. Deprecated APIs remain fully functional until the next major release, giving you or your developers time to migrate your code and update extensions in between releases.

---

[25]https://docs.typo3.org/m/typo3/reference-coreapi/master/en-us/ApiOverview/
ExtensionScanner/Index.html

We caught Sybille Peters, from the University of Oldenburg, during an upgrade and asked her about it. "I'm currently doing an update and our website has been running for years. I don't even know which TYPO3 version it started with, but it's gone through update after update. I would say that the update process of TYPO3, including the Upgrade Wizard, is a really great feature. I'm actually quite excited about it. Especially the extension scanner. The combination of documenting the changes with the changelog, and the extension scanner—it all just works. It's very easy to use and very intuitive."

And if you're so inclined, Sybille explains that "there's also an API where you can write your own update wizards for extensions: If you have your own extensions or third-party extensions, you can go to the update wizard and say 'execute', and it runs your custom update wizard, too."

Upgrading from the command line

Upgrading using the upgrade wizard can be time-consuming for large projects because you have to execute each upgrade step manually. It can also be prone to error if, for example, your TYPO3 installation has a large dataset and hits a problem like the PHP request time-out.

Marcus Schwemer, in his article "Master Challenging TYPO3 Upgrade Projects,"[26] advocates automating as much as possible. He explains

- It's fast. It's quicker to run the upgrade wizards through scripts than clicking through the Install tool.

- It's repeatable. If there is an error in the migration, edit the script and run the migration again.

- It's less error prone. Make a fix in the script each time you hit an error. It won't happen again, and you are done.

You can use the TYPO3 Console[27] extension ("typo3_console") to upgrade from the command line, automating your upgrades to make them reliable and fast. This tool lets you execute all upgrade wizards that are scheduled for execution, making it possible to perform a complete TYPO3 upgrade without any user interaction.

---

[26]https://typo3worx.eu/2018/12/master-challenging-typo3-upgrade-projects/
[27]https://docs.typo3.org/p/helhum/typo3-console/master/en-us/Introduction/Index.html

Daniel Siepmann, web developer for Codappix GmbH, is a fan of TYPO3 Console: "From our point of view it's not possible to do professional TYPO3 projects without the TYPO3 Console because you can automate all the necessary steps in deployment, like clearing caches, running upgrade wizards, and comparing database schema."

Launching and deploying to live

You may start by developing your site locally, but the time will come to share your project with the world. That means deploying it to a web server.

Ideally, you will have thought about your hosting solution early on in your project plan. Clear tool and project-structure choices make deployment easier down the line. With a code repository and a Composer-based setup, you can push your project directly to a modern host using automated build processes.

System requirements

TYPO3 requires a minimum technology stack comprising a web server, PHP, and a database system.[28] The operating system can be Linux, Windows, or macOS—or one of the many common cloud infrastructure setups.

Each layer of the stack and operating system has a lot of configuration options. It is important to optimize each of them for TYPO3.

Web server

At the time of writing, you need a web server with more than 200 MB of disk space and more than 256 MB of RAM.

The web server must be able to run PHP (e.g., Apache httpd, Nginx, Microsoft IIS, Caddy server).

There are some particulars when configuring each of these different server types for TYPO3. See the Web Server Environment settings in the TYPO3 docs[29] to find out more.

---

[28]https://get.typo3.org/version/10#system-requirements

[29]https://docs.typo3.org/m/typo3/guide-installation/master/en-us/In-depth/
  SystemRequirements/Index.html#system-requirements-webserver

PHP

PHP is an open source general-purpose scripting language for web development. PHP scripts can only be executed on a machine that has PHP installed.

For TYPO3, there are several required PHP extensions, and some others are strongly recommended.

For further details, see the PHP Environment settings in the TYPO3 docs.[30]

Database

TYPO3 uses Doctrine DBAL[31] to abstract the database layer from the database management system, so TYPO3 can be used with many common database systems, for example:

- PostgreSQL

- Microsoft SQL Server

- MySQL

- SQLite

- MariaDB

You should set some required and recommended privileges for the database users. See the Database Environment settings in the TYPO3 docs[32] for further detail.

Client browser support

The TYPO3 backend can be accessed with all modern browsers, such as

- Google Chrome (Windows, macOS, Linux)

- Mozilla Firefox (Windows, macOS, Linux)

- Safari on macOS

---

[30]https://docs.typo3.org/m/typo3/guide-installation/master/en-us/In-depth/
SystemRequirements/Index.html#system-requirements-php

[31]https://github.com/doctrine/dbal

[32]https://docs.typo3.org/m/typo3/guide-installation/master/en-us/In-depth/
SystemRequirements/Index.html#system-requirements-database

- Microsoft Edge

- Other modern browsers

It is still possible to use Microsoft Internet Explorer to access the backend, but it is no longer officially supported.

Images

If you would like TYPO3 CMS to process images automatically, you will also need an image processing system installed on the web server. Tools like GraphicsMagick or ImageMagick can scale, resize, and crop images efficiently on the fly at scale.

Moving from local to live

When creating your website and coding, it is common to work in a local development environment that is representative of the live server. Take the time to think about and plan your local-to-live deployment workflow. Here are some examples of technologies you might use. Figure 4-6 shows an example plan of hosting on Amazon.

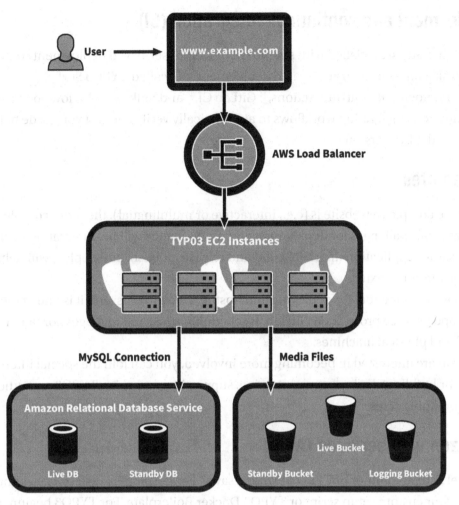

Figure 4-6. *Example AWS hosting diagram*

DDEV

DDEV is a "dev-to-deploy" toolset and hosting solution provider. One of their products, DDEV-Local, is the official, preferred local development environment for TYPO3 and can quickly set up a local Docker-based development environment that works well for TYPO3.

Deployment and continuous integration (CI)

Although many are satisfied with simple Git or Composer-based deployment workflows, TYPO3 also offers its own automated deployment tool called TYPO3 Surf.[33]

Technologies like GitHub Actions,[34] GitLab CI,[35] and Jenkins CI[36] allow you to set up continuous integration workflows to automatically verify and test your code before replacing the live version.

Kubernetes

The more complex a website is (e.g., interactive or multilingual), the more complex the technical challenges for deployment and maintenance will be. Integrating your processes for application upgrade, build and release, publish, and deploy, will help you manage the complexity.

Kubernetes is a tool for deploying and hosting web projects, and it is one of the most active open source projects on GitHub. It schedules, runs, and manages containers on virtual and physical machines.

If you are interested in becoming more involved, you can join the special interest group for building, deploying, maintaining, supporting, and using TYPO3 and other CMSs on Kubernetes.[37]

Amazon web services (AWS)

Michael Schams, author of *TYPO3 Extbase*, says, "For developers: use Docker, either DDEV, your custom setup script or TYPO3 Docker Boilerplate. For TYPO3 beginners or those who need a TYPO3 instance quickly or for test purposes only, try TYPO3-on-AWS."

TYPO3 on AWS[38] is a ready-to-use Debian GNU-/Linux-based server configured with TYPO3 CMS, Apache, and MySQL. It is a stable and secure web hosting solution with full access to the server and to the TYPO3 backend.

---

[33]https://github.com/TYPO3/Surf

[34]https://github.com/features/actions

[35]https://docs.gitlab.com/ee/ci/

[36]https://www.jenkins.io

[37]https://github.com/drud/sig-cms

[38]https://t3rrific.com/typo3-on-aws/

Choosing a hosting provider

TYPO3 GmbH offers an online "Find a Partner" matching service.[39] This tool allows you to search for certified partners based on their location and services, one of them being hosting.

Work out your requirements first, and then shop around. Look for a partner that doesn't just provide a service but that fits your values and feels more like a colleague than a utility provider.

Sybille Peters shares some tips about choosing a host:

- Ideally, choose a host that already has experience with TYPO3.

- Decide what you want to do yourself and what the hoster will do, for example, who will have responsibility for updates and troubleshooting.

- Look at TYPO3 system requirements and make sure the host can fulfill them.

- Consider long-term maintainability, deployment, and version control.

- Ensure the host provides secure SSH access.

- Will you have access to web server logs for troubleshooting?

- Think about what else you might need in the future:

  - Scaling up

  - Search

  - Caching

  - Analytics

  - Image optimization

---

[39]https://typo3.com/services/find-a-typo3-partner

Multisite and centralized site management

TYPO3 makes change management easier because content and settings are managed in a single installation.

The Site Management module (Figure 4-7) helps integrators and site maintainers configure a TYPO3 website:

- Site domains and entry points

- Redirects and routing

- Error handling

- Human-readable and SEO-friendly URLs

- Languages available for the site

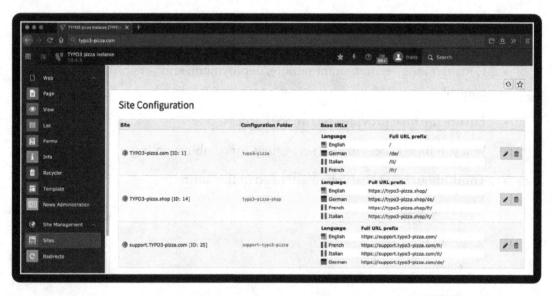

Figure 4-7. *Screenshot of Site Management module taken from TYPO3 official docs*

All the sites within your TYPO3 instance are listed in the Site Management module. These are the same as the root pages with a globe icon in your page tree. Changes to a site in the Site Management module are applied across the whole site at once—meaning they are applied to all subpages of a given root page in the page tree.

Maintaining multisite installations

A well-structured, well-maintained TYPO3 installation with a thousand sites should be just as easy to manage and upgrade as an installation running a single site. The more templates and exceptions from centralized configurations you add, the more attention each site individual will need.

TYPO3 has some powerful features, but the power is best leveraged when you have a structured approach. This starts at the planning stage, before you begin installing or setting up anything.

It is helpful to illustrate your structure with a diagram and document the details. This will help you and your team now, and new team members in the future, to understand the structure when you need to update or override settings.

TypoScript can override and inherit configurations hierarchically, down to a page-by-page basis. To help you maintain a tidy multisite installation, map out the following:

- User group access and permissions

- Content and files shared across sites

- TypoScript configurations, including what is shared, not shared, or overridden

- Page templates that are shared across sites

See Figure 2-8 in Chapter 2 for an example map diagram.

This map will help you quickly find and update configurations and templates and confidently override configurations and templates for a single site (or page).

Maintaining backend languages

Like many popular CMSs, TYPO3's interface has been translated into many languages and can be configured for different users to display the language of their choice.

Figure 4-8 illustrates the TYPO3 backend in English and another language. As shown in these screenshots, if a translation is incomplete, the backend falls back to English.

127

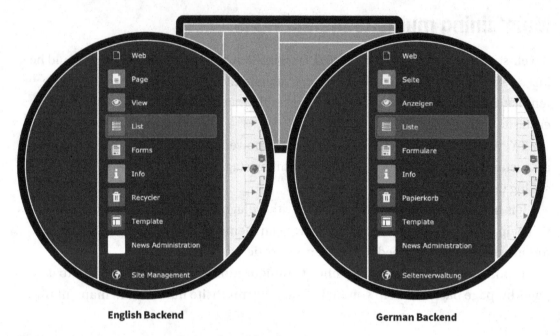

English Backend   German Backend

Figure 4-8. *Screenshot of translated backend*

The translations are hosted on the Crowdin[40] service and are bundled into installable language packages. The TYPO3 community is continually working on adding to and improving the translations. As mentioned in the "Localize Your Backend" section in Chapter 2, translations of the TYPO3 Core are organized by the TYPO3 "Localization with Crowdin" strategic initiative. Crowdin also hosts translations for TYPO3 extensions.

You manage and maintain backed languages in the Maintenance module.

Once you install translation packages on your local TYPO3 instance, you can override and add your own labels to create a seamless user experience.

If you are working in a language that does not have an existing translation in TYPO3, you can add it yourself, either locally within your installation or by contributing a translation to the Crowdin project. Adding a missing translation in your language is a wonderful way to contribute to the project and help others use it. Read more in the "Online Translation with Crowdin" guide.[41]

---

[40]https://crowdin.com/project/typo3-cms

[41]https://docs.typo3.org/m/typo3/reference-coreapi/master/en-us/ApiOverview/
  Internationalization/TranslationServer/Crowdin/OnlineTranslation.html

Remember to check for updates to the language packages regularly to benefit from new and improved translations. You can set up the Scheduler[42] to check and update these for you.

Maintaining translated frontends

You need to add and configure your website languages in TYPO3 to be able to create content translations. The Site Management module is where you define the languages for your content and which languages are available in the frontend. It is also where you specify any fallback rules, which means if content is not available in the current language, an alternative will display.

Chapter 2 in this book covers the single-tree and multitree approaches to multisite configuration for multilingual content and localization. Your choice will affect your flexibility and the effort required to maintain and upgrade your TYPO3 instance over time. Both approaches are valid and can be combined, depending on your needs. The single-tree approach usually results in less maintenance overhead and an easier upgrade path.

The Frontend Localization Guide in the official TYPO3 documentation[43] provides a comprehensive guide to localizing your frontend content.

The translation of frontend content requires time and effort and is an important step to take into account when updating your website content. Depending on the specific use case, some organizations take a phased approach, updating content in one (main) language and releasing translations subsequently. You can, of course, hold off on publishing any new versions of your content until all the translations are ready. In any case, an established, documented workflow is very important for maintaining a multilingual setup. Particularly if you have created language fallback scenarios, it is a good idea to document these and allow extra time for testing before a release.

The localization manager (l10nmgr) and localizer extensions, mentioned in the "Translation Workflow" section in Chapter 2, let you export your content to work with a translation service provider. If you make use of these extensions, factor that work into your upgrade workflow schedule. You'll need to allow time for importing and verifying the translated content.

---

[42]https://docs.typo3.org/c/typo3/cms-scheduler/master/en-us//Introduction/Index.html
[43]https://docs.typo3.org/m/typo3/guide-frontendlocalization/10.4/en-us/Index.html

Find out more in Guide 7: Translating Your Site.

Performance and scalability

Time is money, and in the first few seconds of a visit to your website, performance can mean the difference between customer conversion and abandonment. It's important to configure your site for optimal performance, but it's not "set and forget." You'll need to monitor the speed of your site periodically and keep checking and fine-tuning over its lifetime.

TYPO3 CMS can deliver complex sites with impressive performance. Managing site performance requires a mix of code optimization, server configuration, and caching. External tools and services can help (more on those in the following), but most importantly, a human needs to set it up correctly.

Out of the box, TYPO3 has several key performance boosters:

- **PHP 7 –** The latest version of a fast and performant scripting language

- A unified caching framework that you can optimize for the access pattern of your site

- Built-in configuration options to optimize page load speed (with concatenation, compression, and image resizing), avoid redirects, use a CDN, and more

- The asset collector, which allows custom CSS and JS code to be added multiple times (e.g., in a Fluid ViewHelper) but rendered only once in the output; avoiding duplication and only including the assets that are necessary

In addition to measuring the speed of your site, you'll also want to check in with your users to gauge the perceived performance of your site. Two important user experience (UX) metrics in terms of page loading are First Paint (FP) and First Contentful Paint (FCP). This indicates significant moments in the browser rendering process:

- FP is when the first pixel is drawn on the page.

- FCP (First Contentful Paint) is the moment the first useful data is rendered—the moment when the user can read content on the screen.

In September 2018, an evaluation by HTTP Archive showed that TYPO3 CMS has the fastest First Contentful Paint timing compared to other content management systems.

Performance doesn't only come down to how things are configured. Good coding, following best practices, can make a large difference, too. A common pitfall in TYPO3 is overusing Extbase's object-relational mapping (ORM; how database entries are translated into PHP objects). Object relations can result in hundreds of unnecessary database queries, where a single well-tailored query directly using the database abstraction API would be enough—and much more efficient.

Configuration and settings

To have a performant site, your goals are to minimize the data that is processed and delivered and to do it at the right time. You'll first need a strategy; then you can use TYPO3's tools and configuration options to achieve it.

You can use page analyzers (e.g., Google Lighthouse[44]) and load simulators to check the performance of your website.

Once you know the areas you want to improve, you can fine-tune different settings to speed things up:

- Use TypoScript to enable concatenation and compression of CSS and JavaScript files.

- Check the configuration of your web server, PHP, and database.

- Configure TYPO3's caching to use the fastest available backend.

- Use the latest TYPO3 version and remove unused extensions—they can affect performance.

- Include the CSS files in the page header but mark them for asynchronous load and prioritize with preload.

Optimize your code

During development, you should profile your application regularly. For an initial check, you can use the TYPO3 Admin Panel, which displays the speed of the individual steps when rendering the page. This helps you to identify obvious performance guzzlers.

---

[44]https://developers.google.com/web/tools/lighthouse

Martin Huber, CTO of in2code GmbH, recommends paying attention to the rendering of the menus, because they may require a lot of computing and cause a reduction in performance, depending on their size and navigation depth.

Martin says that another thing to watch out for is having a large number of frontend user groups. TYPO3 generates a separate page cache for each usergroup, even if the content of the page does not differ between the groups. This means a disorganized usergroup policy can affect performance.

Further analysis of the code, primarily the PHP code, is possible with so-called profiling tools. Martin suggests two examples, the free Xhprof[45] and the commercial tool Blackfire.[46]

Caching

The delivery and caching of assets (images and text) contribute to the speed of your website (Figure 4-9). TYPO3 will also cache some configurations, templates, and code to accelerate loading.

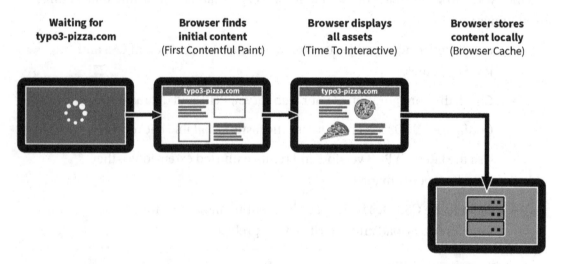

Figure 4-9. *Example of browser caching*

---

[45]https://www.php.net/manual/en/book.xhprof.php
[46]https://blackfire.io

Most browsers will cache assets for your next visit. Content delivery networks (CDNs) are services that cache assets (or pages) and deliver them to the browser. Caching is powerful, but as a website owner, you might want to control when browsers and CDNs rely on the cache and when to freshly request assets from your site. TYPO3 comes with "sensible defaults" out of the box for optimal page load speed, and it is highly configurable, giving you the control you need to make tweaks and improvements.

There are several caches within TYPO3, including the "Core cache" and the "labels cache." In the case of a single page, when TYPO3 displays the page, it also caches the rendered markup (using the "pages cache" and "page section cache"). When an editor makes a change on that page, saving a new content element, for example, TYPO3, clears the cache for the page. The next website visitor to the page triggers a new render, and the result is cached to speed up page load for the next visitor. Benni Mack, TYPO3 Project Lead, expands on this in his article "Caching in TYPO3: Part 1."[47]

The cache entry contains data from all the content and plugins on the page. It takes all relevant URL query-string parameters into account, as well as the current user's login status and their usergroup(s).

TYPO3 caches the output on a per-user-group basis so that, for example, a menu entry that is only accessible to logged-in users can still be retrieved from the cache.

Benni goes on to illustrate what happens when a user visits a TYPO3 website page for the first time:

- All of TYPO3's instructions are fetched.

- All content and all menus are generated.

- All links to other pages are resolved and permission checks are done.

- All referenced images are validated and resized.

This explains why, after a page is cached, loading the page is much faster than the first visit.

---

[47]https://b13.com/blog/caching-in-typo3-part-1-frontend-caches

Make use of extensions to enhance caching of your site:

- Use the scheduler[48] to optimize the caching tables.

- Use a static file cache extension to be able to save a fully cacheable TYPO3 web page to a single prerendered HTML file, bypassing PHP and TYPO3 entirely.

- Use extensions to optimize the size of your images (e.g., "imageautoresize" and "imageoptimizer"). TYPO3 supports responsive images by default.

- Reduce logging and debugging output. A public system in production should never be outputting debug information.

By default, a web page rendered with TYPO3 is stored for 24 hours in the TYPO3 cache, but in the backend, you can choose custom cache lifetimes for pages, from one minute to one month—or to disable caching altogether.

TYPO3 supports these server-side caching technologies, including

- Memcached[49]

- APCu[50]

- Redis[51]

- Varnish[52]

In his article "Caching in TYPO3: Part 1,"[53] Benni Mack says, "Putting the most pressing caches for frontend output into a memory-based cache like Redis or Memcached makes our websites load 30% faster."

A more advanced user can customize TYPO3 to use a different cache backend. Read the Caching Framework documentation[54] to dig deeper into this topic.

---

[48]https://docs.typo3.org/c/typo3/cms-scheduler/master/en-us//Introduction/Index.html
[49]https://memcached.org/
[50]https://www.php.net/manual/en/book.apcu.php
[51]https://redis.io/
[52]https://extensions.typo3.org/extension/varnish/
[53]https://b13.com/blog/caching-in-typo3-part-1-frontend-caches
[54]https://docs.typo3.org/m/typo3/reference-coreapi/master/en-us/ApiOverview/
  CachingFramework/Index.html

You might like to disable caching in your development environment to save you the effort of clearing caches while you're working and developing your site. TYPO3 developer Daniel Goerz explains how in his article "Did You Know?"[55].

CDNs

You can use a content delivery network (CDN) to turbocharge your TYPO3 installation.

A CDN aims to provide high availability and high performance by mirroring large media files and the (more) static parts of your website geographically, so that they are delivered from infrastructure that is geographically closer to your site visitors (Figure 4-10).

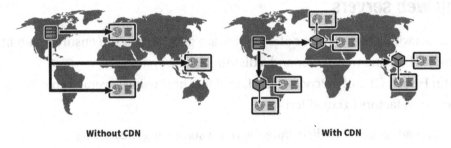

Without CDN   With CDN

Figure 4-10. *Content delivery network*

A CDN typically offers

- HTTP/2 support on all edge servers to help improve speed and optimize content delivery.

- Access to a global network of PoPs (points of presence), reducing latency and allowing site owners to deliver content to users faster.

- Ability to purge by tag, by URL, or purge everything. It only takes a few seconds until the cache is purged on all PoPs.

There are various CDN extensions available in the TYPO3 Extension Repository.

Built scalable and performant

TYPO3 can scale to handle large volumes of traffic while maintaining performance. Its scalable architecture means that it can handle the content management demands and complexity of large multisite and multilingual installations with ease while remaining performant and with minimal impact to high-speed content delivery.

---

[55]https://usetypo3.com/did-you-know.html#c567

A good web hoster can help you find the right technical solutions for your projects' specific performance and scalability needs.

Daniel Siepmann, web developer with Codappix GmbH, talks about one of their customer projects expanding: "For one of our customers, we are working on scaling the TYPO3 installation because it has grown to at least four e-commerce sites. They will add another three shops powered by TYPO3 in the future. We're scaling the infrastructure and adjusting the TYPO3 configuration and the extensions. We are splitting up the extensions and clearly defining the task of each of them, moving code around, and adding further tests."

Scaling web servers

For instances with a high number of page views, a good strategy to ensure reliability is to run on more than one web server and a distributed file system.

Martin Huber, CTO of in2code GmbH, explains how using several web servers introduces new factors to consider:

- A load balancer to distribute the requests among the servers.

- The application files, temporary generated files, and the content (such as images) must be available on all servers.

The common way to achieve this is to deploy the application files directly to the individual servers. This gives additional protection to the application. The files for content and temporary files, on the other hand, must be available on all servers and must exist on a shared file system. This includes the following directories: fileadmin, uploads, typo3temp (up to TYPO3 8), or var (since TYPO3 9).

Scaling the database

To guarantee high performance and reliability for the database, TYPO3 can also use a database cluster. A database cluster consists of several servers, all serving the same data. The cluster keeps the database content synchronized.

Martin Huber suggests considering two clustering technologies: MariaDB Galera[56] and Percona XtraDB Cluster.[57]

---

[56]https://mariadb.com/kb/en/library/what-is-mariadb-galera-cluster/
[57]https://www.percona.com/software/mysql-database/percona-xtradb-cluster

For TYPO3 to communicate with the cluster, you need a proxy in front of it (e.g., ProxySQL[58]). TYPO3 communicates with this proxy as if it were the database server and the proxy forwards the requests to one of the available cluster nodes.

By distributing database queries across multiple nodes, the system remains stable and fast even with many page views. Even if one or more nodes fail, this system can still answer requests.

Independent project reviews

TYPO3 GmbH offers an in-depth project review service that will identify opportunities to optimize performance for your website.

The reviewers are impartial TYPO3 experts. The team does a series of tests on your website to evaluate its performance and assess what can be done to maximize efficiency. The end result is a comprehensive report detailing each area of your website and TYPO3 implementation, with improvement recommendations.

TYPO3 is highly configurable, and sometimes it takes an outside expert with a different perspective to see all opportunities and make your site as fast as it can be. The review will give you recommendations of what to do to achieve optimal performance, maintainability, and scalability.

You don't have to wait until the end of your project to get it reviewed. The team can validate your starting point and determine its efficiency and performance. The review also validates the architecture. You can fail fast, get feedback sooner, and set yourself up for success.

You can download an example project review report here.[59]

System and data security

Security is important and relevant for anyone who is responsible for a publicly accessible website. Everyone involved is responsible for protecting the site against threats to its security and stability. The TYPO3 CMS, with its default security protocols and dedicated security team, makes this task easier.

---

[58]https://www.proxysql.com/
[59]https://typo3.com/services/project-reviews/

Security by default

TYPO3 is a CMS designed with security in mind. It has strict separation between frontend and backend systems and users. The security levels and layers in TYPO3 Core help make TYPO3 websites harder to break into.

However, an application is only as secure as its weakest part. TYPO3's Core Team and all developers contributing extensions are constantly working to make your website as secure as possible. While the hope is that average users don't need to worry about all the moving parts, you should be aware that vulnerabilities can occur not only in the TYPO3 Core and extensions but in every other system they interact with, like PHP, the database, the web server, and the operating system. Refer to Figure 1-1 to see the TYPO3 system layers.

Daniel Siepmann, a web developer with Codappix GmbH, explains some tools that can increase security: "The 'typo3-secure-web' package[60] by Helmut Hummel isolates the backend and the frontend files by placing them in different folders in your web root. This way, you have one place where all your backend executable PHP files are located, and the document root of the webserver contains only entry point scripts and assets. No attackers can access your files directly through the browser."

Benjamin Kott, responsible for the UX design of the TYPO3 backend, describes his setup, "You have to take care that the configuration files of the system are not visible for third parties. I use DDEV to manage my project containers, and I deploy using Deployer."

The TYPO3 Security Team

The TYPO3 Security Team[61] was formed in 2004. The existence of a dedicated team shows how seriously TYPO3 Project views security. The security team members focus on Core, Core components, extensions in the TYPO3 Extension Repository (TER), and infrastructure.

When a security issue has been found, the TYPO3 Security Team follows a policy of *least disclosure*. This means not talking about the issue in public—including mailing lists, forums, Twitter, or any other third-party website until the issue has been resolved and a fix is available. All TYPO3 users are also encouraged to observe responsible disclosure behavior.

---

[60]https://packagist.org/packages/helhum/typo3-secure-web
[61]https://typo3.org/community/teams/security/

When the TYPO3 Security Team receives notification of a potential vulnerability or incident, they first work to isolate the issue and determine what components are affected. The process differs slightly, depending on whether the issue is in the TYPO3 Core or in an extension.

For TYPO3 Core issues, the Security Team works closely with the developers of the appropriate component to verify the problem and devise a solution. The fix is carefully tested and reviewed. A public security bulletin is issued, and an urgent TYPO3 Core update is released.

Any security vulnerabilities uncovered as part of the standard review of TYPO3 are treated as bugs, and therefore work undertaken to resolve them is transparent and open.

When a security issue is found in an extension, the TYPO3 Security Team reaches out to the extension developer. Ideally, the developer acknowledges the security vulnerability and works to deliver a fix to the Security Team. The team reviews the fix and verifies that the problem has been solved before they prepare a security bulletin and coordinate the public announcement with the release of the new extension version.

Unfortunately, extension developers cannot always be reached. In the case where the extension author fails to provide a security fix, all affected versions of the extension are removed from the TYPO3 Extension Repository (TER). A security bulletin is published recommending all users to uninstall the extension.

If an extension developer discovers a security vulnerability in their own extension, it is recommended that they follow this incident handling procedure as well and coordinate the release of the fixed version with the Security Team.

Stay informed

TYPO3 Core security updates, extension security updates, and unmaintained insecure extensions are announced in formal TYPO3 security bulletins.

Each security bulletin contains the

- Version of TYPO3 or extension affected
- Type of issue (e.g., information disclosure or cross-site scripting)
- **Severity** - An indication of how quickly you should act
- Common vulnerability scoring system (CVSS) rating. Further details about CVSS are available in the CVSS user guide[62]

---

[62]https://www.first.org/cvss/user-guide

There is more information about security bulletins in the TYPO3 documentation.[63]

See the "Stay Informed" section of the Introduction for channels and links to keep in touch with information about TYPO3.

Core security and extension security

Historically, most of the known security issues that have arisen in TYPO3 have been found in extensions. The TYPO3 Core has very high-quality and security standards, which are maintained and enforced by teams of developers. Extensions can be written and contributed by anyone, and the code quality can vary.

In the article "The TYPO3 Extbase Book—Interview with the Author,"[64] Michael Schams explained why he included a chapter on security in his book *TYPO3 Extbase*: "Security has always been a hot topic. Compromised websites, stolen sensitive data, and leaked confidential information have a huge impact and can result in significant financial and reputation loss. Looking at the security advisories published by the TYPO3 Security Team in the last few years, most of the vulnerabilities did not occur in the TYPO3 Core but in a variety of TYPO3 extensions. The dedicated chapter 'Security Basics' explains how security processes work in the TYPO3 universe and what typical SQL injection and cross-site scripting (XSS) vulnerabilities look like in an extension. If extension developers understand the background, they know how to avoid these vulnerabilities."

TYPO3 already has a small attack surface. You can further reduce the surface of vulnerability by removing unused extensions.

In operation, TYPO3 distinguishes between activated and deactivated extensions:

- **Activated** extensions are installed and available for use. **Insecure, activated extensions can potentially harm your system:** they are integrated into the system at runtime and can execute code.

---

[63]https://docs.typo3.org/m/typo3/reference-coreapi/master/en-us/Security/
GeneralInformation/Index.html#id1

[64]https://typo3.org/article/the-typo3-extbase-book-interview-with-the-author/

- **Deactivated** extensions' code is present in your system. They are ready for use, but the extensions are not yet installed. **Even deactivated extensions present a potential risk.** Their code may contain malicious or vulnerable functions which, in theory, could be used to attack the system.

As a general rule in software security, you should remove all code that is not being used. In the case of TYPO3, this also means removing any unused extensions. The extension manager can help you do this. You can also use tools with Composer to keep track of versions and updates and scan for unsecure extensions.

Tip   The SensioLabs Security Checker[65] can help. It is a command-line tool that checks if your application uses dependencies with known security vulnerabilities.

The TYPO3 Extension Security Policy[66] has useful information for users downloading extensions, creating extensions, and reporting security issues.

GDPR and privacy-by-design

The General Data Protection Regulation (GDPR) is an important European legislation regarding data privacy. Its advent of GDPR triggered TYPO3 to adopt the principles of privacy-by-design and privacy-by-default in its code and functionality. The TYPO3 Core is GDPR-compliant, and it is easy for developers to build extensions that comply with it and other similar and evolving data privacy laws around the world.

The TYPO3 Core lends itself to compliance because it has

- Nuanced backend settings to configure access control

- Comprehensive audit trails to report on editor actions, for example, to list and revert changes for an entire installation, a site, a page, or a part of the page tree

---

[65]https://github.com/sensiolabs/security-checker
[66]https://typo3.org/community/teams/security/extension-security-policy/

TYPO3 acts defensively when collecting personal data. The strictest privacy settings are applied by default: no cookies are set, all relevant IP addresses are randomized, and third-party media uses the embed URL. In addition, TYPO3 provides tools to assist with the following:

- Access and user management to grant permission to required information only

- Salted user password hashes to prevent password theft

- Set the scheduler[67] to automatically

  - Remove old data such as logs and emails.

  - Anonymize IP addresses in database records after a specified period of time.

- Enforce secure HTTPS/TLS connections for frontend and backend users.

- API to get an anonymized IP address.

Georg Ringer built the TYPO3 GDPR extension,[68] which he offers in both free and paid versions, to control the visibility of information based on user roles and to provide sophisticated data protection, such as pseudonymization and anonymization.

Disclaimer: Even though TYPO3 Core is GDPR-ready, it is your responsibility as the website owner to ensure your website and data storage complies with the legislation. As a website owner, you need to understand what personal data you're capturing and how it is being stored. Users need to grant and be able to withdraw their consent about your storage of their data.

Security reviews

For extra peace of mind, you can hire TYPO3 GmbH to perform an independent security audit on your site as a part of their in-depth project review[69] service.

---

[67]https://docs.typo3.org/c/typo3/cms-scheduler/master/en-us//Introduction/Index.html
[68]https://github.com/georgringer/gdpr
[69]https://typo3.com/services/project-reviews/in-depth-project-review/

This process tests the exposure and vulnerability of your site. The team will analyze the technical condition of your code, as well as the security of your site. The end result is a detailed technical report of findings that includes suggestions concerning implementation, best practices, and next steps.

TYPO3 GmbH does not offer website-building services. Doing so would compete with the agencies and community it represents and is a part of. Instead, it offers products and services supporting and enabling the rest of the community to deliver better websites. The team is expert and discrete. The report provides a system overview, code metrics, and suggestions for improvements, so you can make informed decisions about your site's security.

You don't have to wait until the end of your project to get it reviewed. Likewise, you can get just a part of a project reviewed. The team can validate your security methodology and give you practical advice and recommendations for best practices. You can download an example project review report[70] for more information.

I've been hacked. Now what?

If you suspect your website has been hacked, don't panic—and don't disclose the issue in public (mailing lists, forums, and social media).

Try to identify the nature of the breach. For example, you might notice

- Changed content on your frontend like differences on your home page or downloadable files embedded in your content

- A sudden unusual increase or decrease in site traffic

- Users experiencing antivirus software alerts or browser warnings when visiting your site

It's important to take the website offline. Disable the web server, disconnect it from the Internet, reroute the domain, or all three. It's a good practice to display a "maintenance" page to your visitors for the duration.

Analyze the problem. If you have reasonable grounds for suspecting that the TYPO3 Core or an extension could be the cause, check the security bulletins. If no security bulletin exists for the issue, contact the TYPO3 Security Team.[71] This is a confidential process, and your concerns will be treated with all due seriousness and caution.

---

[70]https://typo3.com/services/project-reviews/
[71]security@typo3.org

When you have identified the breach entry point, undertake a repair and restore process. Then, take preventative measures against future attacks such as changing passwords, applying software updates, changing firewall settings, and implementing an intrusion detection system. Carefully monitor your site in the following months for signs of any new attacks.

You may also need to formally notify relevant stakeholders of the event.

See the "Detect, Analyze, and Repair a Hacked Site" page in the TYPO3 documentation for more information.[72]

Service ecosystem

As a TYPO3 user, you automatically gain access to the vibrant professional TYPO3 community. With a volunteer group of contributors following democratic principles, the TYPO3 community exhibits natural transparency and trust, and lives and breathes the tenets of open source.

In Chapter 1, we covered the TYPO3 community and the organizations that support it. The existence of these groups creates a robust service ecosystem to ensure the quality of your TYPO3 projects. In terms of commercial services, there are many options available to you, including project management, site hosting, upgrading, monitoring performance, and ensuring security.

Whatever your needs, there are resources in the TYPO3 ecosystem to ensure your success.

TYPO3 GmbH services

The TYPO3 GmbH forms the cornerstone of the TYPO3 service agency ecosystem, offering a range of support and services.

TYPO3 GmbH also includes a vetted partner network including specialists available for many industries and use cases from simple to highly complex projects.

---

[72]https://docs.typo3.org/m/typo3/reference-coreapi/master/en-us/Security/
HackedSite/Index.html

You can find an expert partner to provide

- Support

- Coding

- New extensions

- Hosting

- Integrations

- Performance monitoring

- Security analysis

- SEO

The nonprofit TYPO3 Association[73] represents the TYPO3 Project, to ensure its health, value, and sustainability. TYPO3 GmbH[74] was founded by the TYPO3 Association, to steward TYPO3 Association and TYPO3 Project goals; create, support, and promote solutions—products, services, integrations, partnerships, certifications, and education—that enhance and improve the TYPO3 Project ecosystem; and represent the commercial interests of the TYPO3 Project as its official vendor.

The TYPO3 GmbH has a mandate which precludes it from competing with TYPO3 Association member businesses. This means the company won't build your TYPO3 project for you. If you need help to create, launch, or upgrade a TYPO3 site, their "Find Me a Partner" program will help match you with the right agency or freelancer to suit your needs.

Service-level agreements and extended support

One of the main TYPO3 GmbH offerings is commercial service-level agreements (SLAs)[75] and paid extended long-term support (ELTS) for older, otherwise officially unsupported versions of TYPO3 CMS. This is one of the things that sets TYPO3 apart from other open source CMSs: official support. You can purchase the peace of mind that comes with official security patches and regulatory compliance with frameworks like the EU's General Data Protection Regulation (GDPR).

---

[73]https://typo3.org/project/association/

[74]https://typo3.com/services

[75]https://typo3.com/services/service-level-agreements

The team at TYPO3 GmbH will maintain your installation in close collaboration with you or with your digital agency.

With TYPO3, you already get three years of free support by the TYPO3 Core Team and the community. ELTS is three further years of vendor support and a dedicated technical contact from TYPO3 GmbH. It prolongs security and compliance support for your expired version and keeps you legally compliant and up-to-date.

Project reviews

We've mentioned project reviews in this chapter with regard to optimizing performance and ensuring the security of your site.

From reviewing a single extension to a comprehensive project analysis, you can choose the depth of the review. TYPO3 GmbH is fully independent of agencies and their work, so you can trust the results, which are based on best practices for TYPO3 Core.

A project review looks at the use of best practices and relevant issues, including

- Upgradability to the next major version

- Usage of extensions

- Extension upgradability

- Performance

- Assessment of future problems (up to three years in advance)

You can download an example project review report here.[76]

If you are self-managing and self-hosting, you can still access the power of TYPO3 experts by commissioning a project review. You can put the outcomes and recommendations of your report into action yourself or engage someone to do for you.

---

[76]https://typo3.com/services/project-reviews/

Official partners

TYPO3 GmbH manages a network of official TYPO3 GmbH partners.[77] Official partners have to comply with certification and contribution requirements to join and remain certified, which acts as a seal of quality. Partners generally stay up-to-date with TYPO3-related developments and have connections throughout the community. You'll always be able to find someone to suit your project's size, industry, and market.

An official partner agency will be able to offer professional TYPO3 services and deliver high-quality websites, including managing the hosting and maintenance so that you don't have to worry about uptime.

There are full-service agency partners and developer partners with technical know-how. There are also freelance partners for niche projects and expertise, or for when you don't need a full agency. At the time of publishing, a program for official hosting partners is also under consideration.

Find out more about becoming a partner on the TYPO3 website.[78]

Extension support

Your TYPO3 site is probably going to rely on third-party extensions. While TYPO3 GmbH offers SLAs and support for the TYPO3 CMS Core, these services do not cover extensions. These require support and maintenance just as much as the rest of your TYPO3 installation.

Cybercraft GmbH created Coders.Care,[79] which offers a per-extension-SLA model. They work in partnership with extension maintainers and guarantee a quick turnaround on support issues. Extension users get help when they need it; extension developers get support to improve them.

---

[77]https://typo3.com/services/find-a-typo3-partner
[78]https://typo3.com/services/become-a-partner/typo3-partner-program-registration
[79]https://coders.care/

Summary

We've covered a lot in this chapter.

Any CMS solution requires ongoing maintenance. TYPO3 sets you up for success with its excellent, structured support, and community ecosystem. TYPO3 is inherently designed with security and privacy in mind and delivered with sensible default settings in the backend. The transparent, open source approach to development and releases means that you will always know what's on the horizon. A dedicated Security Team is looking out for you.

Built-in to TYPO3 is the capability to elegantly handle multiple site management and multilingual setups; tools for upgrading; and default settings for performance and data privacy.

The community ecosystem offers a transparent approach to development, a highly communicative and dedicated security team, and options for working with others to host and maintain your project.

PART II

Hands-on Guides

The rest of this book is focused on step-by-step tutorials and guides, setting up features that many sites need and showcasing some of the power of TYPO3 CMS.

Each guide starts with a learning objective, so it's clear what the end result will be and what knowledge you will gain by completing each guide's activities.

The guides include

- An introduction with a user requirement, use case, or scenario, so you understand *why*

- Steps to follow to reach the guide's objective

- A list of prerequisites you will need to tackle the guide

- Sample code or material to complete the tasks

- Suggested next steps

- Recommended reference material and official documentation where you can learn more

Each guide is self-contained. You can complete them independently of each other, cherry-picking the ones you want to read to meet your specific needs.

Where relevant, the guides use a fictional scenario where we are creating a website for a book promotion tour. They build on each other, adding different features and functionality to the example site as we go. You can work through the guides sequentially or, if you already have a TYPO3 website, you can use that as a basis for following the steps in the guides.

The final guide, Guide 10: Debugging and troubleshooting, can be used in parallel with the others to investigate unexpected behavior you might encounter along the way.

Guide name	Learning objective	Page number
Guide 1: Installing TYPO3	This guide starts from scratch to having a simple TYPO3 site running on your computer. It uses an extension to create an example website and import demo content into it to explore the backend and start to understand how the CMS works.	153
Guide 2: Creating your first TYPO3 site	This guide picks up from Guide 1 and takes you through downloading and installing a custom frontend theme. Then, it shows you how to configure TYPO3 to use the theme. To do this, you create an extension and get introduced to TypoScript and Fluid.	169
Guide 3: Extending TYPO3	This guide extends the functionality of your site by activating a system extension. You'll also install and activate the popular community-contributed "News" extension.	195
Guide 4: Planning, building, and using content elements	This guide creates a custom content element and introduces the Table Configuration Array (TCA). You'll extend the database and create a Fluid template to render the content element in the frontend.	213
Guide 5: Creating your first stand-alone extension	This guide creates a plugin extension to add functionality to the frontend. You'll gain an understanding of the required directory structure, the TCA, and the power of Extbase.	229
Guide 6: Creating a password-protected members' area	This guide steps you through creating usergroups, restricted content, and a login form so that visitors can log in with a password and access a private area on the site.	255

(continued)

Guide name	Learning objective	Page number
Guide 7: Translating your site	This guide configures your site for multilingual capabilities. It steps you through adding a second language so that you can translate content and adds a language switcher to the website.	267
Guide 8: Configuring content management permissions	This guide creates an editor user with limited backend access to manage content and upload files in the restricted, password-protected area created in Guide 7.	283
Guide 9: Creating a business around TYPO3	This guide is a microhandbook for creating a business around TYPO3. It will show you how to use TYPO3's strengths to target particular market segments and use open source as a unique selling point for your business.	301
Guide 10: Debugging and troubleshooting	Debugging is inevitable, and often knowing where to look takes longer than the fix itself. This guide shows you how to debug TYPO3 quickly and efficiently, using functionality built right into the TYPO3 Core.	311

CHAPTER 5

Guide 1: Installing TYPO3

In this guide, we'll start from scratch and install everything you need to have a simple TYPO3 site running on your computer. This guide is aimed at those who want to see what it's like to install TYPO3 and those who want to explore the backend.

There are various ways to install TYPO3. This guide takes you through one of the easiest and imports demo content so you can get an understanding of how the CMS works. The guide uses a sitepackage to do the heavy lifting, helping you set up and populate an example website.

This guide steps you through installing:

- A local development environment and the infrastructure required for TYPO3
- The TYPO3 package
- A TYPO3 extension that provides a complete sample website

At the end of this tutorial

- You will have a basic website with a backend and a frontend installed on your local computer.
- You will know how to install TYPO3 using the DDEV-Local tool, configure TYPO3 using the Install tool, and download and activate an extension.

Prerequisites

- You need a modern computer, web browser, and an Internet connection.
- This guide assumes that you have some experience using the command line.

© Felicity Brand, Heather McNamee, and Jeffrey A. McGuire 2021
F. Brand et al., *The TYPO3 Guidebook*, https://doi.org/10.1007/978-1-4842-6525-3_5

Considerations before you start

TYPO3 requires a web server, PHP, and a database on your machine. This guide installs DDEV, which supplies a web server and database, so you don't need these on your system before you start. If you have a web server or database running on your machine already, be aware that there may be conflicts. DDEV uses network ports 80 and 443 by default[1], but you can change them if required.

This guide uses Composer to install TYPO3. We recommend it as a best practice, but you can install TYPO3 without using Composer. Refer to the Installation and Upgrade Guide[2] for more information about how to install TYPO3.

Step 1: Setting up a local development environment

The first step is to set up the infrastructure required to support TYPO3. There are several ways to approach this, and you can read more about the different options in Chapter 3.

For this guide, we'll use

- **Docker** - An open source software container technology

- **DDEV-Local** - An open source local development environment that gives us the "AMP stack" (Apache web server, MySQL, PHP) we need to run a website.

- **Composer** - A package manager for PHP that keeps track of dependencies between TYPO3 Core, required frameworks, and extensions. Composer is the recommended tool for installing TYPO3.

All of these tools are available for Linux, macOS, and Windows. This guide presumes you are using Linux or macOS:[3]

1. Open a terminal window, and create a new directory called "demo":

   mkdir demo

---

[1]https://ddev.readthedocs.io/en/stable/

[2]https://docs.typo3.org/m/typo3/guide-installation/master/en-us/Index.html

[3]Using WSL 2 (Windows Subsystem for Linux) should make it possible to use the commands shown here. We have not tested this option in the preparation of this book (https://docs.microsoft.com/en-us/windows/wsl/install-win10).

2. Switch into the new directory:

    `cd demo`

3. Download and install Docker (`https://docs.docker.com/install/`). There are a few steps to this procedure, and the options depend on your operating system.

4. Download and install DDEV-Local (`https://ddev.readthedocs.io/en/stable/`). There are a few steps to this procedure, and the options depend on your operating system.

    ∘ Linux users need to follow postinstall steps.

    ∘ DDEV also recommends using a package manager like Git Bash, Homebrew, or Chocolatey to install it.

5. Confirm that DDEV is available:

    `ddev version`

If you have successfully installed Docker and DDEV-Local, you will see a list of components, versions, and file locations in your terminal. These should include

- DDEV-Local version

- db

- dba

- docker

- docker-compose

- os

- … and a few more

Expected outcome: You now have Docker and DDEV installed.

Step 2: Configuring the project and installing TYPO3 Core

You can find out what files and folders are included in the TYPO3 package in the official TYPO3 documentation[4]:

1. Configure the project to use PHP in a project called "demo":

    ```
    ddev config --project-type typo3 --project-name demo --docroot
    public --create-docroot
    ```

    Press the **Enter** key on each prompt. This will select the defaults for a TYPO3 project with the doc root in the public directory.

2. Download and install the TYPO3 base distribution with the Composer package manager:

    ```
    ddev composer create typo3/cms-base-distribution
    ```

    This shows a warning that the existing content will be deleted. When prompted, select Yes to continue.

3. Start DDEV to start the web server for the new site. This performs some more configuration on your TYPO3 site and gives you the URL of your project:

    ```
    ddev start
    ```

    Your project can be reached at `https://demo.ddev.site`.
    Expected outcome: You now have TYPO3 CMS downloaded and installed.

Step 3: Activating the backend

Now, we will do some work in the browser to activate the TYPO3 backend:

1. In a browser, go to the URL for your site `https://demo.ddev.site`. This redirects to `https://demo.ddev.site/typo3/install.php`.

---

[4]`https://docs.typo3.org/m/typo3/guide-installation/master/en-us/In-depth/ ThePackageInDetail/Index.html#`

The "Installing TYPO3 CMS" page is displayed (Figure 5-1), which is the first step of the TYPO3 installation process.

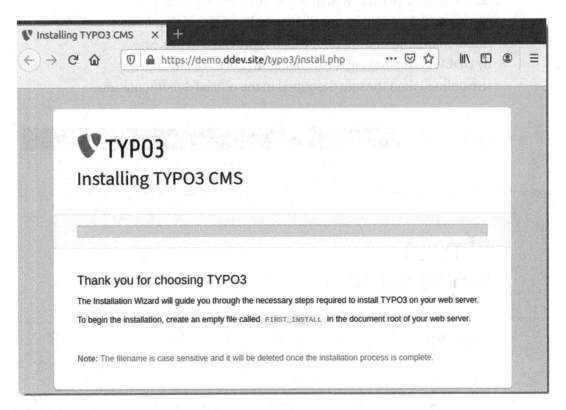

Figure 5-1. *The "Installing TYPO3 CMS" page*

2. To use the Installation Wizard, create a file called "FIRST_ INSTALL" in the root of your TYPO3 Demo project:

    a. In your terminal window, switch into the public directory:

       cd public

    b. Create the file:

       touch FIRST_INSTALL

3. In your browser, refresh the "Installing TYPO3 CMS" page.
   The page updates to show that you have progressed to the
   "Environment Overview" step of the installation process
   (Figure 5-2). The TYPO3 installer is reading information from
   AdditionalConfiguration.php, which is provided in this case
   by DDEV-Local, making the installation process a little more
   streamlined than the one described in the official documentation.

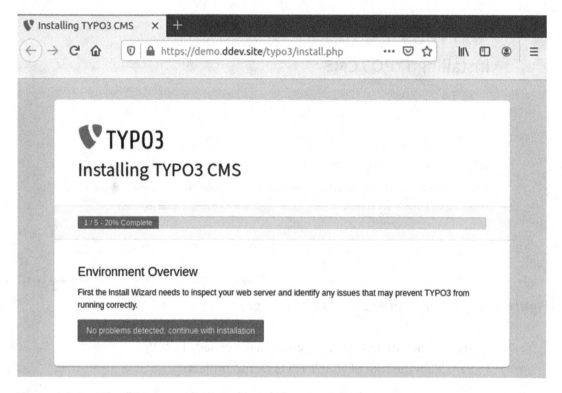

Figure 5-2. The "Environment Overview" step of the installation process

4. Click the **No problems detected, continue with installation**
   button. The page advances to the "Create Administrative User /
   Specify Site Name" step (Figure 5-3).

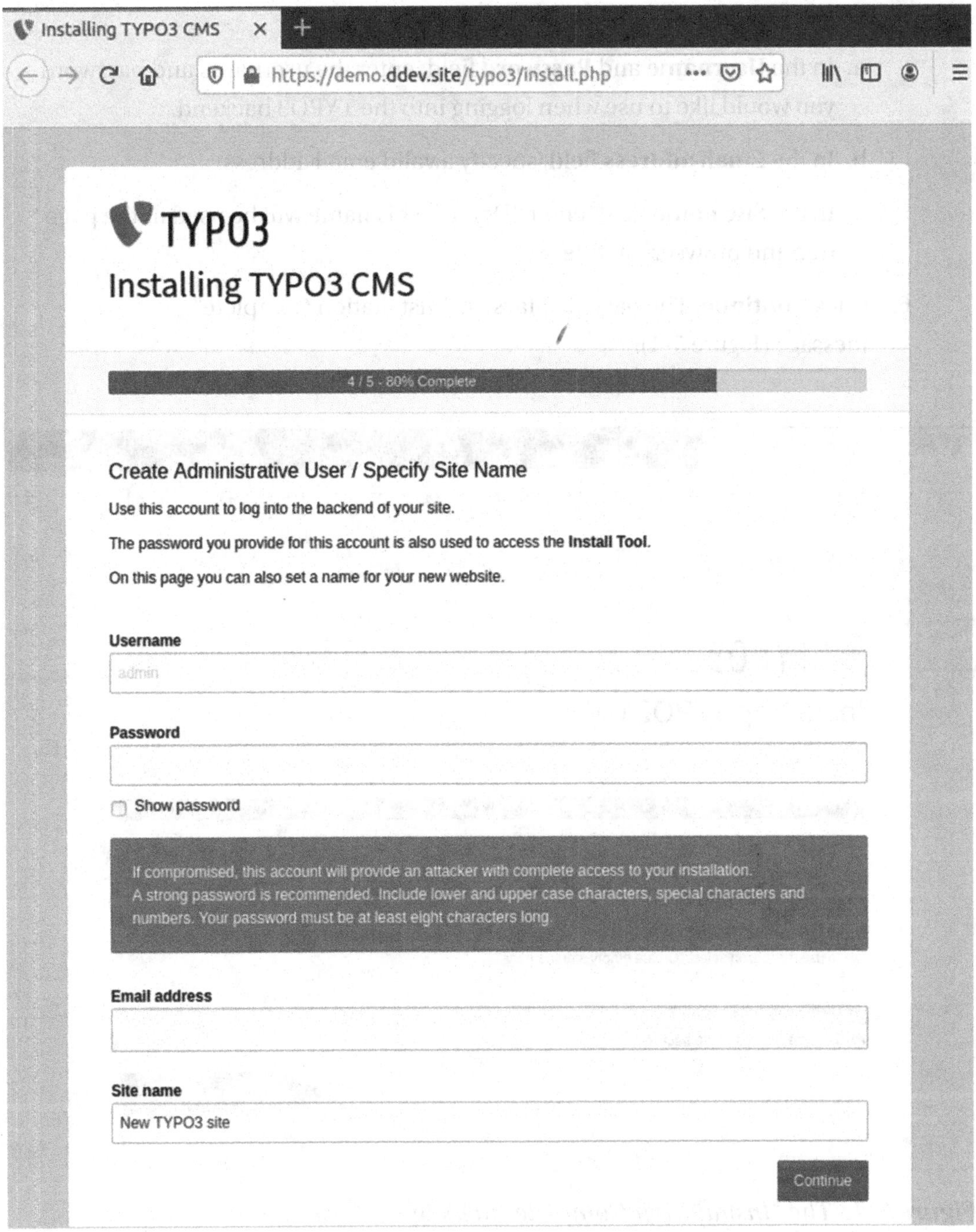

Figure 5-3. *The "Create Administrative User / Specify Site Name" step*

5. Create your site account details:

   a. In the **Username** and **Password** field, enter the username and password you would like to use when logging into the TYPO3 backend.

   b. In the **Email address** field, specify a valid email address.

   c. In the **Site name** field, enter "Demo." This name will be used in the page tree and browser tab title.

6. Click **Continue**. The page displays an "Installation Complete" message (Figure 5-4).

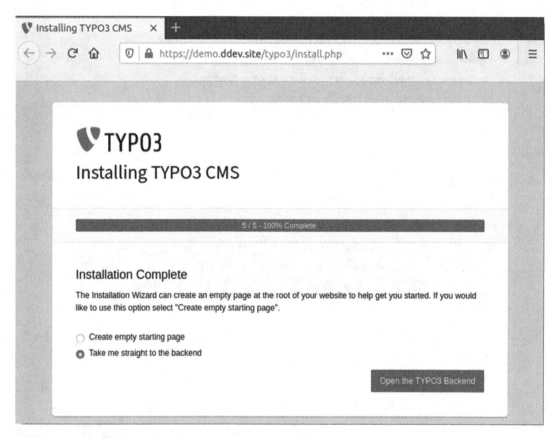

Figure 5-4. *The "Installation Complete" message*

7. We don't need an empty starting page, so leave the default **Take me straight to the backend** option selected.

8. Click the **Open the TYPO3 Backend** button. The browser displays the backend login page (Figure 5-5).

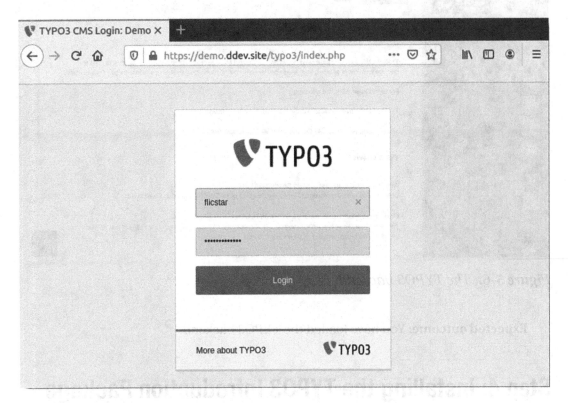

Figure 5-5. *The login page*

9. Log in with the username and password you specified in step 5, and click the **Login** button. The TYPO3 backend will load (Figure 5-6)

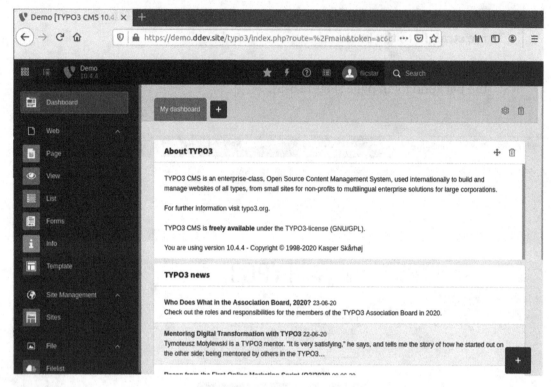

Figure 5-6. *The TYPO3 backend*

Expected outcome: You have loaded the TYPO3 backend.

Step 4: Installing the TYPO3 Introduction Package

Let's look at the frontend URL `https://demo.ddev.site`.

It displays a "Page Not Found" error (Figure 5-7). That's because the installation has no sites or pages, so there is nothing to display yet.

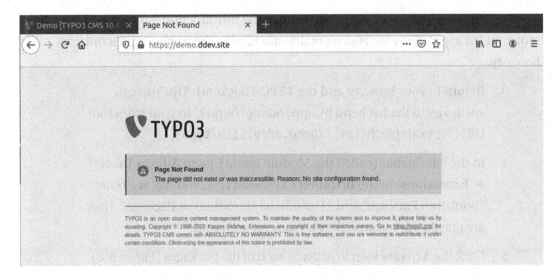

Figure 5-7. *"Page Not Found" error*

When you install TYPO3 from scratch, you have to do some work to configure options and apply a theme before any content can be displayed in the frontend. This is typically done by creating what is called a "sitepackage" in TYPO3.

There are several ways you can approach this:

- Build your own sitepackage from scratch and develop your site in it.

- Install a basic sitepackage that someone else has built and customize it to suit your site's needs.

- Install the Introduction Package and then customize it.

This guide follows the third option, and we will install the Introduction Package (`https://github.com/FriendsOfTYPO3/introduction`). The Introduction Package is a TYPO3 extension that delivers a sample website to demonstrate out-of-the-box features of TYPO3. You will be able to explore the backend administrative tools and functionality, see how content elements are displayed in the frontend, and start customizing your installation—without having to do much configuration beforehand.

1. Switch into your project directory:

    cd -

2. Download the package:

    ddev composer require typo3/cms-introduction

This will download two TYPO3 extensions: the Introduction Package and the Bootstrap Package[5]. The extensions are downloaded to the public/typo3conf/ext/ directory.

3. Return to your browser and the TYPO3 backend. **Tip:** You can always go to the backend by appending "/typo3" to your site's root URL, for example, `https://demo.ddev.site/typo3`.

4. In the left sidebar (called the Module menu), go to **Admin Tools ➤ Extensions**. In the **Installed Extensions** list, you will see both "Bootstrap Package" and "The official Introduction Package." They are grayed out because they are not yet activated.

5. Click the **Activate** icon to activate each of the packages (Figure 5-8).

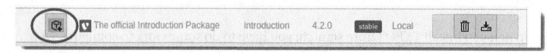

Figure 5-8. *The Activate icon circled in the Extension module*

6. In the Module menu, select **Page**. You will see the "Demo" site at the top of the page tree and, beneath that, a globe icon for the Introduction Package's home page, called "Congratulations." Click it to see its contents (Figure 5-9).

---

[5]If you didn't already have TYPO3 Core installed, this command would also download it as a dependency (the Introduction Package won't run without TYPO3 itself). We've split the process into two parts in this guide to make the steps clear to everyone trying this for the first time. You can install TYPO3 Core and get to work without this package, too.

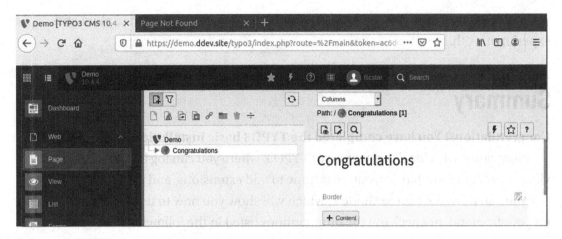

Figure 5-9. *The "Congratulations" home page in the page tree*

7. Go to `https://demo.ddev.site` in your browser and refresh the
    page. After a few seconds, you'll see the Introduction Package
    home page (Figure 5-10).

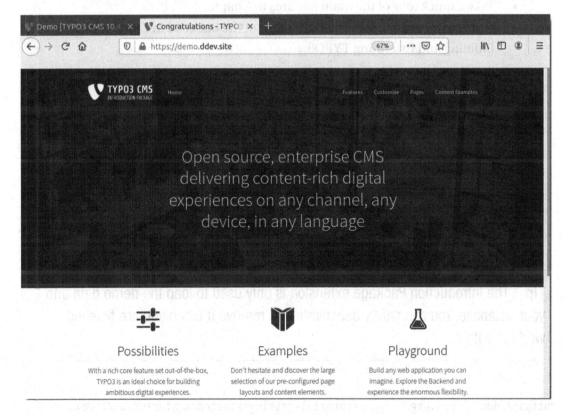

Figure 5-10. *The Introduction Package home page*

Expected outcome: You have an example TYPO3 site that you can explore and experiment with.

Summary

Congratulations! You have completed the TYPO3 basic installation.

Now, you have a local installation of TYPO3, where you can log in to the backend, view examples of frontend layouts, continue to add extensions, and experiment.

You can now move on to Guide 2, which will show you how to use a custom theme for your frontend, or check out the other options listed in the following.

What's next?

Now that you've installed TYPO3, and have a site to work with, you might want to

- Take a quick tour of the main features in Chapter 1, TYPO3 Showroom, or get a more in-depth tour of the backend in Chapter 3, Building and Extending TYPO3.

- Follow the official TYPO3 documentation Getting Started tutorial,[6] which requires having the Introduction Package installed.

- Add version control. It is highly recommended that you keep track of your project, and since the components are managed with Composer, you can add everything to a Git repository to share it or deploy to production servers.

- Move on to Guide 2, the next step in the learning path we designed for you, showing you how to configure a site to use a custom theme.

Tip   The Introduction Package extension is only used to load the demo data into your database. You can safely deactivate and remove it when you are finished working with it.

---

[6]https://docs.typo3.org/m/typo3/tutorial-getting-started/master/en-us/Index. html#start

Resources: Learn more

- The official TYPO3 documentation has detailed instructions for installing TYPO3, both with and without Composer, as well as in-depth instructions for installing for a variety of packages and formats (`https://docs.typo3.org/`).

- You can find the latest release and system requirements at `https://get.typo3.org/`.

- DDEV Documentation includes instructions for installing TYPO3: (`https://ddev.readthedocs.io/en/stable/users/cli-usage/#typo3-quickstart`)

- If you want to start adding more of your own code, see the guide on building a sitepackage and the section in Chapter 3 on TYPO3 development practices.

CHAPTER 6

Guide 2: Creating Your First TYPO3 Site

In Guide 1 (Chapter 5), you learned how to install TYPO3 on your computer and use the sitepackage called "Introduction Package" to render a website.

The Introduction Package is a good way to explore the backend, but probably doesn't look like the website you want to build. You might have your own design in HTML or a theme that you would like to apply to your website.

This chapter picks up from Guide 1, just before installing the Introduction Package, and takes you through downloading and installing a custom theme. The guide shows the steps you need to configure TYPO3 with that theme.

In this guide, you will learn

- How to configure your site

- How to create an extension for your site

- How to add a theme and integrate it into TYPO3 with TypoScript and Fluid

At the end of this tutorial

- You will have your own custom site extension.

- You will have a website using a custom theme.

- You will know how to configure a TYPO3 site and create an empty site extension.

- You will have been introduced to working with TypoScript and Fluid templating.

© Felicity Brand, Heather McNamee, and Jeffrey A. McGuire 2021
F. Brand et al., *The TYPO3 Guidebook*, https://doi.org/10.1007/978-1-4842-6525-3_6

Prerequisites

- You will need an Internet connection and a modern computer with a web browser.

- This guide assumes that you have some experience using the command line.

Considerations before you start

Technical difficulty

This guide gets quite detailed. It is not aimed at general editors or frontend users. It requires some technical ability to understand how files and code tell the software how to behave. No coding is required in this guide (code samples are provided), but an understanding of what that code is doing is necessary in order to benefit the most from this guide.

Time

You'll need a bit of time. The time spent during this initial setup period will save you time later on. Creating an empty site extension gives you the framework for subsequent configuration and easy maintenance of your site.

Roles

Another thing to keep in mind is that people usually play different roles when building a website. Most likely, the same person would not complete all the steps in this guide. You might have a designer to set how things should look, a developer to configure the site, and an editor to add content. We explain the different roles in Chapter 1, "What's in the Box?"

Workspace setup

In these steps, we're going to be using the browser to work in the backend and preview the frontend and the file system to create and edit files. You might like to set up your workspace so that you can view and access all the programs you need. When you make a change in the file system or the TYPO3 backend, you need to refresh the frontend display to see those changes.

Step 1: Creating your page tree

The page tree gives you the framework for your website pages, access, and structure:

1. Run through Guide 1: Installing TYPO3 and create a site called "promotion tour."

    a. Use the project name "promotiontour" instead of "demo" in the ddev config command:

    ```
    ddev config --project-type typo3 --project-name
    promotiontour --docroot public --create-docroot
    ```

    b. Stop after completing "Step 3 Activate the backend."

2. In the backend, navigate to the **Web ➤ Page** module.

3. Right-click Promotion Tour; then select New. You'll see the **Create new Page** screen (Figure 6-1)

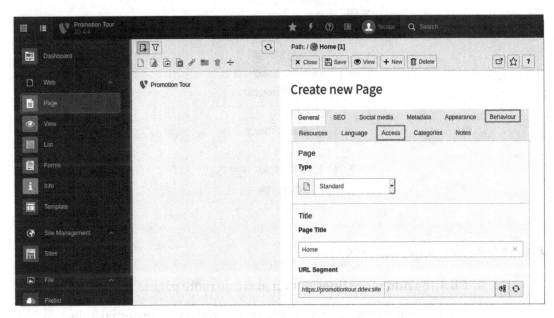

Figure 6-1. *The Create new Page screen, with "Home" as the page title*

4. In the Page Title field, type "Home".

5. Go to the **Behavior** tab, and in the Miscellaneous section, turn on the **Use as Root Page** toggle switch. This will change the icon of the page in the page tree to a globe and make it the root page of your site.

6. Go to the **Access** tab, and in the Visibility section, turn on the **Page visible** toggle switch.

7. Save and close the page.

8. Right-click the home page and select **More options ➤ Create multiple pages**.

9. Create a tree that looks like the following (Figure 6-2):

Figure 6-2. *Example page tree*

   a. Click the **Add more lines** button to create more pages.

   b. Use the **Type** drop-down menu to create folders and external links.

   c. When you are finished, click the **Create pages** button.

   d. Drag and drop pages around in the tree to move them into the appropriate folders.

Expected outcome: You now have a page tree that gives structure to your site.

Step 2: Configuring the site

Set up the basic technical information about the site to make it accessible in the browser (and later online):

1. Navigate to the **Site Management ➤ Sites** module. Notice that TYPO3 has created a site there automatically. This happened when you switched on "Use as Root page" in step 1.5.

2. Click the pencil icon to edit this record. The **Edit Site Configuration** page displays (Figure 6-3).

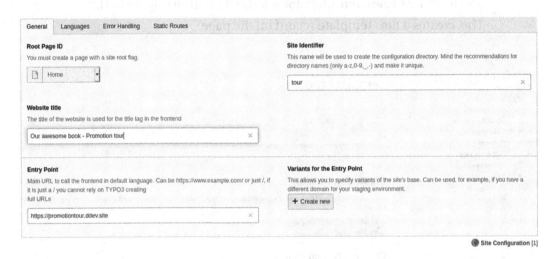

Figure 6-3. *The Edit Site Configuration page*

3. Change the **Site Identifier** from "autogenerated" to "tour."

4. Change the **Entry Point** to "`https://promotiontour.ddev.site`".

5. In the **Website title** field, type "Our awesome book - Promotion Tour."

6. Save and close the record.

Expected outcome: You have now configured the site's URL and title.

Step 3: Adding a TypoScript template

TypoScript is the glue telling TYPO3 *how* to render your website. TypoScript consists of "constants" and "setup." Setup is the actual rendering configuration, whereas constants are generic values that can be inserted into the setup using placeholders, such as maximum image sizes or paths to templates. For more information, see "Using and setting TypoScript" in the TypoScript Template Reference.[1]

In this step, we are going to tell TYPO3 to look for TypoScript in a file in our site extension (which we will create in the next step):

1. Navigate to the **Web ➤ Template** module. Click your home page and then the **Create template for a new site** button (Figure 6-4). This creates a new template record on the page.

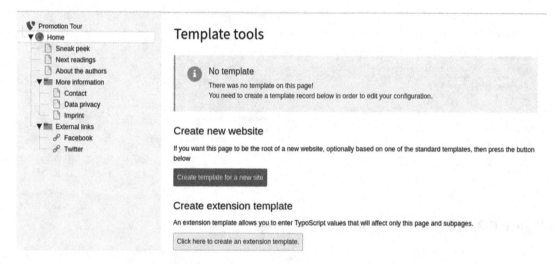

Figure 6-4. *Screen showing the Create template for a new site button*

---

[1]https://docs.typo3.org/m/typo3/reference-typoscript/master/en-us/Index.html

2. In the drop-down menu at the top of the page, select **Info/Modify** (Figure 6-5).

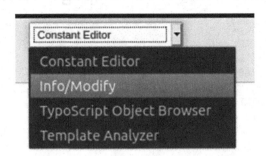

Figure 6-5. *Options in the drop-down menu*

3. Click the pencil icon to edit "Setup" (Figure 6-6).

Template tools

Template information

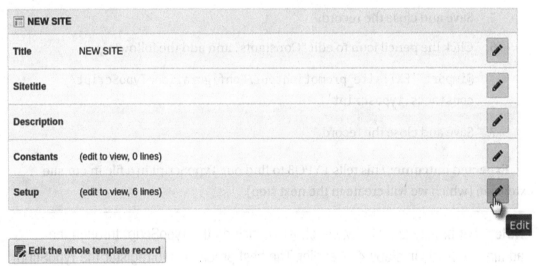

Figure 6-6. *The pencil icon*

You'll see Edit Template "NEW SITE" on page "Home" form (Figure 6-7).

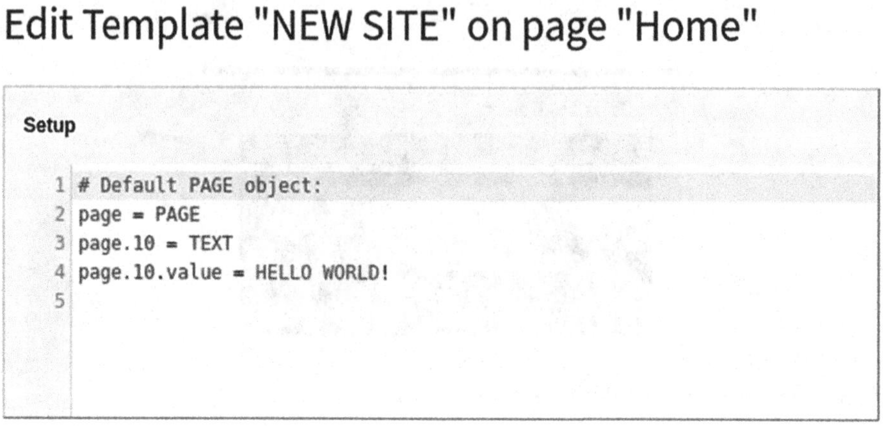

Edit Template "NEW SITE" on page "Home"

```
Setup

1 # Default PAGE object:
2 page = PAGE
3 page.10 = TEXT
4 page.10.value = HELLO WORLD!
5
```

Figure 6-7. *The Setup template*

4. Replace the existing content with

    ```
    @import 'EXT:site_promotiontour/Configuration/TypoScript/setup.
    typoscript'
    ```

5. Save and close the record.

6. Click the pencil icon to edit "Constants", and add the following:

    ```
    @import 'EXT:site_promotiontour/Configuration/TypoScript/
    constants.typoscript'
    ```

7. Save and close the record.

Expected outcome: This tells TYPO3 to find our TypoScript in a file in our site extension (which we will create in the next step).

Note   For brevity and clarity, we chose to include the TypoScript through the admin UI directly in steps 4–7 earlier. The best practice is to register the TypoScript in the sitepackage extension as shown in the TYPO3 extension configuration documentation[2] under "Make TypoScript Available."

---

[2]https://docs.typo3.org/m/typo3/tutorial-sitepackage/master/en-us/
ExtensionConfiguration

Step 4: Creating a site extension

We'll create a site extension to establish a directory structure for TypoScript configuration and other files we need:

1. In the file system for your site, navigate to public/typo3conf/ext/ and create a folder called "site_promotiontour".

2. In this folder, create a file called ext_emconf.php.

3. Paste the following meta information into the file:

```php
<?php
$EM_CONF[$_EXTKEY] = [
    'title' => 'Promotion Tour Site Extension',
    'description' => 'All templates and assets for the website
    promotion tour',
    'category' => 'fe',
    'author' => 'A new TYPO3 star',
    'author_email' => 'nobody@acme.com',
    'state' => 'stable',
    'clearCacheOnLoad' => 1,
    'version' => '1.0.0',
    'constraints' => [
        'depends' =>
            [
                'typo3' => '10.4.0-10.4.99',
                'fluid_styled_content' => '10.4.0-10.4.99'
            ],
        'conflicts' => [],
        'suggests' => [],
    ],
];
```

4. Optionally, you can create an SVG graphic or 64x64 pixel PNG to use as an icon in the Extension Manager module. Create the following new directory, public/typo3conf/ext/ site_promotiontour/Resources/Public/Icons/, and put your file

image into it. Files called Extension.png or Extension.svg will automatically be detected by TYPO3.

5. Go to your TYPO3 backend and navigate to the **Admin Tools ➤ Extensions** module. This is the extension manager, and it lists all installed extensions. The Promotion Tour site extension is disabled and grayed out (Figure 6-8).

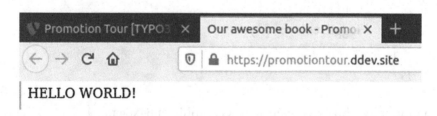

Figure 6-8.   *The disabled, grayed out extension, with the Activate icon circled*

6. Click the **Activate** icon to activate the extension.

7. In the file system for your site, create the following new directory: public/typo3conf/ext/site_promotiontour/Configuration/ TypoScript.

8. Create a file called "setup.typoscript" and paste in the following:

```
page = PAGE
page.10 = TEXT
page.10.value = Hello new world
```

9. In the backend, navigate to the **Web ➤ Page** module, select the home page, and then click the **View web page** icon to preview your website. You should see output shown in Figure 6-9.

> **⚑ Promotion Tour [TYPO3** ×   **Our awesome book - Promo** ×   **+**
>
> ← → C ⌂   🛡 🔒 https://promotiontour.**ddev.site**
>
> HELLO WORLD!

Figure 6-9.   *Website preview*

Expected outcome: This demonstrates how TypoScript influences the display.

Step 5: Including an HTML theme

We would like to use Fluid for templating. You can define everything within the <body> tag using Fluid, but you'll use TypoScript to define how Fluid will work. TypoScript can also be used to configure other parts of the HTML page. Let's see how we do that:

1. Navigate to `https://html5up.net/future-imperfect`, and download the "future imperfect" theme.

2. Extract the contents into

   `public/typo3conf/ext/site_promotiontour/Resources/`
   `Public/External`

3. In the root directory, there is an index.html file. We will take the relevant information from the <head> and the footer JavaScript parts of the index.html and put them into TypoScript. Navigate to your setup.typoscript file and replace the contents with the following:

```
page = PAGE
page {
    meta.viewport = width=device-width, initial-scale=1, user-
    scalable=no
    includeCSS.theme = EXT:site_promotiontour/Resources/Public/
    External/assets/css/main.css
    bodyTag = <body class="is-preload">
    includeJSFooter {
      theme-file1 = EXT:site_promotiontour/Resources/Public/
      External/assets/js/jquery.min.js
      theme-file2 = EXT:site_promotiontour/Resources/Public/
      External/assets/js/browser.min.js
      theme-file3 = EXT:site_promotiontour/Resources/Public/
      External/assets/js/breakpoints.min.js
      theme-file4 = EXT:site_promotiontour/Resources/Public/
      External/assets/js/util.js
      theme-file5 = EXT:site_promotiontour/Resources/Public/
      External/assets/js/main.js
    }
}
```

```
10 = FLUIDTEMPLATE
10.templateRootPaths.10 = {$page.templates.templateRootPath}
10.partialsRootPaths.10 = {$page.templates.partialRootPath}
10.layoutRootPaths.10 = {$page.templates.layoutRootPath}
10.templateName = Default
10.dataProcessing {
    1 = TYPO3\CMS\Frontend\DataProcessing\SiteProcessor
    1.as = site
    10 = TYPO3\CMS\Frontend\DataProcessing\MenuProcessor
    10 {
        levels = 1
        as = headerMenu
    }
}
}
```

4. Next, create a new file in the same folder called constants.
   typoscript. This file contains TypoScript constants (see "Step 3:
   Adding a TypoScript template"). Paste in the following:

```
# page
page.templates {
    layoutRootPath = EXT:site_promotiontour/Resources/Private/
    Layouts/Page/
    partialRootPath = EXT:site_promotiontour/Resources/Private/
    Partials/Page/
    templateRootPath = EXT:site_promotiontour/Resources/Private/
    Templates/Page/
}
# content
styles.templates {
    layoutRootPath = EXT:site_promotiontour/Resources/Private/
    Layouts/ContentElements/
    partialRootPath = EXT:site_promotiontour/Resources/Private/
    Partials/ContentElements/
```

```
templateRootPath = EXT:site_promotiontour/Resources/Private/
Templates/ContentElements/
}
```

5. Everything else within the \<body\> tag of the index.html file can be put into a Fluid template. Copy the "index.html" file, and paste it into the following new directory:

    ```
    public/typo3conf/ext/site_promotiontour/Resources/
    Private/Templates/Page
    ```

6. Rename the file to Default.html.

7. Edit the file to remove the opening and closing HTML, head, and body tags. Retain the contents of the body tag.

Expected outcome: In your browser, refresh the preview of the website. You should see the content of the Default.html file with beautiful styling. Clear the browser cache and refresh the preview if you don't.

Note   For brevity and clarity, we have included CSS and JavaScript through TypoScript in step 3 earlier. You can also use the Fluid view helpers f:asset.css[3] and f:asset.script[4] to include the files. This way, the files will only be included if the template is rendered—ideal for content elements.

Step 6: Replacing the theme content with dynamic parts

In this step we'll build the navigation menu for the website in Fluid. We'll also make the website logo dynamically link to the home page:

1. In the file system for your site, go to the Fluid template (Default. html) that we created in the previous step.

---

[3]https://docs.typo3.org/other/typo3/view-helper-reference/10.4/en-us/typo3/fluid/latest/Asset/Css.html

[4]https://docs.typo3.org/other/typo3/view-helper-reference/10.4/en-us/typo3/fluid/latest/Asset/Script.html

2. Edit the file, and replace the <header> tag with the following to insert the navigation menu:

```
<header id="header">
    <h1><f:link.page pageUid="1">{site.configuration.
    websiteTitle}</f:link.page></h1>
    <nav class="links">
        <ul>
            <f:for each="{headerMenu}" as="menuItem">
                <li class="{f:if(condition: menuItem.active,
                then:'active')}">
                    <a href="{menuItem.link}" target="
                    {menuItem.target}" title="{menuItem.
                    title}">{menuItem.title}</a>
                </li>
            </f:for>
        </ul>
    </nav>
    <nav class="main">
        <ul>
            <li class="menu">
                <a class="fa-bars" href="#menu">Menu</a>
            </li>
        </ul>
    </nav>
</header>
```

Tip   In some areas, the text is replaced with braces "{}". These are placeholders (also known as "object accessors") for the variables we set in TypoScript. Braces are also used for view helpers in a shorthand syntax: {f:if(condition: active, then: 'active')} is the same as <f:if condition="{active} "><f:then>active</f:then></f:if>.

---

3. Replace the Links section with the following:

```
<!-- Links -->
<section>
    <ul class="links">
        <f:for each="{popoverMenu}" as="menuItem">
            <li class="{f:if(condition: menuItem.active,
            then:'active')}">
                <a href="{menuItem.link}" target="{menuItem.
                target}" title="{menuItem.title}">
                    <h3>{menuItem.title}</h3>
                    <p>{menuItem.subtitle}</p>
                </a>
            </li>
        </f:for>
    </ul>
</section>
```

4. Navigate to the backend and look at the page tree. The navigation
    menu of your website mirrors the page tree, but does not render
    the folders. To display the subpages of the "More information"
    folder, we need to find out the page ID.

5. Hover over the folder icon in the page tree to display the ID. In this case, it is id=5 (Figure 6-10).

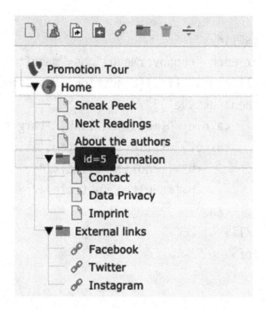

Figure 6-10. *The ID shown when the cursor is hovered over an item in the page tree*

6. In the file system, navigate to the setup.typoscript file. We need to add the page ID of the "More information" folder to our TypoScript. In our case, the page ID is 5, so we specify that toward the end, where it says "special.value = 5". Add the following to the 10.data Processing section:

```
10.dataProcessing {
    1 = TYPO3\CMS\Frontend\DataProcessing\SiteProcessor
    1.as = site
    10 = TYPO3\CMS\Frontend\DataProcessing\MenuProcessor
    10 {
            levels = 1
            as = headerMenu
        }
    20 = TYPO3\CMS\Frontend\DataProcessing\MenuProcessor
    20 {
            special = directory
            # Replace 5 below with the page ID
```

```
            special.value = 5
            as = popoverMenu
        }
    }
```

Expected outcome: In your browser, refresh the preview of the website. You should see the pages of your page tree displayed as a menu across the top of the page, with the three line "hamburger" contextual menu displaying the subpages of the "More information" folder (Figure 6-11).

OUR AWESOME BOOK - PROMOTION TOUR   SNEAK PEEK   NEXT READINGS   ABOUT THE AUTHORS   ≡

Figure 6-11. *The navigation menu*

Tip   Best practice is to use constants to specify page IDs. If you would like to test your skills, try moving the page ID into a TypoScript constant. If your constant is called "informationPid," you can reference it in the TypoScript above like this:

```
special.value = {$informationPid}
```

Step 7: Creating content

In this step we'll add some simple text and image content:

1. In the backend, navigate to the **Web ➤ Page** module. Select the "Home" page in your page tree and then click the **+ Content** button (Figure 6-12).

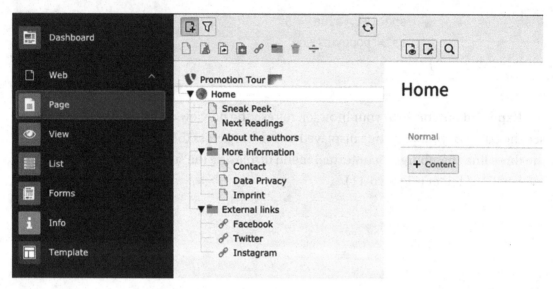

Figure 6-12. *The "Home" page selected on the page tree and the + Content button*

The Create new content element window displays (Figure 6-13).

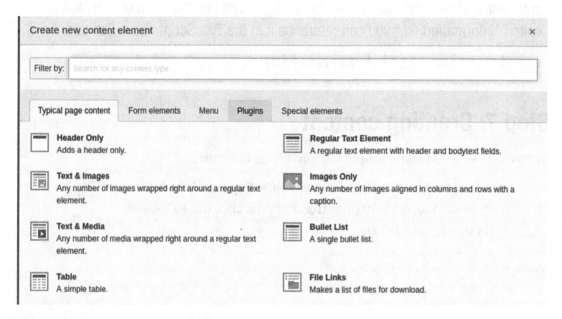

Figure 6-13. *The Create new content element window*

2. Select **Text & Images. The Create new Page Content on page "Home"** screen displays (Figure 6-14).

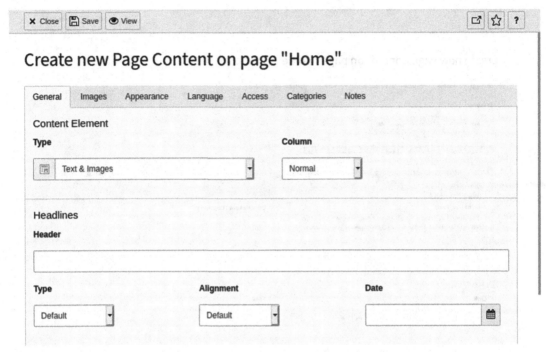

Figure 6-14. *The Create new Page Content on page "Home" screen*

3. In the **Header** field, type "Have you heard about our book?".

4. In the **Text** field, type a few sentences.

5. Go to the **Images** tab. We will upload an image from your computer. Feel free to download a royalty-free image from unsplash.com for this exercise.

6. Click **Select & upload files**, browse, and choose an image
    (Figure 6-15).

Figure 6-15. *The Select & upload files button*

Content elements can hold a variety of metadata, like a header
and permissions. Explore the tabs to get familiar with the editing
form and see what options are available.

7. Save and close the content element record.

8. Click the **View web page** icon to preview the website. You'll notice
    that the content we just added is not displaying. We need to
    instruct our Fluid template to display it.

9. In your file system, navigate to the Default.html file. Within the "<div id="main">" tag, add the following line:

```
<!-- Main -->
<div id="main">

    <f:cObject typoscriptObjectPath="styles.content.get" />
```

We have defined where our content should be rendered, but haven't yet defined how this content should be rendered. To do that, we need to include the rendering definitions from Fluid Styled Content into our TypoScript template.

TYPO3 comes with a handful of predefined content element types (see Guide 4 for building custom content element types), like "Text" and "Text w/ Image". The system extension "Fluid Styled Content" contains default rendering definitions, templates, and TypoScript telling TYPO3 how to render these Content Types on your website.

10. In your file system, navigate to your site extension's constants. typoscript file, and add the following line at the beginning of the file:

```
@import 'EXT:fluid_styled_content/Configuration/TypoScript/
constants.typoscript'
```

11. Similarly, add the following line at the beginning of the setup. typoscript file:

```
@import 'EXT:fluid_styled_content/Configuration/
TypoScript/setup.typoscript'
```

You can read more about adding TypoScript in the TypoScript Template Reference guide[5] in the official documentation.

Expected outcome: In your browser, refresh the website. You should see that the content is rendered, but it is not yet using the themes from the future imperfect template (Figure 6-16).

---

[5]https://docs.typo3.org/m/typo3/reference-typoscript/master/en-us/UsingSetting/
Entering.html#include-typoscript-files

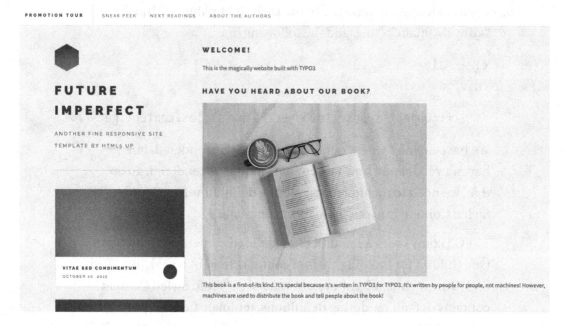

Figure 6-16. *Preview of the website*

Step 8: Styling the content

In the previous step, we got our content to display, but they're still using the default rendering definitions for Fluid Styled Content. We need to override them in order to use those of the future imperfect theme.

You can view the Fluid Styled Content documentation[6] to understand what styles TYPO3 ships by default.

Fluid is built with partials (reusable HTML snippets), templates (for each page or content element, or each plugin), and a set of layouts that you can use.

The best practice is to not modify Fluid Styled Content's templates directly. We only modify what we need to change, and keep the rest untouched. This makes it easier to upgrade TYPO3.

You can define multiple directory paths where Fluid will look for templates. If it can't find a template in one location, it will continue, looking in other paths.

Our TypoScript setup already defines our paths. We can look into the Fluid Styled Content extension and copy the files we need into our site extension:

---

[6]https://docs.typo3.org/c/typo3/cms-fluid-styled-content/master/en-us/

1. In your file system, navigate to public/typo3/sysext/fluid_styled_ content (Figure 6-17).

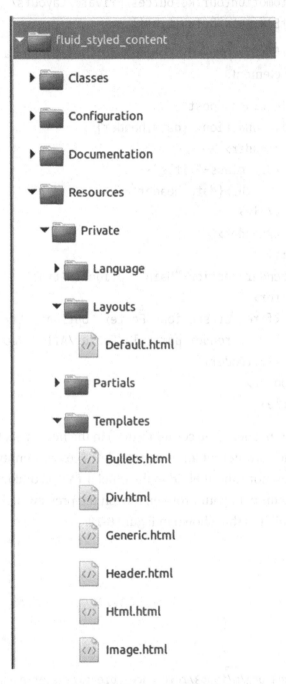

Figure 6-17. *The contents of the fluid_styled_content folder*

2. Copy the Layouts/Default.html file, and paste it into this directory in our site extension:

    ```
    site_promotiontour/Resources/Private/Layouts/
    ContentElements/Default.html
    ```

3. Edit the file to replace the content with the layout for a single content element:

```
<article class="post">
    <f:if condition="{data.header}">
        <header>
        <div class="title">
            <h2>{data.header}</h2>
        </div>
        </header>
    </f:if>
    <f:render section="Main" optional="true" />
    <footer>
        <f:render section="Footer" optional="true">
            <f:render partial="Footer/All" arguments="{_all}" />
        </f:render>
    </footer>
</article>
```

We render the "header" (the content's title) in the header section. After it comes the main section, which is different for every template (i.e., content type). Finally, we render the footer. Find out more about Fluid in the official TYPO3 documentation.[7]

Expected outcome: In your browser, refresh the preview of the website. You should see something similar to that shown in Figure 6-18.

---

[7]https://docs.typo3.org/m/typo3/reference-coreapi/master/en-us/ApiOverview/Fluid/
Index.html

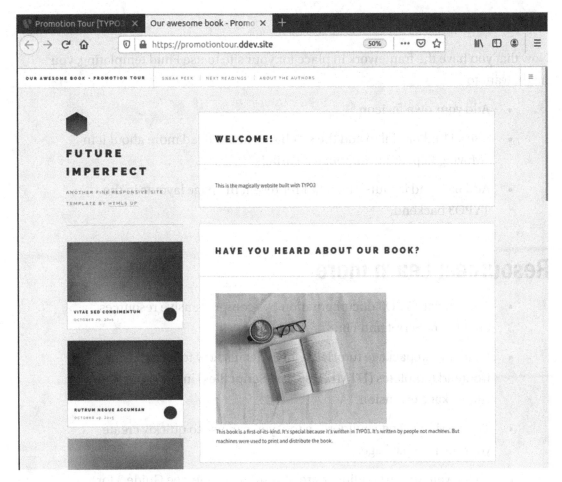

Figure 6-18. *Preview of the website*

Summary

Congratulations! You have created the foundation for a TYPO3 website, which uses a site extension, TypoScript, and Fluid templating to render a custom theme.

Now, you can further tailor the theme to customize the design of the website.

What's next?

Now that you have the framework in place for your site to use Fluid templating, you might want to

- Add your own favicon.[8]

- Use a Fluid partial to add the sidebar content. Read more about it in "Moving Repeating Snippets to Partials."[9]

- Add backend layouts[10] to better represent the page layouts in the TYPO3 backend.

Resources: Learn more

- The official TYPO3 documentation has comprehensive resources about TypoScript and Fluid.

- Read the sitepackage tutorial[11] which details how to turn a set of frontend templates (HTML, CSS, JavaScript files) into a stand-alone sitepackage extension.

- Try the sitepackage builder[12]–a tool you can use to quickly create your own sitepackage.

- If you want to start adding more of your own code, see Guide 3 for building a site extension and Guide 4 for building a custom content element.

---

[8]https://wiki.typo3.org/Add_your_own_favicon

[9]https://docs.typo3.org/m/typo3/book-extbasefluid/master/en-us/8-Fluid/3-moving-repeating-snippets-to-partials.html

[10]https://docs.typo3.org/m/typo3/reference-coreapi/master/en-us/ApiOverview/BackendLayout/Index.html

[11]https://docs.typo3.org/m/typo3/tutorial-sitepackage/master/en-us/Index.html

[12]https://www.sitepackagebuilder.com/

CHAPTER 7

Guide 3: Extending TYPO3

In Guide 1, we installed TYPO3 and in Guide 2 we created a site. This guide introduces you extensions, the mechanism for customizing TYPO3 websites to do what you need. We extend the functionality of your demo site from Guide 2 by activating a system extension. We also install and activate a third-party extension.

This guide is aimed at those who want to see how to extend the functionality of a TYPO3 site to meet your needs.

Chapter 3 covers extensions. Extensions are clearly confined code additions, such as plugins, backend modules, application logic, skins, and third-party integrations. The TYPO3 Core framework interacts with system and community-contributed extensions via the TYPO3 extension API. The TYPO3 core and extensions interact with each other seamlessly and operate as a single, unified system.

TYPO3 comes with a range of system extensions that you can choose to activate. They cover a variety of features, such as workspaces, scheduling, and reports.

You can extend your site further by adding community-contributed extensions or building your own. While you can upload their extensions to any version-control repository (e.g., GitHub), the TYPO3 Extension Repository (TER)[1] is the platform's official extension catalog, and this guide will only look at the TER. Every TYPO3 extension is identified by a unique extension key.

---

[1]https://extensions.typo3.org/

© Felicity Brand, Heather McNamee, and Jeffrey A. McGuire 2021
F. Brand et al., *The TYPO3 Guidebook*, https://doi.org/10.1007/978-1-4842-6525-3_7

This guide is about how to choose, install, and activate an extension. It steps you through

- Activating a system extension

- Browsing the TER and reviewing community-contributed extensions

- Downloading and installing an extension

In this guide, we build on the site created in Guide 2. We add the news extension and create a blog on the website.

At the end of this tutorial...

- You will have a website where you can create chronologically organized content like blog posts and news articles.

- You will know how to activate a system extension.

- You will know how to browse the TER, assess, and choose community-contributed extensions.

- You will know how to install and activate extensions.

Prerequisites

- You will need a modern computer, web browser, and an Internet connection.

- **A TYPO3 site –** This guide assumes you have completed Guide 2 from this book, but any TYPO3 site can be used.

Considerations before you start

This guide follows on from Guide 1, which installs TYPO3 via a Composer. This means extensions need to be installed using the same tool. The following steps are our recommended approach, but not the only way to install extensions. You can also use the extension manager and packages from the TER. You can read how to install extensions without Composer in the official TYPO3 documentation[2].While the TER is the official catalog of extensions, Packagist[3] is the default Composer package repository, and you can find TYPO3 extensions there, too.

Step 1: Activating a system extension

Extensions are managed in the backend via the Admin Tools ➤ Extensions module.

You can use this procedure to activate or deactivate any extension. For now, we will focus on the system extension "Advanced file metadata" (extension key: filemetadata). This extension adds a number of additional metadata fields to files, such as author, publisher, and geo coordinates:

1. For comparison, let's look at an image file before we activate the extension.

   a. Go to the File ➤ Filelist module.

   b. Find an image.

   c. Click the hyperlinked name of the image file to view its metadata (Figure 7-1).

---

[2]https://docs.typo3.org/m/typo3/tutorial-sitepackage/master/en-us/ ExtensionInstallation/Index.html

[3]https://packagist.org/explore/?type=typo3-cms-extension

Figure 7-1. *The image metadata screen*

2. The data for this file is divided into two tabs: General and
    Categories. The general fields available for the image are
    alternative text, description, and title (Figure 7-2).

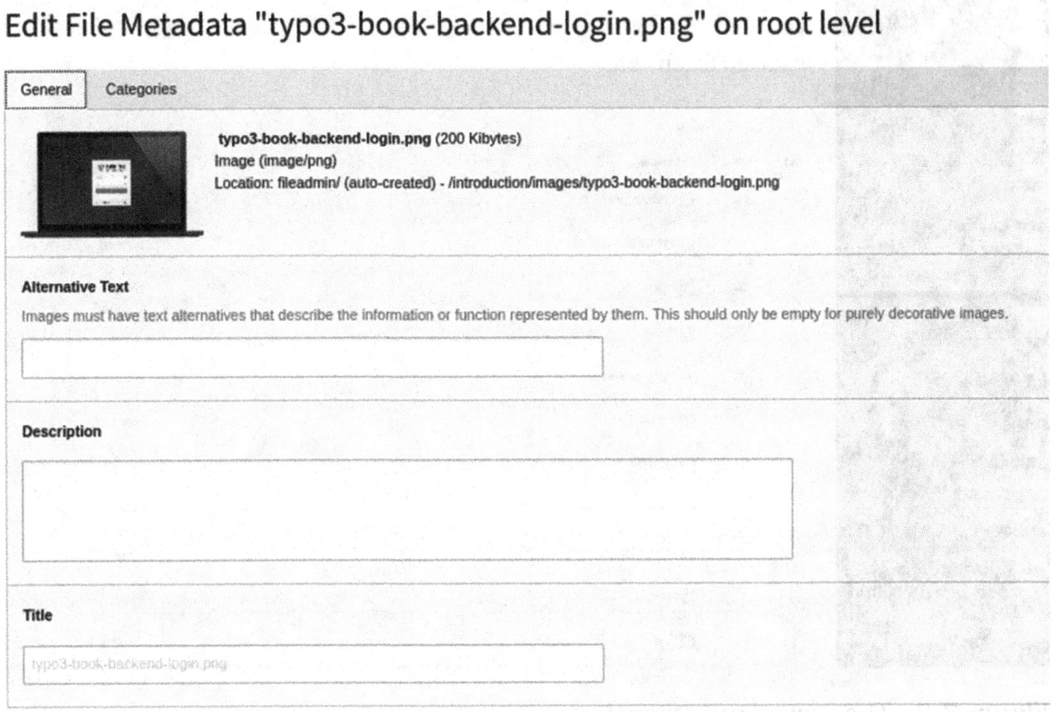

Edit File Metadata "typo3-book-backend-login.png" on root level

Figure 7-2. *The General tab for file metadata*

3. Navigate to the **Admin Tools ➤ Extensions** module. Notice that the extension is grayed out, and the A/D icon has a plus sign, indicating that it can be activated (Figure 7-3).

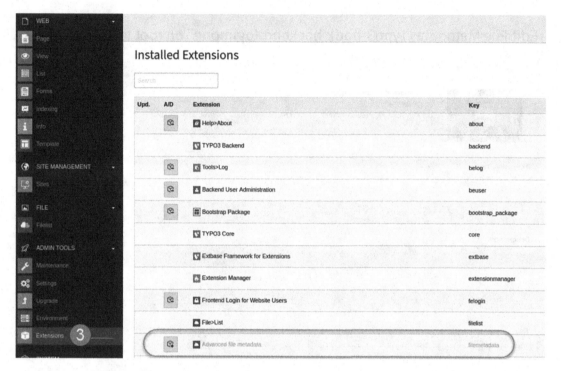

Figure 7-3. *The grayed out extension*

4. Click the icon to activate the extension. The icon changes to display a minus sign to indicate that it can be deactivated.

5. Let's go back and look at our image file to see what has changed:

   a. Go to the File ➤ Filelist module.

   b. Find an image.

   c. Click the hyperlinked name of the image file to view the metadata.

You will see additional fields and new tabs have been added. The fields available in the General tab now include keyword, ranking, and download name (Figure 7-4). The Metadata and Camera Data tabs let you include much richer information about the file.

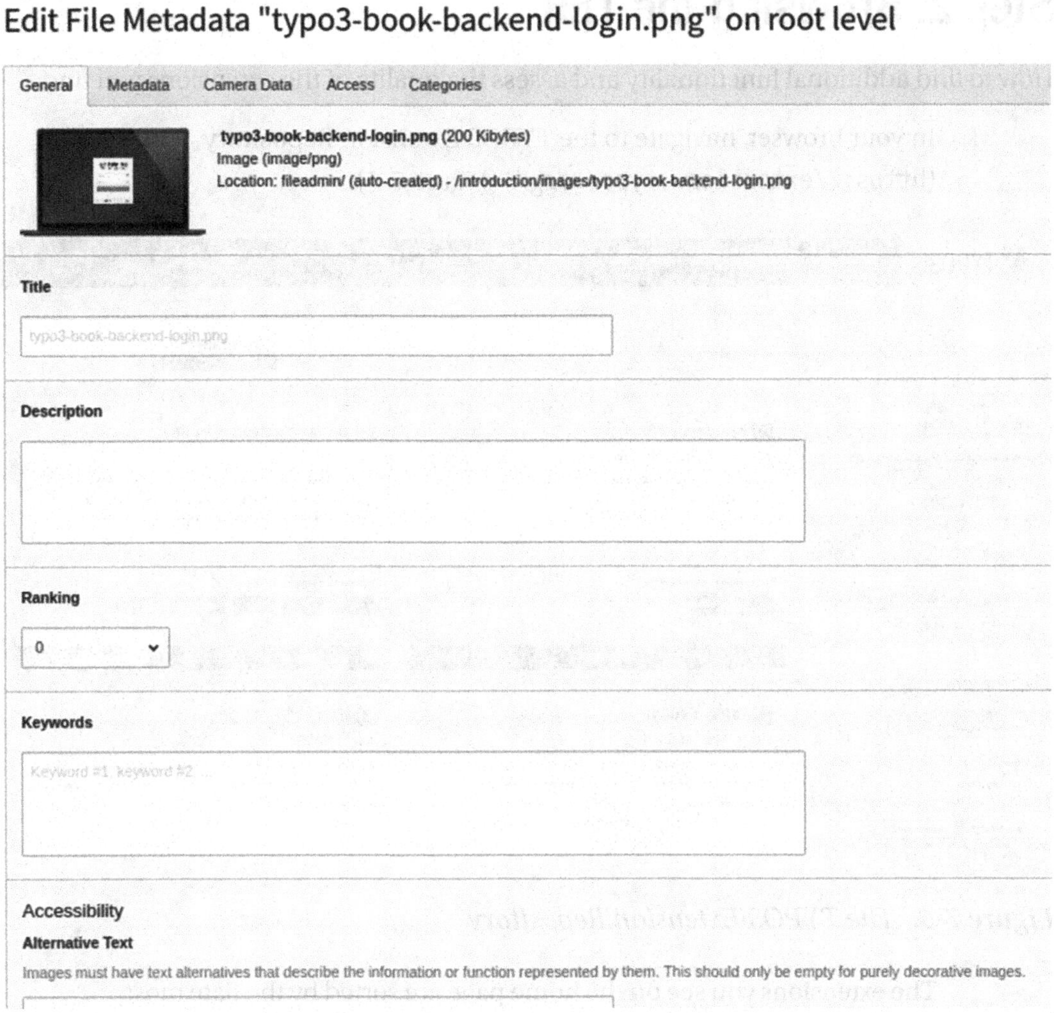

Edit File Metadata "typo3-book-backend-login.png" on root level

Figure 7-4. *Extra metadata fields displayed on the General tab*

Expected outcome: In the Extension module, the "Advanced file metadata" extension is activated and no longer grayed out. Now, the system extension is activated and can record a wide variety of metadata for your files.

Step 2: Browsing the TER

How to find additional functionality and assess the quality of the extensions you find

1. In your browser, navigate to the TYPO3 Extension Repository
   (https://extensions.typo3.org/) (Figure 7-5).

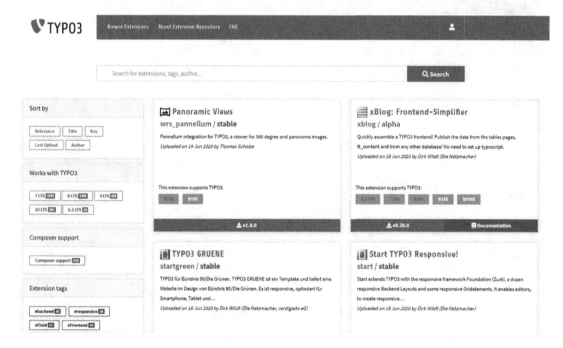

Figure 7-5. *The TYPO3 Extension Repository*

The extensions you see on the home page are sorted by the date most
recently added, changed, or updated. Extensions are displayed with
some standard information and categorization, for example:

- Name
- Status (beta or stable)
- Description
- Author
- TYPO3 version compatibility
- Download button
- Link to documentation

You can narrow the result by searching for keywords or by using the filters on the left side of the page.

2.   In the Search box at the top of the screen, type "news". The first result will probably be the "News system" extension (extension key: news) by Georg Ringer (Figure 7-6).

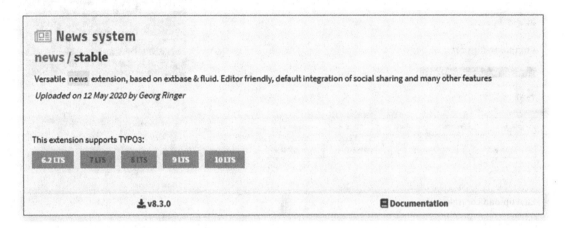

Figure 7-6. *The "News system" extension*

3.   Click the title to see more information about it. Each extension has a details page displaying further information, including instructions for installation using the zip file and Composer (Figure 7-7).

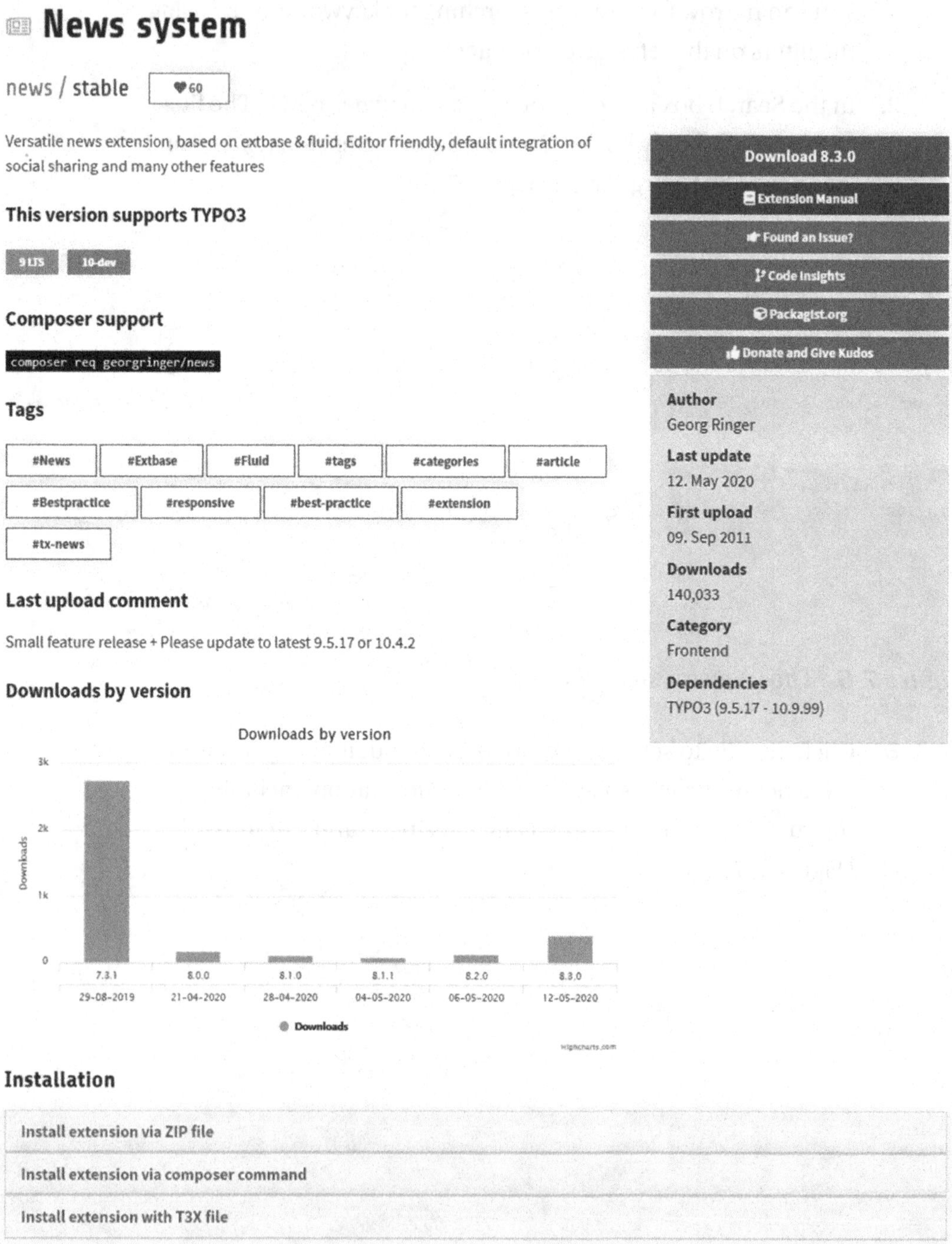

📇 News system

news / stable   ♥ 60

Versatile news extension, based on extbase & fluid. Editor friendly, default integration of social sharing and many other features

This version supports TYPO3

9 LTS   10-dev

Composer support

```
composer req georgringer/news
```

Tags

| #News | #Extbase | #Fluid | #tags | #categories | #article |

| #Bestpractice | #responsive | #best-practice | #extension |

| #tx-news |

Last upload comment

Small feature release + Please update to latest 9.5.17 or 10.4.2

Downloads by version

Download 8.3.0

📖 Extension Manual

📣 Found an Issue?

⅟ Code Insights

🌐 Packagist.org

👍 Donate and Give Kudos

Author
Georg Ringer

Last update
12. May 2020

First upload
09. Sep 2011

Downloads
140,033

Category
Frontend

Dependencies
TYPO3 (9.5.17 - 10.9.99)

Downloads by version

Installation

Install extension via ZIP file
Install extension via composer command
Install extension with T3X file

Figure 7-7. *Detail page for the "News system" extension*

How to choose good extensions

The TER houses many and varied extensions, some of which may be of a higher quality than others. Here is Stefan Busemann's advice about how to choose good extensions:

- Take a look at the documentation. A good extension will provide documentation that is more than just a README file. The documentation should contain, for example, a list of configuration options and contact details to get support.

- The extension should clearly state which TYPO3 version it is built for; the version constraint must be set.

- Check when the extension was the last updated. Compare it to the first upload date. If an extension received its last update a long time ago, it may be not the best solution because it indicates that there aren't frequent updates. On the other hand, if the updates are too many or too frequent, it could be a bad sign, too (many bug fix releases, e.g., could mean poor initial quality). Use your judgment.

- It is good if the extension has a company behind it. This is often a sign of quality and commitment to the extension.

- Is it stable or beta?

- Look at the number of downloads by version. Popularity can be an indicator of quality. The more developers, agencies, and sites that use a particular extension, the more broadly useful its functionality and the more eyes it has had on its code.

Expected outcome: Now you can navigate to the TER, search for extensions based on their name or function, and analyze how suitable the extension is for you.

Step 3: Installing the news extension

This guide follows on from Guide 2, which installs TYPO3 via Composer. This means that we will use Composer to install extensions:

1. Go to the directory where the root composer.json file is located for your site (called project root).

2. Open a terminal window and type: `composer require georgringer/news`

3. Wait for it to install, then in your TYPO3 backend, go to the Admin Tools ➤ Extensions module, and activate it.

   Expected outcome: In the Web module menu, there is now a new module called "News Administration." This module lets you create chronologically organized content like news articles or blog posts.

Note   The preceding composer requires command works for extensions registered on Packagist. At the time of writing, some extensions, however, are registered in the deprecated TYPO3 Composer Repository, instead. In the case you want to use one, follow the instructions for installing extensions from TYPO3 Composer Repository.[4]

Step 4: Configuring the news extension

Now that the extension is activated, we need to do some configuration. This section dives into detail. You can find out more in the comprehensive documentation[5] about how to configure and use the news extension.

---

[4]https://get.typo3.org/misc/composer/repository
[5]https://docs.typo3.org/p/georgringer/news/master/en-us/Introduction/Index.html

First, we need to include the News TypoScript in the site template to be able to render the content:

1. Navigate to the Web ➤ Template module.

2. Select the root page of the site.

3. In the drop-down list at the top of the page, select **Info/Modify** (Figure 7-8).

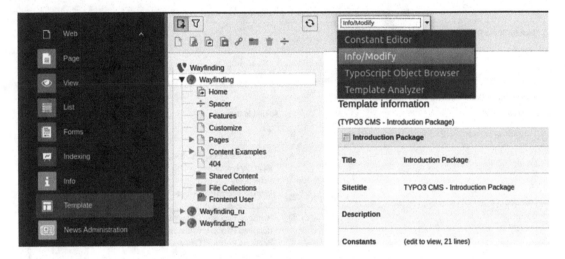

Figure 7-8. *The drop-down list at the top of the page screen*

4. Click the **Edit the whole template record** button (Figure 7-9):

    a. Go to the **Includes** tab.

    b. In the **Available Items** list, click "News (news)." The extension is added to the **Selected Items** list.

    c. Save and close.

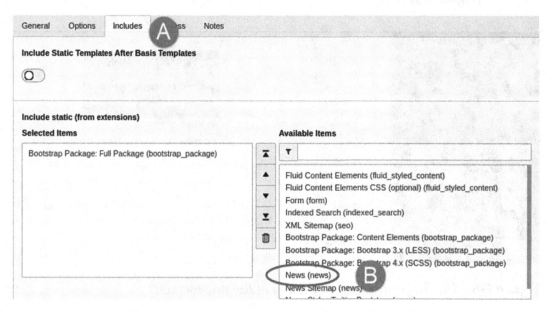

Figure 7-9. *The Includes tab*

Next, we need to create news records, so they can be shown in the frontend.

5. Navigate to the Web ➤ List module, and click **Create new record** (Figure 7-10).

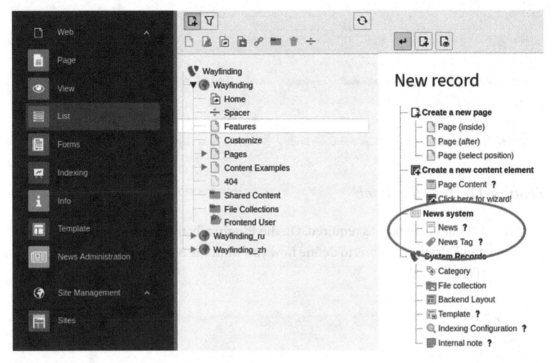

Figure 7-10. *The New record screen*

6. Click **News** to create a new news category. Fill out the details as required and save the record. Refer to the extension documentation[6] for more information.

    Finally, we need to add a plugin to a specific page so that we can render news content.

7. Navigate to the Web ➤ Page module.

8. Select a page and click **Content** to add a new content element.

---

[6]https://docs.typo3.org/p/georgringer/news/master/en-us/UsersManual/HowToStart/Index.html

9. On the **Plugins** tab, select **News system** (Figure 7-11).

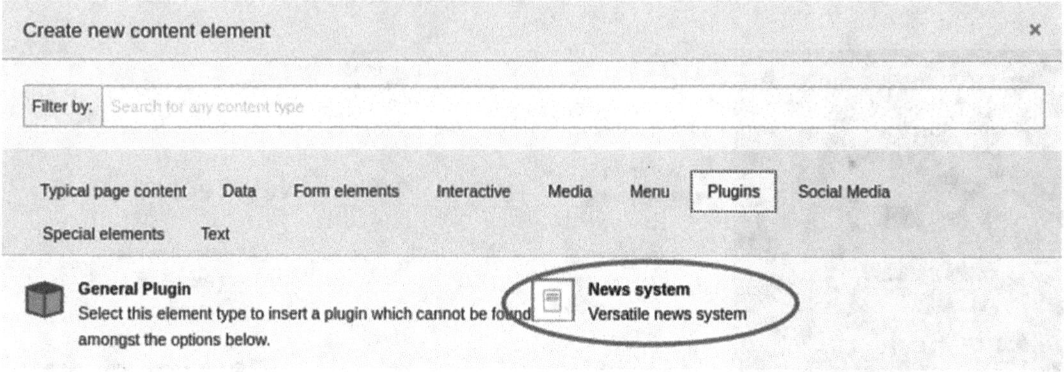

Figure 7-11. *The Plugins tab*

10. Fill out the details as required. On the **Plugin** tab, there are configuration options to define how you want the News to display (Figure 7-12).

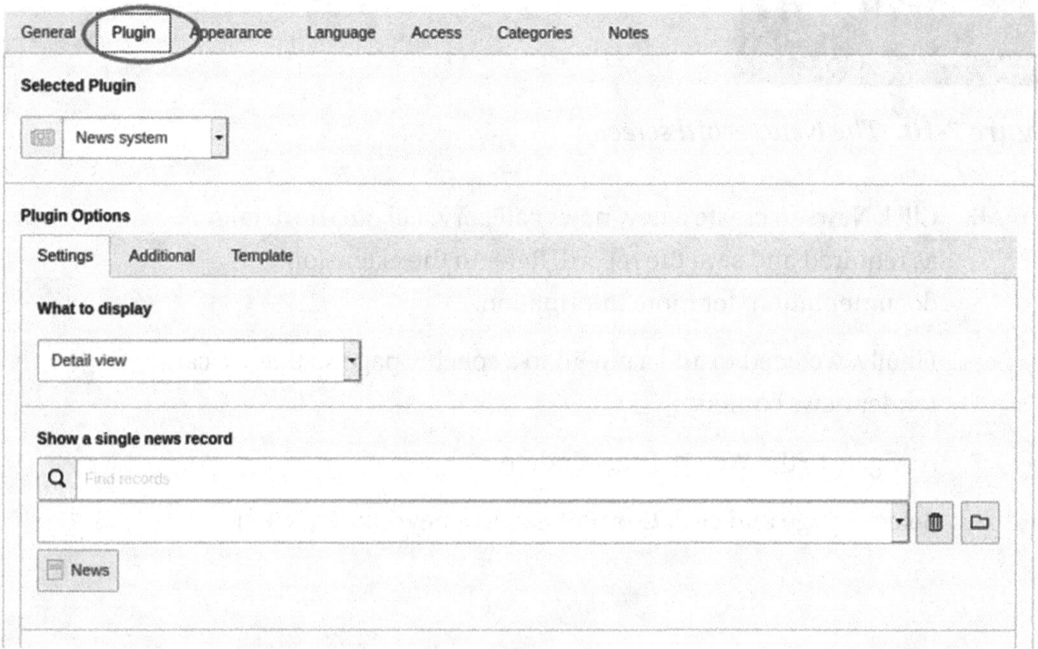

Figure 7-12. *Configuration options on the Plugin tab*

Tip   In step 4 earlier, we edit the template record to include the News extension's TypoScript template. This can also be done using TypoScript only—and from within your site extension. This way the TypoScript is always included. Where do you think you can find the News extension's TypoScript, and how can you include it in your site extension? **Hint:** Look for "@include" and the file paths in the TypoScript of the previous chapter.

Summary

Congratulations! You now know how to install and activate new extensions to capture extra metadata for your files and add news articles to your site.

You can continue to add extensions to add functionality to your site—either to change the backend experience (like adding a living style guide[7]) or to add features to the frontend.

What's next?

Now that you've had some experience with system and community-contributed extensions, you might want to learn about building your own extension:

- See Guide 5: Create your first extension.

- Read Chapter 3, which includes a section about building custom extensions.

Resources: Learn more

You can find the official manual for *Developing TYPO3 Extensions with Extbase and Fluid* in the TYPO3 documentation.[8]

---

[7]https://github.com/TYPO3/styleguide
[8]https://docs.typo3.org/m/typo3/book-extbasefluid/master/en-us/   211

Guide 4: Planning, Building, and Using Content Elements

This guide builds on the site created in Guide 2 and the extension added in Guide 3. It shows you how to create a custom content element.

TYPO3 comes with some content types that you can use right away, like text and images, but you can also build content types that are exactly suited to your site's particular needs.

A custom content element could be a "quote" element if you plan to build a website around quotes from celebrities or a "teaser" element displaying a teaser text and a link to another page for a news website.

A content element is in its essence a representation of static data, and it will not be suitable for a social media feed, or a dynamic list of upcoming events. In these cases, using a plugin is more appropriate (see Guide 5).

Building on our book promotion website from Guide 2, we would like to create a content element to present quotes from notable readers. We could use a combination of text and media content elements, but with a custom content element, we will have something that is exactly fit for purpose, making the editors' job more efficient.

The steps required to build a custom content type are

- Create a content type (add it to "tt_content" table) and define the required fields.

- Extend the "New Content Element" window so that editors can easily select the new content type.

- Create a template to render the content type.

213

© Felicity Brand, Heather McNamee, and Jeffrey A. McGuire 2021
F. Brand et al., *The TYPO3 Guidebook*, https://doi.org/10.1007/978-1-4842-6525-3_8

At the end of this tutorial...

- You will have a basic understanding of TCA, "tt_content," and where content is stored in the database.

- You will know how to create a custom content type.

- You will know how to make the custom content type available for editors to use.

- You will be able to render a custom content type with a template.

- You will know where to look up information about the TCA configuration.

Prerequisites

- You will need a modern computer, web browser, and an Internet connection.

- **A TYPO3 site –** This guide assumes you have completed Guides 2 and 3 from this book, but any TYPO3 site with a custom extension can be used.

Considerations before you start

Guide 3 demonstrates building a custom site extension called "site_promotiontour." This guide creates a content type that is specifically for the promotion tour website, so we'll build it into the site extension. Another approach would be to create an extension for each content type so that you can reuse them in multiple TYPO3 installations, but we won't show that in this guide.

Step 1: Exploring TYPO3 content types

Let's have a look at the content elements that come out of the box with TYPO3 and get an idea about how and where they are stored in the system:

1. In your backend, navigate to the **Web ➤ Page** module. Select the "Home" page in your page tree and then click the **+ Content** button.

2. The **Create new content element** window displays (Figure 8-1).

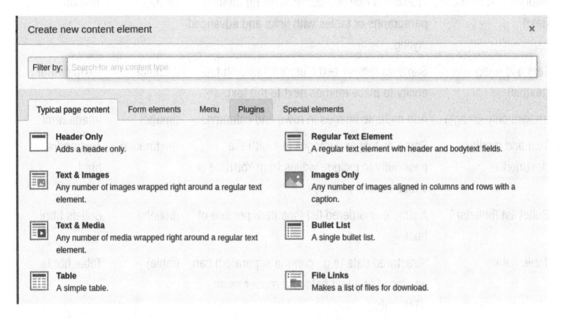

Figure 8-1. *The Create new content element window*

3. Explore the available Content Types listed in Table 8-1:

Table 8-1. *Available content types*

Content type	Description	(CType identifier)	Fluid template file
Typical page content			
Header only	Renders a heading. This is included in all other content types, but if you only need to display a heading, use this content type.	header	Header.html
Regular text element (text)	Provides a rich text editor allowing multiple paragraphs or tables with links and advanced styling.	(text)	Text.html
Text and images (textpic)	Same as regular text element, but with the ability to place images next to the text.	(textpic)	Textpic.html
Images only (image)	Add multiple images in rows and columns.	(image)	Image.html
Text and media (textmedia)	Same as text and images but with the possibility to include videos from YouTube or Vimeo next to text.	(textmedia)	Textmedia. html
Bullet list (bullets)	A simple unordered list (one item per line of text).	(bullets)	Bullets.html
Table (table)	Structured data (e.g., comma separated) can be placed in a text field and render as an HTML table.	(table)	Table.html
File links (uploads)	A list of downloads—either single files or files from a folder or file collection.	(uploads)	Uploads.html
Menu			
Menu	Create a menu of pages. The different menu options are described in the "Menus" section of the content elements based on Fluid section of the TYPO3 documentation.[1]		

(continued)

---

[1]https://docs.typo3.org/c/typo3/cms-fluid-styled-content/master/en-us/
ContentElements/Menu/Index.html

Table 8-1. (*continued*)

Content type	Description	(CType identifier)	Fluid template file
Special elements			
Divider	A horizontal divider line.	(div)	Div.html
Plain HTML	Allows the editor to add plain HTML directly. This can be useful for iFrame integration or HTML snippets.	(html)	Html.html
Insert records	Reference and render existing content elements from the same or other pages.	(shortcut)	Shortcut.html
Plugins			
Custom plugins	For rendering custom logic or specific database records.	(list)	List.html

Common information on TCA and tt_content

An important part of TYPO3 is the Table Configuration Array (TCA). It defines how (and if) fields of a database table are displayed in the backend and what kind of restrictions apply to their content. The database tables you'll work with in this guide are

- "pages" (Pages in the page tree)

- "tt_content" (content elements)

Each table contains the properties "uid" (the ID of a record) and "pid" (the uid of the parent page, where the record is stored). You'll find detailed information about other common database fields in "TYPO3 Explained: Database Structure"[2] in the TYPO3 documentation.

---

[2]https://docs.typo3.org/m/typo3/reference-coreapi/master/en-us/ApiOverview/
Database/DatabaseStructure/Index.html

A selection of other TYPO3 database tables using TCA:

- Backend users and editors (in the database tables "be_users" and "be_groups").

- Frontend users ("fe_users" and "fe_groups", see Guide 7).

- System-wide categories.

- Files. File metadata is stored in "sys_file", and the connections where they are used are stored in a relational table called "sys_file_reference."

A "tt_content" record represents a content element or a version of it. The field `CType` contains the content element type. Each content type defines its own editable fields through the TCA and its own rendering template.

It's possible to rely on existing database fields when you create a custom content type, but you can also extend the tt_content table, adding new fields. We advise against reusing fields for dissimilar data (a title text field shouldn't be used for referencing a record UID in another content element type). However, reusing a "header" field for headline text across content element types makes switching between types easier.

Expected outcome: You have an understanding of the different content elements that come with TYPO3 and where they are stored in the database.

Step 2: Create new content type

To create a new content type, we extend the tt_content TCA with our new content element. This means we must create a new declaration for such a type. We'll create new files and then rebuild TYPO3's caches to make the new content type available.

Always make a plan before creating a new content element. Decide what fields are required, which fields should be editable, and how you would like the content element to look in the frontend.

For the quote element, we'll make the CType identifier "bookquote."

Requirements

- The actual quote (we'll use the existing database field "bodytext").

- The author of the quote. Let's use the "header" field for this (because it is a single line).

- An image of the author. We can use the existing field "assets," which is used for image content types.

This step requires writing a small amount of PHP code:

1. In your file system, go to the site_promotiontour extension and create a file called bookquote.php in site_promotiontour/Configuration/TCA/Overrides.

2. To register the "bookquote" content typeType, and the fields displayed with it, edit the file and paste in the following:

```php
<?php
call_user_func(static function () {
// Adds another option to the dropdown representing the field
"CType" of the tt_content table.
\TYPO3\CMS\Core\Utility\ExtensionManagementUtility::addTcaSelectItem(
    'tt_content',
    'CType',
    // The first entry is the menu item label, the second is the
    value stored in the database.
    ['What other people are saying?', 'bookquote'],
    // This content type will show up after the "HTML" content
    type in the dropdown menu.
    'html',
    'after'
);

// The following defines which fields should be visible, and in
which order.
$GLOBALS['TCA']['tt_content']['types']['bookquote'] = [
    'showitem' => '
```

```
                    --div--;LLL:EXT:core/Resources/Private/Language/
                Form/locallang_tabs.xlf:general,
                    --palette--;;general,
                    bodytext;Quote,
                    header;Author,
                    assets;Image of the author,
                --div--;LLL:EXT:frontend/Resources/Private/
                Language/locallang_ttc.xlf:tabs.appearance,
                    --palette--;;frames,
                    --palette--;;appearanceLinks,
                --div--;LLL:EXT:core/Resources/Private/Language/
                Form/locallang_tabs.xlf:language,
                    --palette--;;language,
                --div--;LLL:EXT:core/Resources/Private/Language/
                Form/locallang_tabs.xlf:access,
                    --palette--;;hidden,
                    --palette--;;access,
                --div--;LLL:EXT:core/Resources/Private/Language/
                Form/locallang_tabs.xlf:categories,
                    categories,
                --div--;LLL:EXT:core/Resources/Private/Language/
                Form/locallang_tabs.xlf:notes,
                    rowDescription,
                --div--;LLL:EXT:core/Resources/Private/Language/
                Form/locallang_tabs.xlf:extended,
                ',
        'columnsOverrides' => [
            'bodytext' => [
                'config' => [
                    'rows' => 3
                ]
            ]
        ]
    ];
});
```

3. Now, we need to add the content type to the "New Content Element" window. In the root of the site_promotiontour directory, create a file named "ext_localconf.php."

4. Paste in the following code:

```php
<?php

\TYPO3\CMS\Core\Utility\ExtensionManagementUtility::addPageTSConfig('
    mod.wizards.newContentElement.wizardItems {
        common.elements.bookquote {
            title = Book Quote
            description = What other people are saying
            tt_content_defValues.CType = bookquote
            iconIdentifier = content-text
        }
        common.show := addToList(bookquote)
    }
');
```

5. Now, go to the backend in your browser. At the top right of the screen, click the lightning bolt icon and then select **Flush all caches**.

6. In the page tree, select the "Home" page, and add a new content element. The **Create new content element** window displays (Figure 8-2).

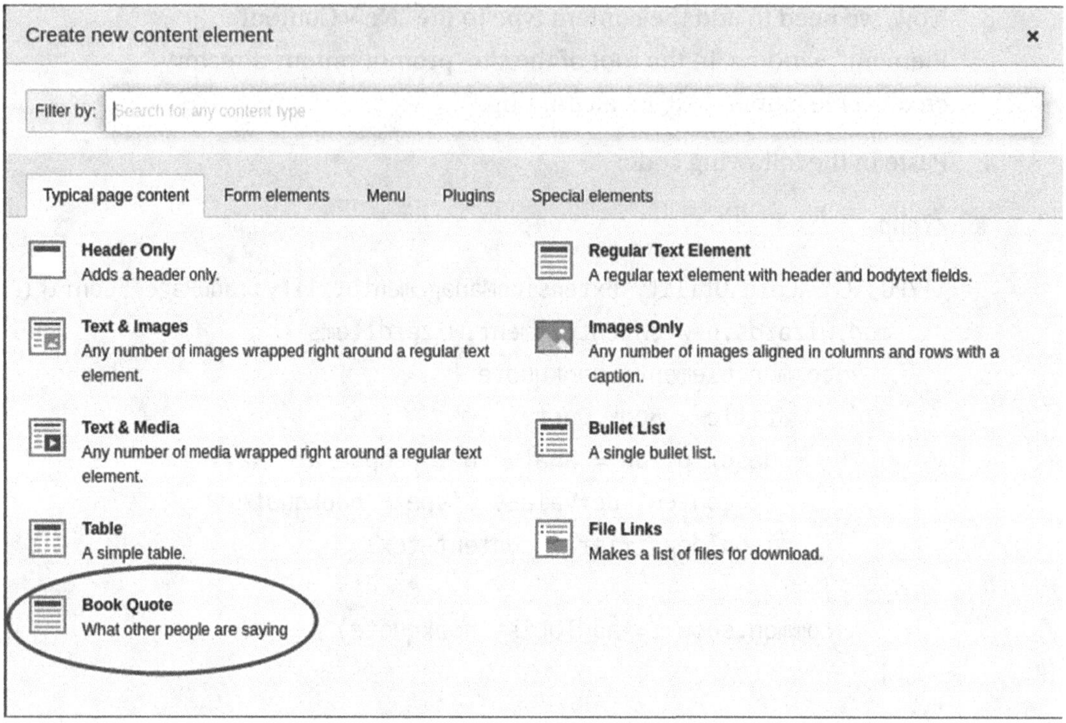

Figure 8-2. *Expected outcome: The Create new content element window now includes the Book Quote element*

Tip   In step 4, we included the PageTS code directly for clarity and brevity. The best practice is to put the code in a file and include that file using the "@import" you have seen used in previous chapters.

```
\TYPO3\CMS\Core\Utility\ExtensionManagementUtility::addPageTSConfig(
'@import "[PATH]"');
```

Tip   In step 5, we flushed the caches via the lightning bolt icon. The Install tool's cache flushing[3] can also come in handy in some cases, when the simpler option hasn't cleared out everything.

---

[3]https://docs.typo3.org/m/typo3/guide-installation/10.4/en-us/Upgrade/
RemoveTemporaryCacheFiles/Index.html

Step 3: Using the content type

Now, we'll put our new content type into action on our site, adding a very simple piece of content:

1. In the **Create new content element** window, select the **Book Quote** element.

2. Add some content in the **Quote** and **Author** fields (Figure 8-3).

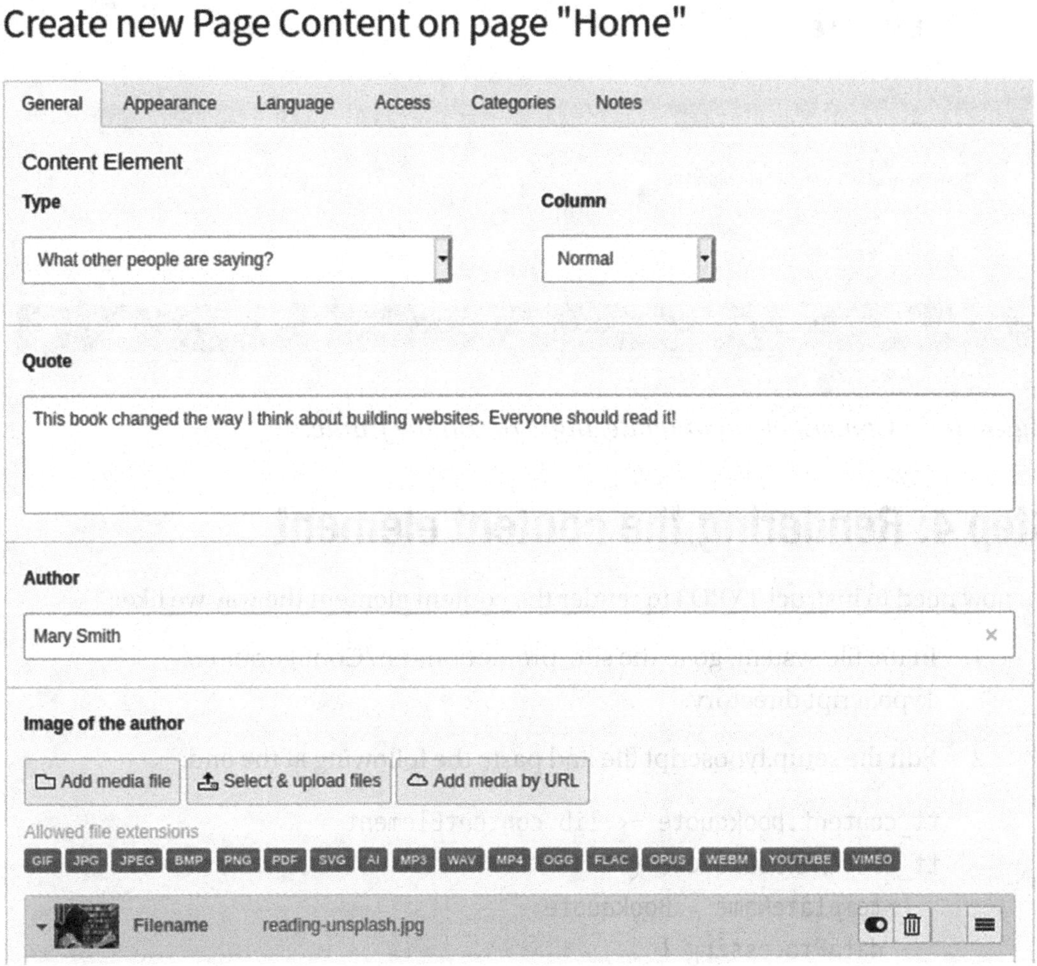

Create new Page Content on page "Home"

General	Appearance	Language	Access	Categories	Notes

Content Element

Type   **Column**

What other people are saying?   ▼   Normal   ▼

Quote

This book changed the way I think about building websites. Everyone should read it!

Author

Mary Smith   ✕

Image of the author

📁 Add media file   📤 Select & upload files   ☁ Add media by URL

Allowed file extensions

GIF JPG JPEG BMP PNG PDF SVG AI MP3 WAV MP4 OGG FLAC OPUS WEBM YOUTUBE VIMEO

▾ [thumbnail] Filename   reading-unsplash.jpg   ◐ 🗑   ≡

Figure 8-3. Fields in the Book Quote content element

3. Upload an image file from your computer to use as an image of the author. You can find royalty-free images at unsplash.com.

4. Save and close the page.

Expected outcome: If you view the website, an error message will tell you that there is no rendering definition for the element, shown in Figure 8-4.

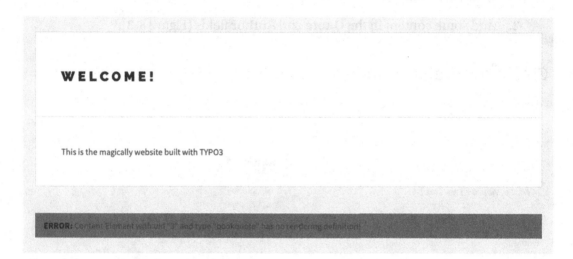

Figure 8-4. *Content element rendering error on the frontend*

Step 4: Rendering the content element

We now need to instruct TYPO3 to render the content element the way we like:

1. In the file system, go to the site_promotiontour/Configuration/ TypoScript directory.

2. Edit the setup.typoscript file and paste the following at the end:

```
tt_content.bookquote =< lib.contentElement
tt_content.bookquote {
    templateName = Bookquote
    dataProcessing {
        10 = TYPO3\CMS\Frontend\DataProcessing\FilesProcessor
```

```
10 {
    references.fieldName = assets
    as = assets
  }
 }
}
```

This means that we inherit the default rendering from Fluid Styled Content and use a template file called "Bookquote.html" (the ".html" extension is added automatically), but also resolve images for the author as the property "assets".

3. Create a file called Bookquote.html in site_promotiontour/
    Resources/Private/Templates/ContentElements/ with this
    content:

```
<article class="post">
    <f:if condition="{data.header}">
        <header>
            <div class="title">
                <h2>{data.header}</h2>
            </div>
        </header>
    </f:if>
    <div class="row">
        <div class="col-9">
            <p>This is what {data.header} said about our book:</p>
            <blockquote>{data.bodytext}</blockquote>
        </div>
        <div class="col-3">
            <div class="image">
                <f:image image="{assets.0}" maxHeight="200" />
            </div>
        </div>
    </div>
</article>
```

4. Go to your browser and preview the home page.

Expected outcome: The book quote element is rendered (Figure 8-5).

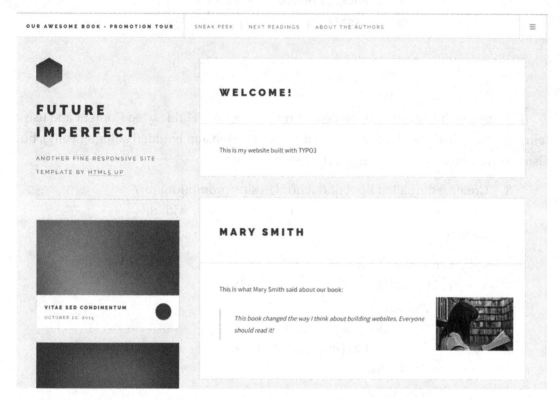

Figure 8-5. *The Book Quote content element rendered on the frontend*

Tip   As in previous sections, we are including the code in step 2 directly for clarity and brevity. The best practice, which also makes code more readable in big installations, is to put the code in its own file and then include it from setup. typoscript include using the "@import" you have seen used before.

Summary

Congratulations! You have created a new content element and used it in your website. First, we planned the fields for the new content type, and then we added it as content type in the tt_content table. Next, we added it to the **New Content Element** window, so that it was available for editors to work with. Finally, we created a template to render the new content type in the frontend.

What's next?

Now that you're done creating a new custom content element, you might like to

- Create another content element.

- View the entire TCA configuration. You'll need to activate the system extension "lowlevel", and then navigate to the **System ➤ Configuration ➤ TCA** module.

Resources: Learn more

- Read the TCA Reference guide[4] to learn more about the many options possible.

- Read Chapter 2 in this book to find out more about content elements and the TYPO3 editing experience.

---

[4]https://docs.typo3.org/m/typo3/reference-tca/master/en-us/Introduction/Index.html

CHAPTER 9

Guide 5: Creating Your First Stand-Alone Extension

Guide 3 explained the extensibility of TYPO3 using extensions, and in Guide 4, we built custom content types to extend TYPO3's content element rendering. A lot of TYPO3's flexibility comes through the extension API, which allows you to add functionality without changing the core.

In this guide, we'll create an extension to display reading dates for our promotion tour, with the option to show only the next three upcoming events based on the current date. In TYPO3, extensions that contain dynamic functionality for the frontend are called "plugins."

The results of this guide can also be achieved more rapidly by using the extension called "extension builder."[1] It will create the Table Configuration Array (TCA), domain models, controllers, and controller actions for you. This guide steps you through how it all works in detail, so that you understand the concepts underlying the system.

Most plugins are built with a model-view-controller (MVC) framework called "Extbase". Plugins can load data from anywhere, such as the database or external sources like an RSS feed or Twitter stream. Published extensions already provide a wide range of features, such as forums, guest books, and ecommerce functionality.

---

[1]At the time of writing, extension builder does not yet officially support TYPO3 v10, but the development branch is already being used with TYPO3 v10, so we expect this to change soon. Find out more at `https://github.com/FriendsOfTYPO3/extension_builder`.

© Felicity Brand, Heather McNamee, and Jeffrey A. McGuire 2021
F. Brand et al., *The TYPO3 Guidebook*, https://doi.org/10.1007/978-1-4842-6525-3_9

In the MVC pattern, the model is a representation of the data structure, the view (in TYPO3's case, a Fluid template) handles display, and the controller and its actions handle output, user input, and changes to the model data. You can read more about it in the book *TYPO3 Extbase: Modern Extension Development for TYPO3 CMS with Extbase and Fluid*[2] by Michael Schams or in the documentation for Extbase and Fluid.[3]

At the end of this tutorial...

- You will know how to create an extension and its required directory structure.

- You will understand the basic concepts of the TCA.

- You will know how records can be edited if there is a TCA in place.

- You will see how custom records are output with the power of Extbase.

Prerequisites

- You will need a modern computer, web browser, and an Internet connection.

- A TYPO3 site. This guide assumes you have completed Guides 2, 3, and 4 from this book, but any TYPO3 site can be used.

Considerations before you start
Technical difficulty

This guide gets quite detailed. It is not aimed at general editors or frontend users. No coding is required (code samples are provided). To benefit the most from it, you'll need some knowledge of file formats and PHP code. This will help you understand what is happening and how to tell the software to behave when you're doing your own work later.

---

[2]https://leanpub.com/typo3extbase-3rd-edition-en
[3]https://docs.typo3.org/m/typo3/book-extbasefluid/10.4/en-us/

Workspace setup

In these steps, we're going to be using the browser to work in the backend and to preview the frontend and the file system to create and edit files. When we make a change in the file system or the TYPO3 backend, we will refresh the frontend display to see those changes.

Step 1: Create the extension structure

First, we create a new extension and establish a folder structure for the files we need. We'll keep it very simple here. In a real-life situation, you will want to integrate more closely with Composer and your Git repository:

1. In the file system for your site, navigate to public/typo3conf/ext/, and create a folder called "promotionevents".

2. In this folder, create a file called ext_emconf.php.

3. Paste the following metainformation into the file:

```php
<?php

$EM_CONF[$_EXTKEY] = [
    'title' => 'Promotion Tour: Upcoming Events',
    'description' => 'Manage upcoming events and display them on
    your website',
    'category' => 'fe',
    'author' => 'A new TYPO3 star',
    'author_email' => 'nobody@acme.com',
    'state' => 'alpha',
    'clearCacheOnLoad' => 1,
    'version' => '1.0.0',
    'constraints' => [
        'depends' =>
            [
                'typo3' => '10.4.0-10.4.99'
            ],
```

```
            'conflicts' => [],
            'suggests' => [],
        ],
    ];
```

Expected outcome: In your TYPO3 backend, the **Admin Tools ➤ Extensions** module shows the Promotion Events site extension as disabled and grayed out.

Step 2: Add a custom data structure

Next, we will create a custom database table so that we can manage records that are not bound to the content.

Let's define the fields that are relevant for a single "promotion event":

- A title

- A simple description (with rich text editing capabilities)

- The event date (we'll call it "promotiondate")

- The start time for the event

- A single-line text field for the location

- A link to the location (e.g., the website of the bookstore or coffee shop where the event is taking place)

All fields will be mandatory, except for the description:

1. In the "promotionevents" directory, create a file called "ext_tables.sql".

2. Paste the following contents:

```
CREATE TABLE tx_promotionevents_domain_model_event (
    title varchar(200) DEFAULT '',
    description text DEFAULT '' NOT NULL,
    promotiondate DATE,
    promotiontime TIME,
    location varchar(200) DEFAULT '',
    locationlink varchar(1024) DEFAULT ''
);
```

The database table is called "tx_promotionevents_domain_
model_event", where "tx_" is a prefix that stands for "TYPO3
extension". Next comes the extension name; then the "_domain_
model_" is best practice for Extbase extensions, as well as the
model name "event".

3. Now, we need to set up the Table Configuration Array (TCA) so
    that TYPO3 knows how each database field should be rendered in
    the backend. Navigate to the "promotionevents" directory; create
    a new directory called "Configuration" and one called "TCA"
    inside it (giving you this directory structure: promotionevents/
    Configuration/TCA).

4. In this directory, create a file called tx_promotionevents_domain_
    model_event.php. The file name must use the name of the
    database table plus the ".php" file type extension.

5. Paste the following into the file:

```php
<?php

return [
    'ctrl' => [
        # A text for TYPO3 listings
        'title' => 'Promotion Tour Events',
        # The main label for TYPO3 listings, plus alternative
        fields which should be shown along
        'label' => 'promotiondate',
        'label_alt' => 'headline,promotiontime',
        'label_alt_force' => true,
        # order records in TYPO3's Backend by the date
        'default_sortby' => 'promotiondate DESC',
        # an icon for the records in TYPO3 Backend, custom icons
        can be registered as well
        'typeicon_classes' => [
            'default' => 'mimetypes-x-sys_note'
        ],
```

```
        # TYPO3 will automatically create control-fields in the
        database here
        'tstamp' => 'updatedon',
        'crdate' => 'createdon',
        'cruser_id' => 'createdby',
        'enablecolumns' => [
            'disabled' => 'hidden'
        ]
    ],
    # definition of each field from ext_tables.sql
    'columns' => [
        'title' => [
            'label' => 'Title',
            'config' => [
                'type' => 'input',
                'size' => 50,
                'max' => 200,
                'eval' => 'required'
            ],
        ],
        'description' => [
            'label' => 'Additional information',
            'config' => [
                'type' => 'text',
                'renderType' => '',
                'cols' => 80,
                'rows' => 15,
                'enableRichtext' => true,
            ]
        ],
        'promotiondate' => [
            'label' => 'Date of the Event',
            'config' => [
                'type' => 'input',
                'renderType' => 'inputDateTime',
```

```
                'eval' => 'date,required',
                'dbType' => 'date',
        ]
    ],
    'promotiontime' => [
        'label' => 'Start time of the Event',
        'config' => [
                'type' => 'input',
                'renderType' => 'inputDateTime',
                'eval' => 'time,required',
                'dbType' => 'time',
        ]
    ],
    'location' => [
        'label' => 'Location',
        'config' => [
                'type' => 'input',
                'size' => 50,
                'max' => 200,
                'eval' => 'required'
        ],
    ],
    'locationlink' => [
        'label' => 'Optional Link to the location',
        'config' => [
                'type' => 'input',
                'renderType' => 'inputLink',
                'size' => 50,
                'max' => 1024,
                'fieldControl' => [
                    'linkPopup' => [
                        'options' => [
                            'title' => 'LLL:EXT:frontend/Resources/
                            Private/Language/locallang_ttc.
                            xlf:header_link_formlabel',
```

```
                    ],
                ],
            ],
            'softref' => 'typolink'
        ]
    ],
],
# define the order on how the fields should be shown in TYPO3s
Backend Editing view
'types' => [
    1 => [
        'showitem' => '
            title,
            promotiondate,
            promotiontime,
            location,
            locationlink,
            description,
            '
    ]
]
];
```

Read the TCA Reference guide[4] to learn more about the many available options.

With this TCA information, TYPO3 will generate some additional metafields automatically (such as unique ID, page ID, creation date, etc.) once the extension is activated, which we'll do in step 3.

Expected outcome: You have created two new files, "ext_tables.sql" and "tx_promotionevents_domain_model_event.php" that configure a table and fields for a new, custom record type in the database.

---

[4]https://docs.typo3.org/m/typo3/reference-tca/master/en-us/Introduction/Index.html

Step 3: Activate the extension and add events

Now, it's time to turn on what we've built and add some data to it:

1. Go to the TYPO3 backend and navigate to the **Admin Tools ➤ Extensions** module. This is the extension manager; it lists all installed extensions. The "promotionevents" extension should appear in the list, though deactivated and grayed out (Figure 9-1).

Figure 9-1. *The deactivated "promotionevents" extension, with the Activate button circled*

2. Click the **Activate** button to activate the extension.

3. Navigate to the **Page ➤ List** module and create a new page.

4. Set the **Type** to "Folder" and give it the title "Promotion Events," and then save and close (Figure 9-2).

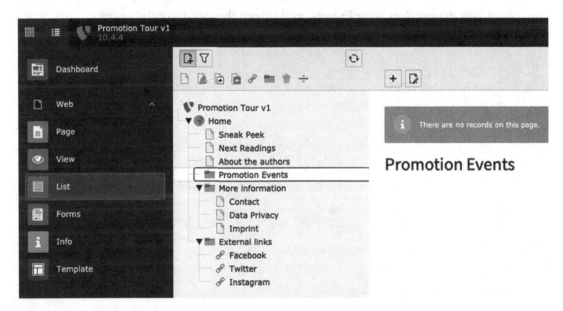

Figure 9-2. *The Promotion Events folder in the page tree*

5. In the page tree, select the Promotion Events folder you just created, and then click the + button (**Create New Record**). A list of the possible records you can create is displayed (Figure 9-3).

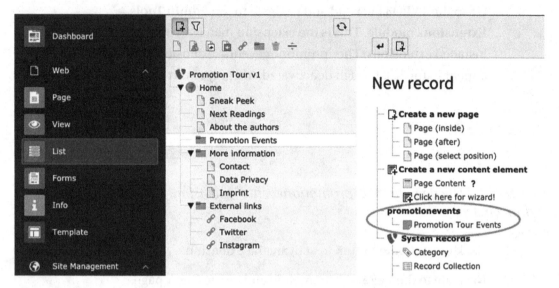

Figure 9-3. *The possible records you can create in the Promotion Events folder, with the Promotion Tour Events record circled*

6. Click **Promotion Tour Events**, and fill out the details of the event. It might look something like Figure 9-4.

Create new Promotion Tour Events on page "Promotion Events"

Headline

A reading session with Emma Banton   ×

Date of the Event

26-08-2020   📅

Start time of the Event

19:00   📅

Location

Casper's Little Coffee Shop, Lisboa, Portugal   ×

Optional Link to the location

https://www.caspers-coffee-shop.dev/   ×   ✂   🔗

Additional information

Normal   ▾ | **B** *I* x₂ x² | ☰ ☰ | ☰ ☰ | " | ☰ ☰ ☰ ☰ | ⊕ ⊗ |

✂ ⬚ ▦ ▦ ▦ | I_x | ↰ ↱ | ABC▾ | ▦▾ ☰ Ω ↔ | ⤢ | ⌨ Source

This is the first time Emma will be in front of a small crowd reading from her latest book. Don't miss it. Please RSVP as Casper's Little Coffee Shop only has a limited auditorium of 1000 people. Don't forget: Tip generously.

Figure 9-4. *A Promotion Tour Events record*

7. Save and close the event record.

8. Create another five events with dates in the future.

Expected outcome: Your **Promotion Events** folder lists a number of future events.

Step 4: Create the plugin

To create the plugin, we need to register it in two places:

- The **Create New Content Element** window, so that editors can add Promotion Events to a page.

- The output definition (TypoScript and Fluid) to specify how the Promotion Events should be rendered on the website.

1. In the extension directory, create a new file in the directory Configuration/TCA/Overrides called "plugins.php". The name of the file does not matter here, but the folder structure is important.

2. Paste in the following:

```php
<?php
defined('TYPO3_MODE') or die();

\TYPO3\CMS\Extbase\Utility\ExtensionUtility::registerPlugin(
    'promotionevents', // Extension Name
    'Upcoming', // Plugin identifier
    'Upcoming Promotion Events', // Label
    'EXT:promotionevents/Resources/Public/Icons/Extension.png'
    // Icon
);
```

3. In the root directory of the "promotionevents" extension, create a file named "ext_localconf.php".

4. Paste the following code:

```php
<?php
defined('TYPO3_MODE') or die();

\TYPO3\CMS\Extbase\Utility\ExtensionUtility::configurePlugin(
    'promotionevents',  // Extension Name
    'Upcoming', // Plugin identifier
    [
        // A group of all controllers and actions for this plugin
        \PromotionTourWebsite\PromotionEvents\Controller\
        EventsController::class => 'upcoming,detail'
```

```
    ],
    [
        // No uncacheable plugin actions
    ]
);
```

Note This file references a PHP class that does not exist yet, but we will create it soon.

---

5. In your browser, go to the TYPO3 backend. At the top right of the screen, click the lightning bolt icon and select **Flush all caches**.

6. Go to the **Web ➤ Page** module and select the "Next Readings" page in the page tree.

7. Click the **+ Content** button. The **Create new content element** window displays.

8. Go to the **Plugins** tab and select **General Plugin** (Figure 9-5).

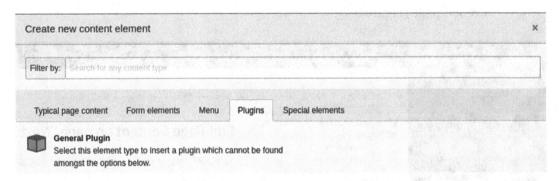

Figure 9-5. *The Plugins tab on the Create new content element window*

The **Create new Page Content** screen displays.

9.   In the **Plugin** tab, click the **Selected Plugin** menu, and choose "Upcoming Promotion Events" (Figure 9-6).

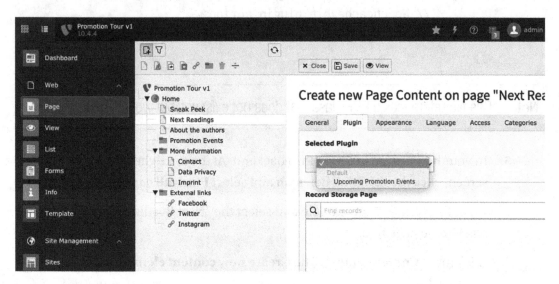

Figure 9-6.   *The Selected Plugin menu on the Plugin tab*

10.   In the **Record Storage Page** field, find and select the "Promotion Events" page (Figure 9-7).

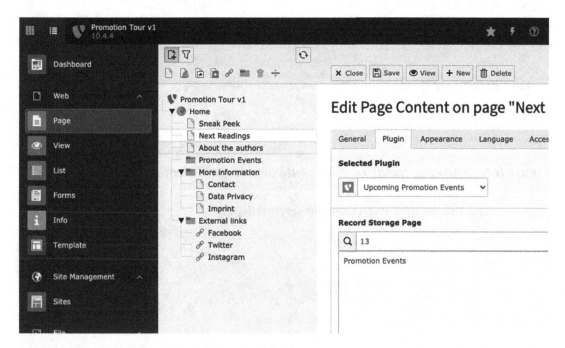

Figure 9-7.   *The Record Storage Page field*

11.   Save and close the content element record.

   If you view this page in the frontend, you should see the message
   "Oops, an error occurred!". This is because we haven't created the
   TypoScript and the PHP class yet.

12.   In your file system, create the following directory in the extension
   root folder Classes/Controller/.

13.   Create a file called "EventsController.php" and paste in the following:

```php
<?php

namespace PromotionTourWebsite\PromotionEvents\Controller;

use TYPO3\CMS\Extbase\Mvc\Controller\ActionController;

class EventsController extends ActionController
{
    public function upcomingAction()
    {

    }
}
```

14.   In Guides 1 and 2, we installed TYPO3 via Composer, which
   means the class cannot be found until we declare it in a composer.
   json file. In a real-life project, you would use a composer.json
   file within the extension. For the sake of brevity, you can add the
   following to the composer.json file in our root project directory
   instead:

```json
"autoload": {
    "psr-4": {
        "PromotionTourWebsite\\PromotionEvents\\":
        "public/typo3conf/ext/promotionevents/Classes"
    }
},
```

15. In a terminal, run "composer dumpautoload" via the
     command line.

16. In the file system, create the template file public/typo3conf/
     ext/promotionevents/Resources/Private/Templates/Events/
     Upcoming.html, and add this HTML code to it to test the output
     on the frontend:

```
<h2>Upcoming Events</h2>
<ul>
    <li>Event a</li>
    <li>Event b</li>
    <li>Event c</li>
</ul>
```

17. Go to the TYPO3 backend in your browser. At the top right of the
     screen, click the lightning bolt icon and select **Flush all caches**.

Expected outcome: When reloading the Next Readings page, your website will look
something like Figure 9-8.

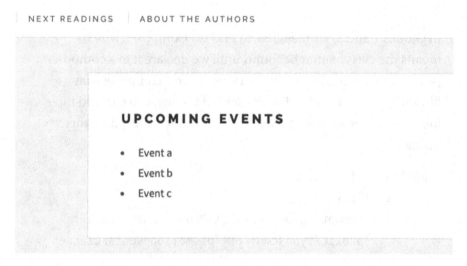

Figure 9-8. *Placeholder events listed on the frontend*

Step 5: Fetch content from the database

We are now rendering static content from the template file. Let's make the plugin load the events we added in step 3 from the database. We need to create a domain model PHP class that can represent a single event, and a repository PHP class to fetch the domain model objects representing the database records:

1. For the domain repository PHP class, create a folder in the "promotionevents" root directory called Classes/Domain/ Repository/.

2. In this folder, create a file called "EventRepository.php" with the following content:

```php
<?php

namespace PromotionTourWebsite\PromotionEvents\Domain\Repository;

use TYPO3\CMS\Extbase\Persistence\QueryInterface;
use TYPO3\CMS\Extbase\Persistence\Repository;

class EventRepository extends Repository
{
    public function findUpcoming()
    {
        $query = $this->createQuery();
        $query->greaterThan(
            'promotiondate',
            new \DateTime()
        );
        // Show the next three events
        $query->setLimit(3);
        $query->setOrderings(['promotiondate' =>
        QueryInterface::ORDER_ASCENDING]);
        return $query->execute();
    }
}
```

We've created a new PHP class which has one method, which we've called "findUpcoming()."

3. Next, we place the domain model in the Classes/Domain/Model/ directory. Create a file called "Event.php" with the following content:

```php
<?php

namespace PromotionTourWebsite\PromotionEvents\Domain\Model;

use TYPO3\CMS\Extbase\DomainObject\AbstractEntity;

class Event extends AbstractEntity
{
    /**
     * @var string
     */
    protected $title;

    /**
     * @var string
     */
    protected $description;

    /**
     * @var \DateTime
     */
    protected $promotiondate;

    /**
     * @var \DateTime
     */
    protected $promotiontime;

    /**
```

```php
 * @var string
 */
protected $location;

/**
 * @var string
 */
protected $locationlink;

/**
 * @return string
 */
public function getTitle(): string
{
    return $this->title;
}

/**
 * @return string
 */
public function getDescription(): string
{
    return $this->description;
}

/**
 * @return \DateTime
 */
public function getPromotiondate(): \DateTime
{
    return $this->promotiondate;
}

/**
 * @return \DateTime
 */
```

```php
    public function getPromotiontime(): \DateTime
    {
        return $this->promotiontime;
    }

    /**
     * @return string
     */
    public function getLocation(): string
    {
        return $this->location;
    }

    /**
     * @return string
     */
    public function getLocationlink(): string
    {
        return $this->locationlink;
    }
}
```

Extbase's persistence logic will automatically recognize and fill the properties with the correct data.

4. Now, we need to instruct the controller action, to fetch the upcoming events from the repository and hand the records over to the view—which is in our case using the "Upcoming.html" fluid template. In the promotionevents/Classes/Controller folder, we adapt the EventsController.php so that the contents of the file look like this:

```php
<?php

namespace PromotionTourWebsite\PromotionEvents\Controller;

use PromotionTourWebsite\PromotionEvents\Domain\Repository\
EventRepository;
use TYPO3\CMS\Extbase\Mvc\Controller\ActionController;
```

```php
class EventsController extends ActionController
{
    /**
     * @var EventRepository
     */
    protected $eventRepository;

    public function __construct(EventRepository $eventRepository)
    {
        $this->eventRepository = $eventRepository;
    }

    public function upcomingAction()
    {
        $upcomingEvents = $this->eventRepository->findUpcoming();
        $this->view->assign('upcomingEvents', $upcomingEvents);
    }
}
```

5. In the public/typo3conf/ext/promotionevents/Resources/Private/
    Templates/Events/ directory, adapt the contents of the Fluid
    template to render the upcoming event data. Modify the contents
    of the "Upcoming.html" file to look like this:

```html
<h2>Upcoming Events</h2>
<ul>
<f:for each="{upcomingEvents}" as="event">
    <li>{event.title} at {event.location} on <f:format.date
format="d.m.Y">{event.promotiondate}</f:format.date></li>
</f:for>
</ul>
```

6. Go to the TYPO3 backend and flush all caches.

Expected outcome: When you refresh the Next Readings page, you should see a list
of the next three upcoming events based on the current date, looking something like
Figure 9-9.

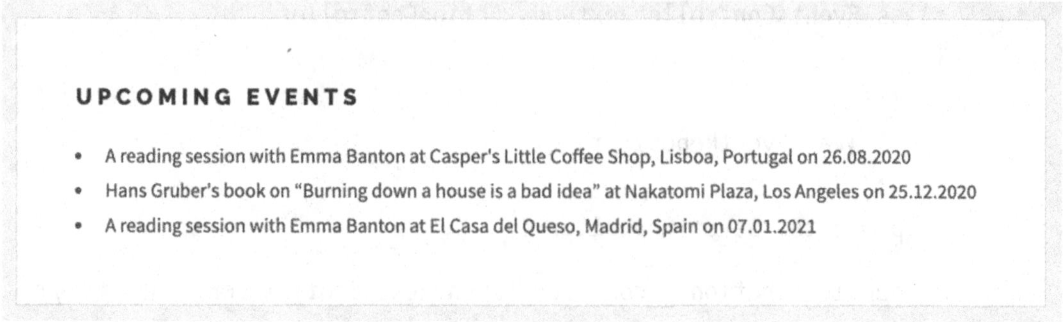

UPCOMING EVENTS

- A reading session with Emma Banton at Casper's Little Coffee Shop, Lisboa, Portugal on 26.08.2020
- Hans Gruber's book on "Burning down a house is a bad idea" at Nakatomi Plaza, Los Angeles on 25.12.2020
- A reading session with Emma Banton at El Casa del Queso, Madrid, Spain on 07.01.2021

Figure 9-9. *List of upcoming events displayed on the frontend*

Step 6: Create a detail view for an event

Now, let's create a link from each event to a page displaying all the event information, including the description text.

In step 4, along with the "upcoming" action, we also specified a "detail" action in the "ext_localconf.php" file:

```
// A group of all controllers and actions for this plugin
\Example\PromotionEvents\Controller\EventsController::class =>
 'upcoming,detail'
```

So all we need to create is

- A new detailAction method in the controller PHP class

- A new Detail.html Fluid template

- A link to the detail action in the Upcoming.html Fluid template

The controller's detailAction method will receive the event as an argument, and we'll hand it off to the view. Everything else is handled by Extbase automatically:

1. In the classes/controller directory, update the EventsController. php file to look like the following:

```
<?php

namespace PromotionTourWebsite\PromotionEvents\Controller;

use PromotionTourWebsite\PromotionEvents\Domain\Model\Event;
```

```php
use PromotionTourWebsite\PromotionEvents\Domain\Repository\
EventRepository;
use TYPO3\CMS\Extbase\Mvc\Controller\ActionController;

class EventsController extends ActionController
{
    /**
     * @var EventRepository
     */
    protected $eventRepository;

    public function __construct(EventRepository $eventRepository)
    {
        $this->eventRepository = $eventRepository;
    }

    public function upcomingAction()
    {
        $upcomingEvents = $this->eventRepository->findUpcoming();
        $this->view->assign('upcomingEvents', $upcomingEvents);
    }

    public function detailAction(Event $event)
    {
        $this->view->assign('event', $event);
    }
}
```

2. Create a new Fluid template file in Resources/Private/Templates/
    Events/ called "Detail.html" to render all details:

```html
<h2>{event.title}</h2>
<p>
    Location: {event.location}<br>
    <f:if condition="{event.locationlink}">
        <f:link.typolink parameter="{event.locationlink}">Location
        details</f:link.typolink>
    </f:if>
</p>
```

```
<p>
    <f:format.date format="d.m.Y">{event.promotiondate}</f:format.
    date> - starts at <f:format.date format="H:i">{event.
    promotiontime}</f:format.date>
</p>
<f:format.html>{event.description}</f:format.html>
```

Remember, we can access all the properties we defined in the event model in the Fluid template using the {event. propertyName} syntax.

3. Update the Upcoming.html file to link to the detail action:

```
<h2>Upcoming Events</h2>
<ul>
<f:for each="{upcomingEvents}" as="event">
    <li>
        {event.title} at {event.location} on <f:format.date
        format="d.m.Y">{event.promotiondate}</f:format.date><br>
        <f:link.action action="detail" arguments="{event:
        event}">More details</f:link.action>
    </li>
</f:for>
</ul>
```

4. Go to the TYPO3 backend and flush all caches.

Expected outcome: When you refresh the Next Readings page, you should see that each event now includes a link to view more details (Figure 9-10).

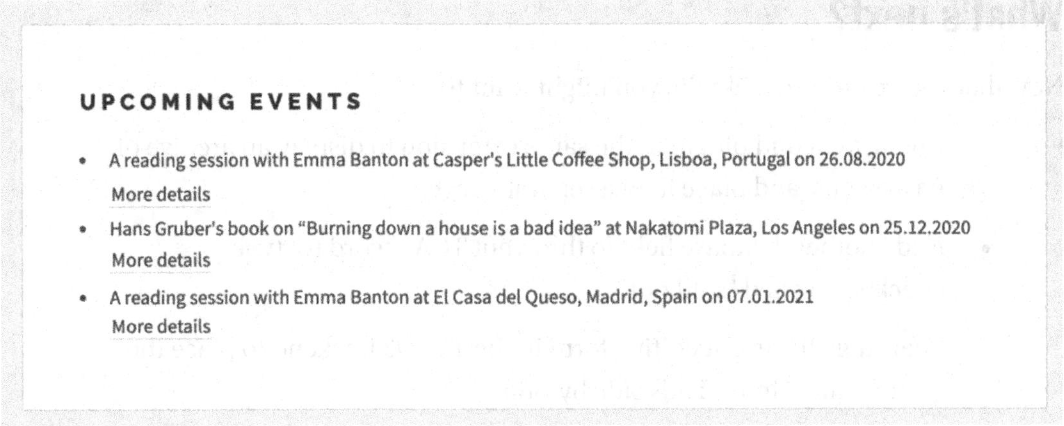

UPCOMING EVENTS

- A reading session with Emma Banton at Casper's Little Coffee Shop, Lisboa, Portugal on 26.08.2020
  More details
- Hans Gruber's book on "Burning down a house is a bad idea" at Nakatomi Plaza, Los Angeles on 25.12.2020
  More details
- A reading session with Emma Banton at El Casa del Queso, Madrid, Spain on 07.01.2021
  More details

Figure 9-10. Each upcoming event now includes a link to more details

When you click one of the links, a page displaying more details and the description for the event should load (Figure 9-11).

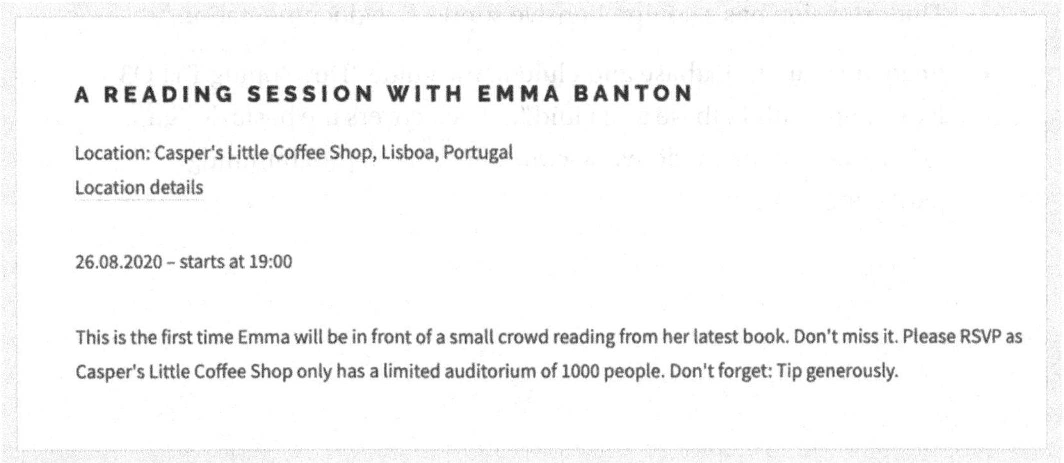

A READING SESSION WITH EMMA BANTON

Location: Casper's Little Coffee Shop, Lisboa, Portugal
Location details

26.08.2020 – starts at 19:00

This is the first time Emma will be in front of a small crowd reading from her latest book. Don't miss it. Please RSVP as Casper's Little Coffee Shop only has a limited auditorium of 1000 people. Don't forget: Tip generously.

Figure 9-11. More details displayed about an event

Summary

Congratulations! You have created a dynamic extension for the frontend called a plugin. Now that you understand the basic Extbase model-view-controller (MVC) concept, you can continue to add functionality to your plugin.

What's next?

Now that you've created a plugin, you might want to

- Create a second plugin in the same extension to display an archive of past events, and place it on a separate page.

- Add another database field to the event TCA record (of type checkbox) called "sold out."

- Rearrange the event editing form in the TYPO3 backend to place the "Date" and "Time" fields side by side.

Resources: Learn more

- Find out more about the extension called "extensionbuilder."[5] It has a graphical interface and can generate TCA, models, repositories, and language files to help you build Extbase-based TYPO3 extensions. This extension has a comprehensive supporting documentation.[6]

- Read more about Extbase and Fluid in the guide "Developing TYPO3 Extensions with Extbase and Fluid,"[7] which covers the basic design principles and the model-view-controller (MVC) programming paradigm.

---

[5]https://github.com/FriendsOfTYPO3/extension_builder
[6]https://docs.typo3.org/p/friendsoftypo3/extension-builder/master/en-us/
[7]https://docs.typo3.org/m/typo3/book-extbasefluid/master/en-us/

CHAPTER 10

Guide 6: Creating a Password-Protected Members' Area

TYPO3 ships with everything you need to build a members' area on your website. You can use a password-protected area to show your clients work in progress, to host downloadable files, or to offer exclusive content and build a sense of community.

In this guide, we'll add a members' area to an existing website—the promotion tour website we created in Guide 2. The area will contain some premium content that should only be available for logged-in users who are members.

The basic authentication process and the functionality to create users and groups are included in TYPO3's core. In order to leverage this functionality, you need a login form. TYPO3 comes with a system extension called "felogin" (frontend login) that provides login, logout, and password reset functionality.[1]

At the end of this tutorial, you will have...

- A frontend usergroup and a single user
- Access-restricted content requiring a login
- A login form

---

[1] https://docs.typo3.org/c/typo3/cms-felogin/master/en-us/

© Felicity Brand, Heather McNamee, and Jeffrey A. McGuire 2021
F. Brand et al., *The TYPO3 Guidebook*, https://doi.org/10.1007/978-1-4842-6525-3_10

Prerequisites

- You will need a modern computer, web browser, and an Internet connection.

- A TYPO3 site. This guide assumes you have completed Guides 2, 3, and 4 from this book, but any TYPO3 site can be used.

- The core extension "felogin" must be installed and enabled.

Step 1: Create a frontend usergroup and user

Access is granted to groups, rather than individual users, in TYPO3. Conceptually, you can think in categories of users—authors, moderators, editors, etc.—and the tasks they need to complete to plan access rules. Practically, planning these groups means lots less work and less risk compared to trying to track access for many individuals. So, the first step in this guide is to create a frontend group and add users to it:

1. In the TYPO3 backend, navigate to the **Web ➤ List** module.

2. Above the page tree, make sure the page with a plus sign is selected. A list of page types—including a folder—should be displayed below it.

3. Drag the folder icon down to just under the Promotion Events folder. The folder will appear in the page tree with an icon indicating that it is disabled.

4. Name it "Users & Groups". The result should look like Figure 10-1.

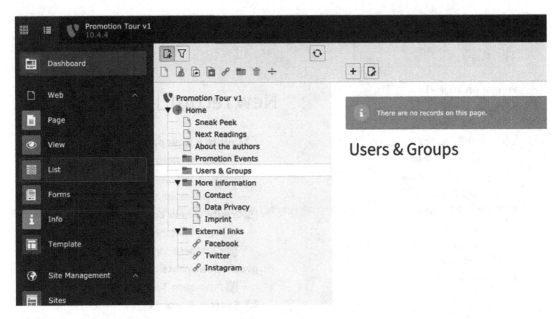

Figure 10-1. *The Users & Groups folder in the page tree*

5. Right-click the folder and choose **Enable** from the context menu.

6. Click the "+" **Create new record** button at the top of the screen to create a new record.

7. Select **Website Usergroup** (see Figure 10-2).

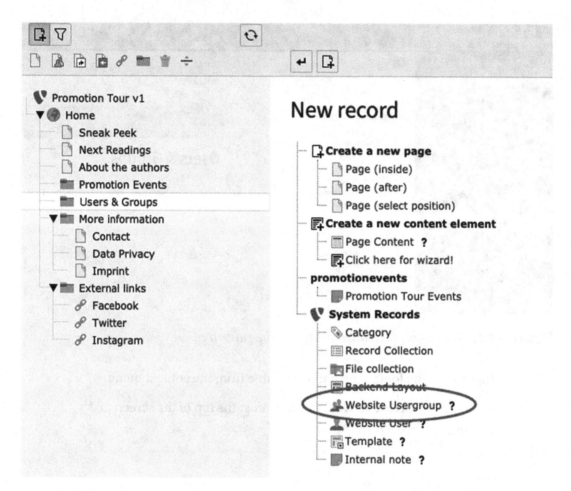

Figure 10-2. *The list of new records you can create, with the Website Usergroup record circled*

8. In the **Group Title** field, type "Members". This name can be changed at any time.

9. Save and close the record.

10. Click the "+" **Create new record** button again, and this time
     create a **Website User** record (shown in Figure 10-3).

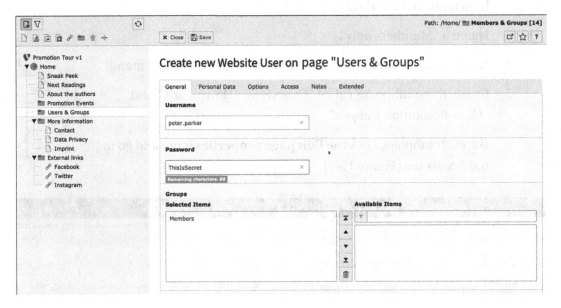

Figure 10-3. *Fields completed in the Website User record*

11. In the **Username** field, type "peter.parker".

12. In the **Password** field, specify a password. Passwords are not
     stored as plain text in the TYPO3 database but as one-way hashes.

13. In the **Groups** section in the **Available Items** list, select
     "Members". It is automatically added to the **Selected Items** list.

14. Save and close the record.

Expected outcome: You have a frontend usergroup called members with one user
assigned to it.

Step 2: Create access-restricted content

Next, we'll create access-restricted content for the members' area, which is content that
only logged-in users can view:

1. In the **Web ➤** Page module, above the page tree, make sure the
    icon at the top left, the "page with a plus sign," is selected. A list of
    page types should be displayed below it.

2. Drag the new page icon down to just above the Promotion Events folder. The page will appear in the page tree with an icon indicating that it is disabled.

3. Name it "Members only".

4. Right-click the page and choose **Enable** from the context menu.

5. Create three subpages called "Overview," "Downloads," and "High-Resolution Images."

6. For each subpage, click the **Edit page properties** icon, and go to the Access tab (Figure 10-4).

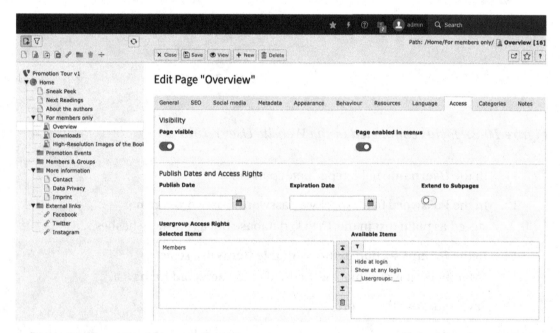

Figure 10-4. *The Access tab used to editing page properties*

7. Toggle the **Page visible** switch to enable the pages.

8. In the **Usergroup Access Rights** section, click "Members." This moves our newly created usergroup to the **Selected Items** list.

9. Save and close. The page icon in the page tree will change, indicating that this page is access-restricted.

10. Navigate to the **Web ➤ Page** module and edit the Overview page. Add some basic content (Figure 10-5).

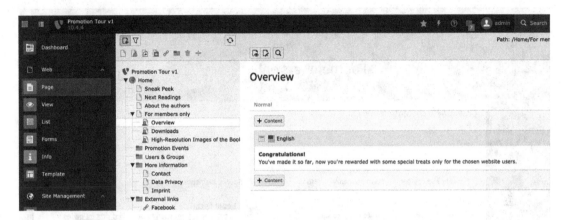

Figure 10-5. *Basic content added on the Overview page*

Expected outcome: When you view your website, you can see "Members only" in the navigation menu, but with no content on it, and no subpages. This is because we're not yet logged in as a website user. In order to log in, we first need to create a login form.

Step 3: Adding a login form

TYPO3 comes with a system extension called "felogin," which we can use for the login form. We need to make sure it's activated and then add the form to a page:

1. Navigate to the **Admin Tools ➤ Extensions** module, and check that the "felogin" extension is activated.

2. Navigate to the **Web ➤ Pages** module and select the "Members only" page.

3.   Click the **+ Content** button, and on the **Form elements** tab, select
     Login form (Figure 10-6).

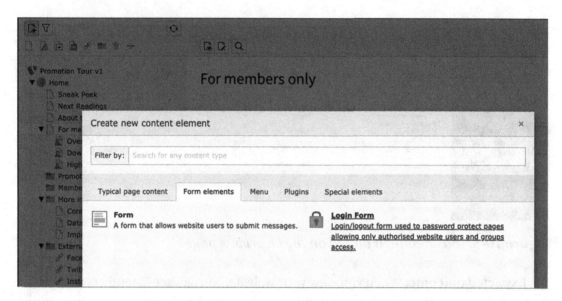

Figure 10-6. *The Form elements tab of the Create new content element window*

4.   Go to the **Plugin** tab. You'll see three tabs under **Plugin Options**.

5.   In the **General** tab, in the **User Storage Page** section, select the
     "Users & Groups" folder.

6. On the **Redirects** tab, in the **Redirect Mode** section, click "After Login (TS or Flexform)." It is added to the **Selected Items** list (Figure 10-7).

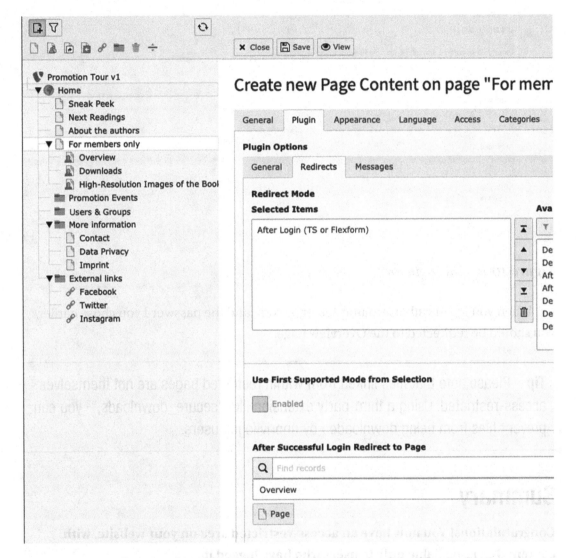

Figure 10-7. *The completed fields on the Redirects tab of the Plugin Options screen*

7. In the **After Successful Login Redirect to Page** section, search for and select the "Overview" page.

8. Save and close the page.

Expected outcome: Go to your website and refresh the "Members Only" page. You should see the login form on the page, as shown in Figure 10-8.

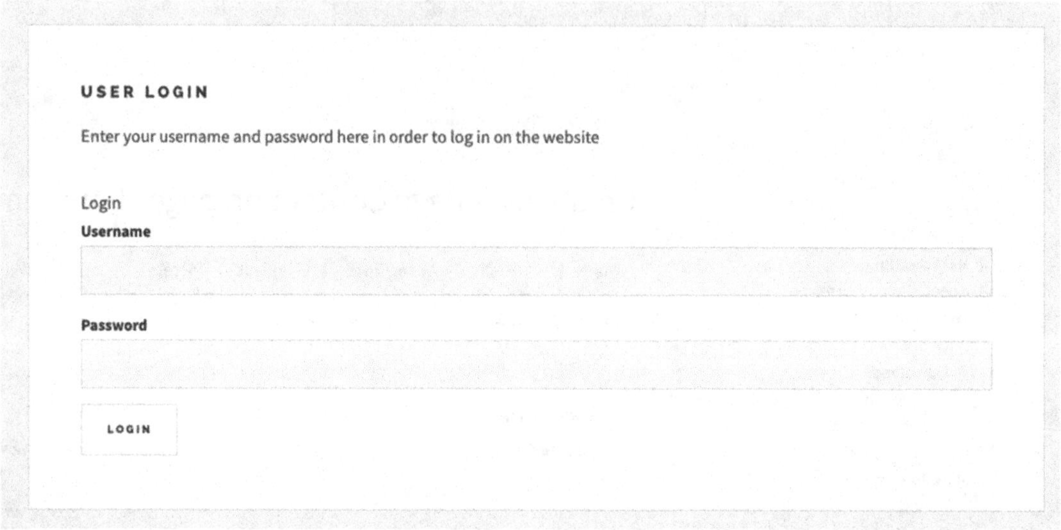

Figure 10-8. *The login form*

When you log in with username "peter.parker" and the password you chose earlier, you should be redirected to the Overview page.

Tip   Please note that files linked from within restricted pages are not themselves access-restricted. Using a third-party extension like "secure_downloads,"[2] you can prevent files from being downloaded by unprivileged users.

Summary

Congratulations! You now have an access-restricted area on your website, with content that is available only to users who have logged in.

TYPO3 allows us to build access-restricted areas very quickly, without having to be a programmer. Access restriction can be applied per page, but also per content element. Access-restricted pages and content elements will only be visible after a successful login.

---

[2]https://extensions.typo3.org/extension/secure_downloads/

> **Tip**   It is possible to restrict a certain part of the page tree to one usergroup and another part to another. You can assign multiple usergroups to one user to give access to various restricted-access areas on your website.

What's next?

Now that you have created a frontend usergroup and a login form, you might like to

- Create another usergroup and another restricted area.

- Create an entire website where all the content is available only after successful login.

- Explore extensions that will manage the login process. With community-contributed extensions for remote login via LDAP, OAuth 2.0, or SAML Authentications, it is possible to store passwords completely outside TYPO3.

- Change the text in the password reset email for the login form.

Resources: Learn more

- This procedure is also described in the Editor's Tutorial[3] in the official TYPO3 documentation.

- The frontend login for website users (felogin) extension comes with comprehensive documentation.[4]

- Take the next step and explore the community-contributed extensions that provide plugins for user registration and forum functionality. This allows you to extend the login and password reset functionality included in TYPO3 Core to build and manage a community of frontend users.

---

[3]https://docs.typo3.org/m/typo3/tutorial-editors/master/en-us/AccessControl/Login/Index.html

[4]https://docs.typo3.org/c/typo3/cms-felogin/master/en-us/Introduction/Index.html

CHAPTER 11

Guide 7: Translating Your Site

Adding multilingual capabilities to a TYPO3 website does not require any programming skills. It can all be configured directly from the TYPO3 backend.

In this guide, we're going to add a language to the website we created in Guide 2, "Promotion Tour." We'll add Spanish as a new language, and add Spanish translations of our existing content.

TYPO3 stores translated records, such as content elements, as separate database records. A number of database fields are used to identify the language and the record it was translated from. Usually this is referred to as the "sys_language_uid" or the "languageId." Language ID zero represents the default language of the site.

For our case, we have an English website (language ID zero), and we would like to add a new language (Spanish), so editors can translate content into this language.

At the end of this tutorial, you will have...

- A website with pages and content in English and Spanish.

- An option in the menu on your website to switch between languages.

Prerequisites

- You will need a modern computer, web browser, and an Internet connection.

- A TYPO3 site. This guide assumes you have completed Guides 2, 3, and 4 from this book, but any TYPO3 site can be used.

© Felicity Brand, Heather McNamee, and Jeffrey A. McGuire 2021
F. Brand et al., *The TYPO3 Guidebook*, https://doi.org/10.1007/978-1-4842-6525-3_11

Step 1: Adding a new language

We'll add the Spanish language to the TYPO3 instance:

1. In the TYPO3 backend, navigate to the **Web ➤ List** module.

2. In the page tree, select the root page of your TYPO3 installation. You'll find it at the top of your page tree with the TYPO3 logo as an icon. In our example, it is called "promotion tour" (Figure 11-1).

3. Click the "+" **Create new record** button at the top of the screen to create a new record.

4. Select **Website Language** (Figure 11-1).

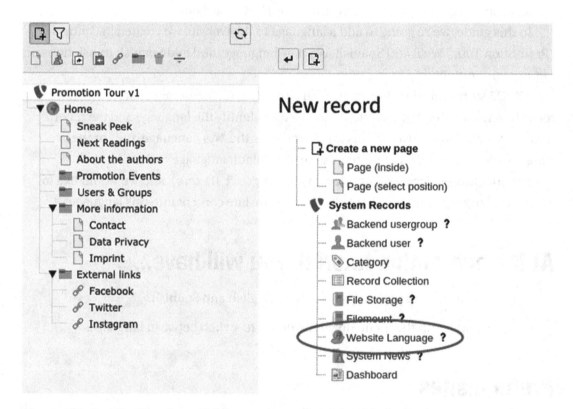

Figure 11-1. *The list of available new records with Website Language record circled*

5. In the **Language** field, type "Spanish".

6. In the **Select language** list, select "Spanish, Castilian."

7. In the **Select flag icon** list, select "es" (Figure 11-2).

Figure 11-2. *The fields for the Website Language record*

8. Save and close the record.

Expected outcome: You have added a record for Spanish to your TYPO3 instance. If it is the first language you add, Spanish will be assigned language ID 1.

Step 2: Assigning the language to a site

One TYPO3 instance can have multiple sites, each with different languages. You need to configure the language for each site to activate the translation mode:

1.   Navigate to the **Site Management ➤ Sites** module (Figure 11-3), and click the pencil icon to edit the main site configuration.

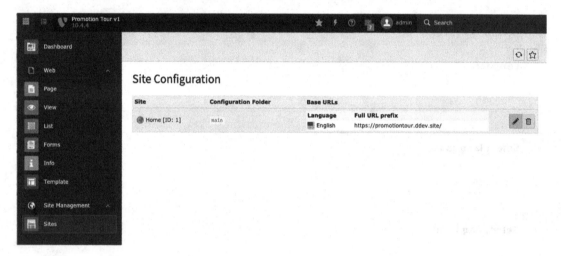

Figure 11-3. *The Sites module*

2. On the **Languages** tab, select Spanish. Scroll down to see the
    fields that become available and need configuration (Figure 11-4).

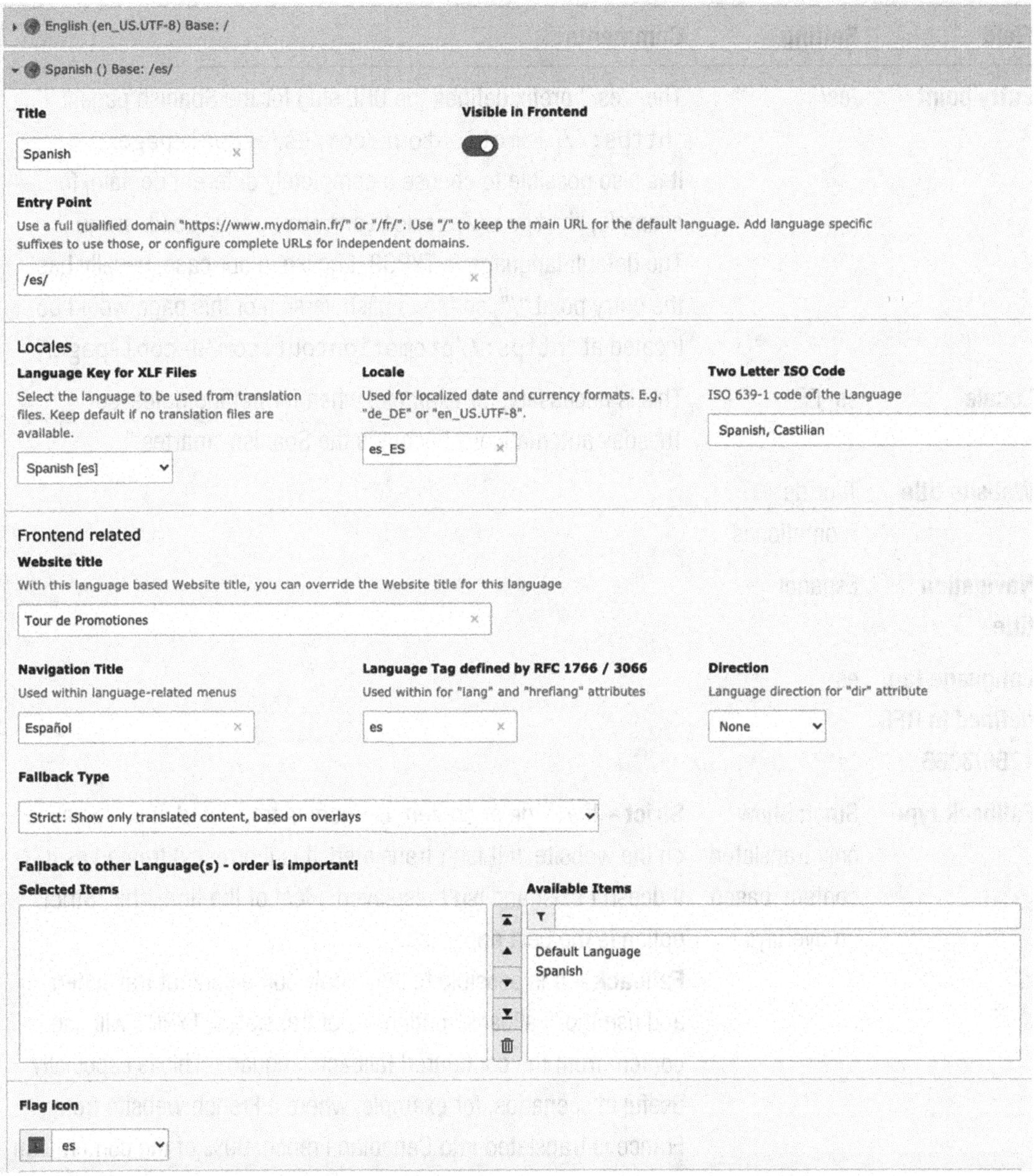

▸ ● English (en_US.UTF-8) Base: /

▾ ● Spanish () Base: /es/

Title

| Spanish | × |

Visible in Frontend

Entry Point

Use a full qualified domain "https://www.mydomain.fr/" or "/fr/". Use "/" to keep the main URL for the default language. Add language specific
suffixes to use those, or configure complete URLs for independent domains.

| /es/ | × |

Locales

Language Key for XLF Files

Select the language to be used from translation
files. Keep default if no translation files are
available.

| Spanish [es] | ⌄ |

Locale

Used for localized date and currency formats. E.g.
"de_DE" or "en_US.UTF-8".

| es_ES | × |

Two Letter ISO Code

ISO 639-1 code of the Language

| Spanish, Castilian |

Frontend related

Website title

With this language based Website title, you can override the Website title for this language

| Tour de Promotiones | × |

Navigation Title

Used within language-related menus

| Español | × |

Language Tag defined by RFC 1766 / 3066

Used within for "lang" and "hreflang" attributes

| es | × |

Direction

Language direction for "dir" attribute

| None | ⌄ |

Fallback Type

| Strict: Show only translated content, based on overlays | ⌄ |

Fallback to other Language(s) - order is important!

Selected Items

Available Items

| ▼ |

Default Language
Spanish

Flag icon

| ▦ | es | ⌄ |

Figure 11-4. *The fields on the Languages tab*

271

3. Configure the fields as shown in Table 11-1.

Table 11-1. *Languages tab fields*

Field	Setting	Comments
Entry point	/es/	The "/es/" prefix defines the URL slug for the Spanish pages: "`https://promotiontour.com/es/a-cool-page.`" It is also possible to choose a completely different domain, for example, "`https://promotiontour.es/a-cool-page.`" The default language in TYPO3, English in our case, usually has the entry point "/", so the English version of this page would be located at "`https://promotiontour.com/a-cool-page.`"
Locale	es_ES	This is necessary, for example, when formatting dates, so Tuesday automatically becomes the Spanish "martes."
Website title	Tour de Promotiones	
Navigation title	Español	
Language tag defined in RFC 1766/3066	es	
Fallback type	Strict: Show only translated content, based on overlays	**Strict** – If a page or content element is translated, it is displayed on the website. If it isn't translated, it is (correctly) treated as if it doesn't exist and isn't displayed. Most of the time, the "Strict" option is the best approach. **Fallback** – It is possible to leave only some content translated and use the "Fallback" option. If not translated, TYPO3 will use content from the configured fallback language. This is especially useful in scenarios, for example, where a French website from France is translated into Canadian French. 90% of the content can probably be left untranslated and fall back to the French original. **Free** – The "Free" option refers to an approach where we're not actually talking about translations anymore. Each language can have entirely separate, different content.

4. Save and close the record.

Expected outcome: You now have two languages configured for your site: Spanish and, the default, English.

Tip   Language fallback handling only applies to text content, not media or images, nor URL handling. Using the Filelist module, you can localize your media assets' metadata for each language. See multilingual websites with TYPO3 in Chapter 2 for more information.

Step 3: Translating pages and content

There are two different methods for translating content in TYPO3: "translate" and "copy." In this guide we'll use the "translate" method, which creates a direct connection between the original language and translation. The "copy" method allows the translated text to diverge from the original. The option you choose has an impact on the editing workflow (can you use different modes for each page/language combination), and it is difficult to revert the decision once made. For information about each method and how they work, see the "Translation workflow" section in Chapter 2:

1. Navigate to the **Web ➤ Page** module, and select the "Home" page in the page tree.

2. At the top of the page, there is a drop-down menu containing the options "Columns" and "Languages" (Figure 11-5). Select "Languages."

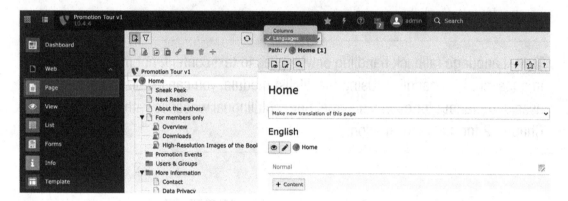

Figure 11-5. The drop-down menu at the top of the Page module screen

3. In the **Make new translation of this page** drop-down, select "Spanish."

4. Translate the title of the "Home" page.

5. Save and close the page. You'll see a second column with the Spanish version of the page (Figure 11-6).

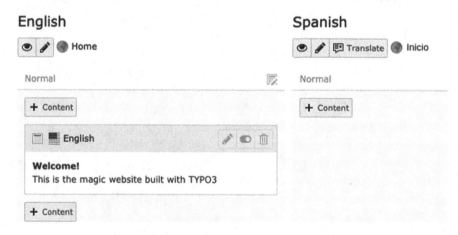

Figure 11-6. A column of content per language

6. At the top of the Spanish column, click the **Translate** button. The **Localize page** wizard displays (Figure 11-7).

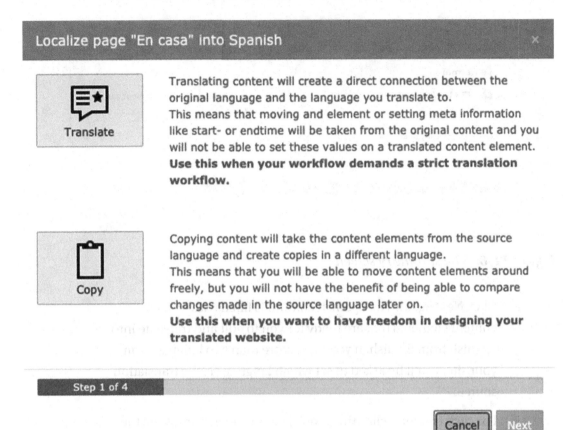

Figure 11-7. *The **Localize page** wizard*

7. Select the **Translate** option, and then click **Next**. A summary screen displays, as shown in Figure 11-8.

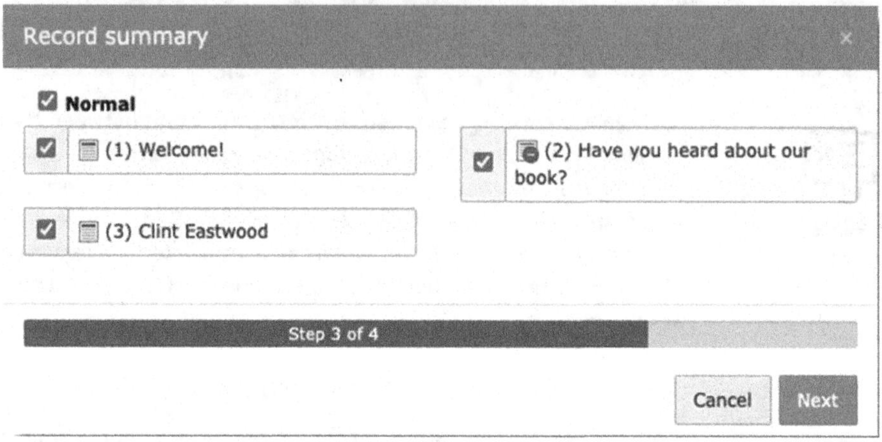

Figure 11-8. The summary screen

8. Click **Next** again. The Spanish column is filled with hidden content elements that are ready for you to edit and translate into Spanish from English. If you have more than two languages on your site, you'll be asked to set which language is the translation source.

9. For each element, click the pencil icon to edit and translate the text. All content is prefixed with "[Translate to Spanish]" so you know what needs to be translated.

When you've translated some content, your page should look something like Figure 11-9.

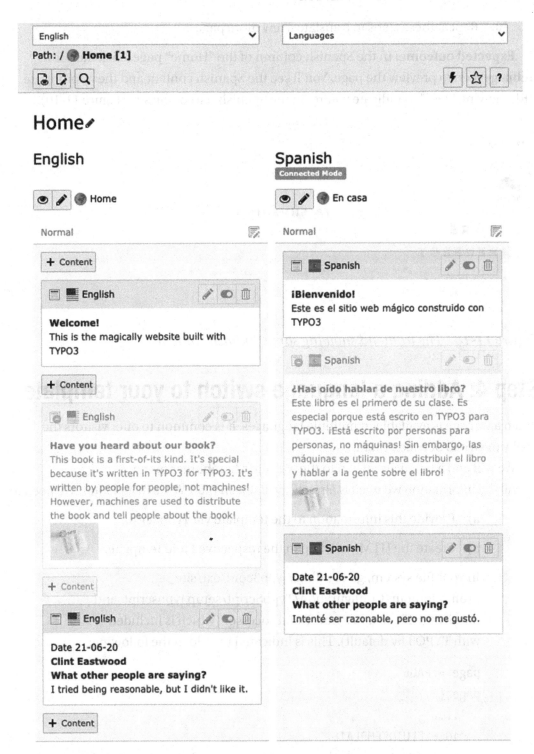

Figure 11-9. *Some English content elements translated into Spanish*

10.   Repeat these steps to translate a few more pages.

Expected outcome: In the Spanish column of the "Home" page, click the **View webpage** icon to preview the page. You'll see the Spanish content and the appropriate URL showing "/es/" to indicate you're on the Spanish part of the site (Figure 11-10).

Figure 11-10. *The frontend showing some Spanish content*

Step 4: Adding a language switch to your template

When a website is available in multiple languages, it is common to offer visitors the ability to switch between them.

We will add a language switch to the website's hamburger menu.

All the information we need is already available in the TYPO3 installation. We need to

a)   Provide this information to the template via TypoScript.

b)   Create the HTML markup in the respective Fluid template.

1.   In your file system, go to public/typo3conf/ext/site_promotiontour/Configuration/TypoScript/setup.typoscript, and modify the file to add a new DataProcessor (which is included with TYPO3 by default). This is indicated in bold in the following:

```
page = PAGE
page {
    ...
    10 = FLUIDTEMPLATE
    10.templateRootPaths.10 = {$page.templates.templateRootPath}
```

```
10.partialsRootPaths.10 = {$page.templates.partialRootPath}
10.layoutRootPaths.10 = {$page.templates.layoutRootPath}
10.templateName = Default
10.dataProcessing {
    1 = TYPO3\CMS\Frontend\DataProcessing\SiteProcessor
    1.as = site
    10 = TYPO3\CMS\Frontend\DataProcessing\MenuProcessor
    10 {
        levels = 1
        as = headerMenu
    }
    20 = TYPO3\CMS\Frontend\DataProcessing\MenuProcessor
    20 {
        special = directory
        special.value = 5
        as = popoverMenu
    }
    30 = TYPO3\CMS\Frontend\DataProcessing\LanguageMenuProcessor
    30.as = languageMenu
}
}
```

Now, all information about a page and possible other variants of
the page in different languages is now available as "languageMenu"
in the Page Template Fluid file. For more information about
dataProcessing and the LanguageMenuProcessor, see the
TypoScript Template Reference.[1]

2. Go to public/typo3conf/ext/site_promotiontour/Resources/
    Private/Templates/Page/Default.html, and add the following code
    after the `<section id="menu">` HTML snippet as indicated in
    bold in the following:

```
<section id="menu">
    ...
```

---

[1]https://docs.typo3.org/m/typo3/reference-typoscript/master/en-us/ContentObjects/
Fluidtemplate/DataProcessing.html

```
<!-- Links -->
<section>
    <ul class="links">
        <f:for each="{popoverMenu}" as="menuItem">
            <li class="{f:if(condition: menuItem.active,
            then:'active')}">
                <a href="{menuItem.link}" target="{menuItem.
                target}" title="{menuItem.title}">
                    <h3>{menuItem.title}</h3>
                    <p>{menuItem.description}</p>
                </a>
            </li>
        </f:for>
    </ul>
</section>

<!-- Actions -->
<section>
    <ul class="actions stacked">
        <f:for each="{languageMenu}" as="menuItem">
            <f:if condition="{menuItem.active} == 0">
                <li><a href="{menuItem.link}" class="button
                large fit">Switch to {menuItem.
                navigationTitle}</a></li>
            </f:if>
        </f:for>
    </ul>
</section>

</section>
```

3. Go to the TYPO3 backend in your browser. At the top right of the
   screen, click the lightning bolt icon, and then select **Flush all
   caches**.

Expected outcome: Refresh your browser to view the Home page. The hamburger
menu icon displays a **Switch to Español** button, shown in Figure 11-11.

Figure 11-11. *The hamburger menu circled on the frontend, and the menu showing the Switch to Español button*

Summary

Congratulations, your website is now available in two languages!

Your editors can manually translate your content, and your website visitors can switch between languages.

What's next?

Now that you've added a language to your website, you might like to

- Repeat the steps in this guide to add a third language.

- Explore the community-contributed extension called "l10nmgr"[2] that can export your content into standardized formats for common translation memory systems [TMS], like Trados, and import translated content again.

---

[2]https://extensions.typo3.org/extension/l10nmgr/

Resources: Learn more

- Find out more about the single-tree and multitree approach to translation in the "Approaches to multisite configuration" section in Chapter 2.

- The official TYPO3 Frontend Localization Guide[3] provides comprehensive information about creating a website in multiple languages.

---

[3]https://docs.typo3.org/m/typo3/guide-frontendlocalization/master/en-us/Index.html

CHAPTER 12

Guide 8: Configuring Content Management Workflow and Permissions

TYPO3's powerful permission system can allow teams of editors, even thousands of them, to manage content through the backend. Administrators have fine-grained control over who can see and edit what content, determined by a number of factors, including user role, language, location within the page tree, and more.

As an administrator or integrator, you should take care that the options and fields provided fit editors' everyday workflow. Providing too many options can add complexity and slow things down, while too many limitations can block the creative process.

In this guide, using the promotion tour website we created in Guide 2, we'll create a usergroup for the editor role, configure it to only be able to manage content and upload files in the restricted, password-protected area we created in Guide 7, and then create an editor user to test the permissions.

TYPO3 permission basics

In TYPO3, you can control permissions for the frontend output to site visitors and, in the backend, for administrators, system maintainers, and editors.

283

There are three types of backend users:

1. **Editors**, following the principle of least privilege, don't have any permissions to see or change anything, unless explicitly granted.

2. **Administrators (admins)** can see and do anything related to content within a TYPO3 installation. For example, this role can create additional editors and administrators, can modify permissions, and see all system-relevant settings.

3. **System maintainers** can do anything an admin can. In addition, this role has access rights to change TYPO3 installation-wide and low-level settings for maintaining database consistency, handling TYPO3 updates, and more.

When installing TYPO3, an administrator with system maintainer permissions is automatically created. This guide will focus on the editor role and the permissions needed to have a limited set of options available in TYPO3.

Permissions are set on a group basis. Editors should be assigned to a usergroup, giving all users in that group the same permissions. This is especially useful when your project is growing and you need many people as editors or other jobs. Since we also say "all users with the editor role," it's helpful to give your groups meaningful names.

At the end of this tutorial, you will have...

- A file mount to a specific folder in the file system to allow access to files

- A backend usergroup with one backend user assigned

- Permissions for the usergroup, restricting access to the file mount

Prerequisites

- You will need a modern computer, web browser, and an Internet connection.

- A TYPO3 site. This guide assumes you have completed Guides 2, 3, 4, and 7 from this book, but any TYPO3 site can be used.

Step 1: Creating the file mount

For our promotion tour website, we want to have editors who are able to manage content for a limited part of the website—the restricted members' only area that we created in Guide 7. We configure a "file mount" to give a usergroup access to a specific folder in the file structure:

1. In the TYPO3 backend, navigate to the **File ➤ Filelist** module.

2. Click the main folder "fileadmin/" and then click the "+" **Create new record** button at the top of the module (Figure 12-1).

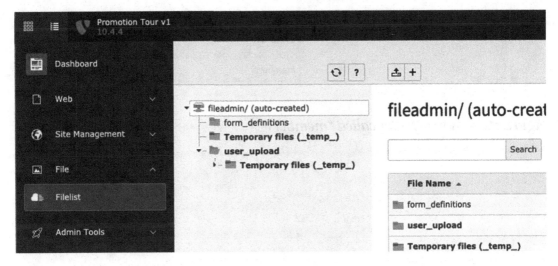

Figure 12-1. *The Filelist module and page tree*

3. Add a new folder called "members" (Figure 12-2).

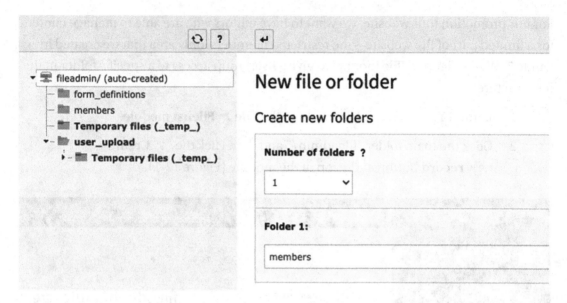

Figure 12-2. *A new folder called "members"*

4. Go to the **Web ➤ List** module, and select the Promotion Tour root page in the page tree.

5. Click the "+" **Create new record** button on the very top of the module, and select "Filemount" (Figure 12-3).

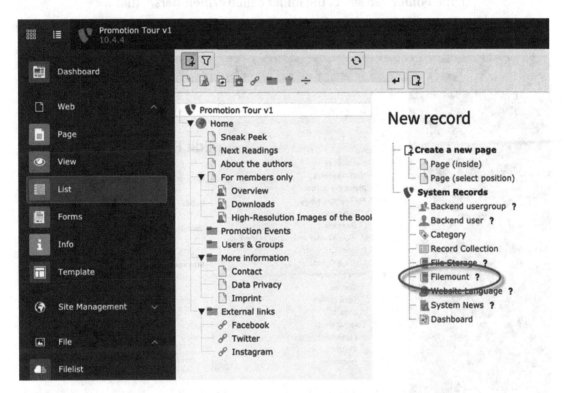

Figure 12-3. *The list of new record options, with "Filemount" circled*

6. Configure the file mount as follows:

    ◦ In the **Label** field, type "Member area".

    ◦ In the **Storage** list, select "fileadmin".

    ◦ In the **Folder** list, select the folder called "/members/" that we just created (Figure 12-4).

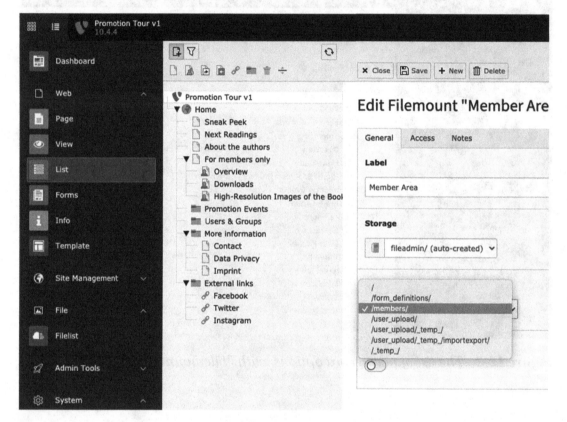

Figure 12-4. *The fields configured for Filemount*

7. Save and close the record.

Expected outcome: You now have a file mount called "Member area" for the promotion tour site.

Step 2: Creating a backend user group

Before we create an editor user, we'll create a usergroup and set the permissions for all users that are attached to that group.

When setting permissions, there are a lot of options. Doing this on a per-group basis lets admins control the activities of classes of users, defined by their usergroups. This is best practice and makes for more efficient and more secure user management, as you don't need to set these options for each user over and over again:

1. Go to the **System ➤ Backend Users** module.

2. In the drop-down list at the top of the screen, select "Backend user groups" (Figure 12-5).

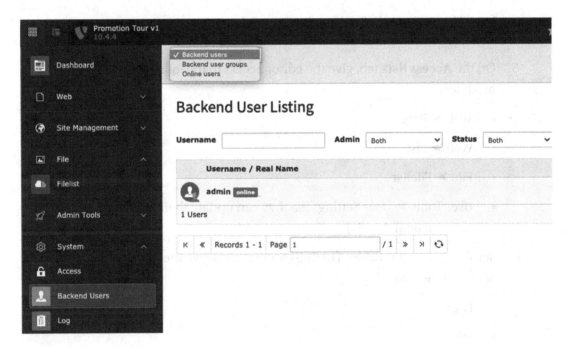

Figure 12-5. *The drop-down list at the top of the screen of the Backend Users module*

3. Click the "+" **Create new record** button.

4. On the **General** tab, in the **Grouptitle** field, type "Member Area Managers" (Figure 12-6).

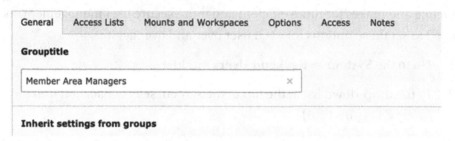

Figure 12-6. *The Grouptitle field on the General tab*

5. On the **Access lists** tab, give the editor access to the following modules:

    o   Web ➤ Page

    o   Web ➤ List

    o   File ➤ Filelist

    o   User Tools ➤ User Settings (so they can update their password and personal details)

6. Scroll down to the **Tables (listing)** section, and give the editor access to the following:

    o   Page

    o   File

    o   File collection

    o   File metadata

    o   File reference

    o   Page content

7. Scroll down and tick the **Toggle all** box (Figure 12-7) for the
    following sections:

    ◦ **Page types**

    ◦ **Allowed excludefields**

    ◦ **File reference**

    ◦ **File collection**

    ◦ **Page**

Figure 12-7. *The Toggle all box for sections on the Access lists tab*

8. On the **Mounts and Workspaces** tab (Figure 12-8), do the following:

    ◦ In the **DB Mounts** section, select the "For members only" page.

    ◦ In the **File Mounts** section, select "Member area."

    ◦ In the **Fileoperation permissions** section, tick the **Toggle all** box.

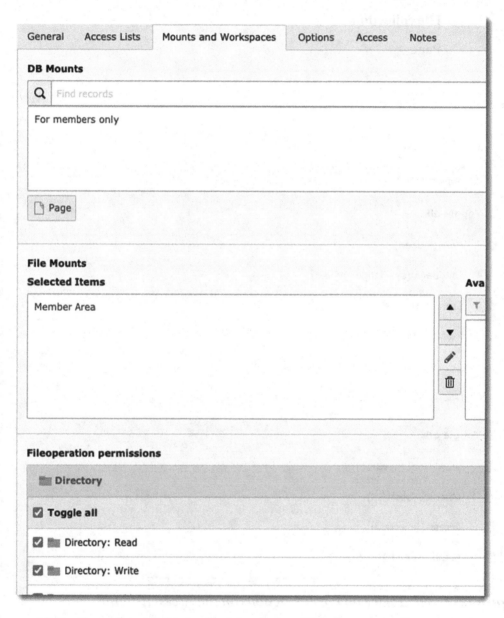

Figure 12-8. *Completed fields in the Mounts and Workspaces tab*

9.   Save and close the record.

Expected outcome: You now have a backend usergroup called "Member Area Managers."

Tip   In this step, for clarity and brevity, we created a usergroup expressly for the members' area editors. Permissions are cumulative and inheritable in TYPO3; a user has all the permissions granted to all usergroups they belong to. The best practice is to create a usergroup for general access permissions for all users. Then, add a sub-usergroup on top of that, granting additional permissions for editors. If we were putting this project site into production, we would add a further subgroup, extending the editors group, adding the permissions for the members' area editors.

For more on this topic, see the "Configure user permissions" section of Chapter 3, which includes a visual metaphor (Figure 3-5) that we find helpful in explaining this concept. The image is taken from the article "Creating TYPO3 Backend Usergroups Your Clients Will Love"[1] by Desirée Lochner at b13. It provides useful information about designing well-organized backend usergroups.

---

[1]https://b13.com/blog/creating-typo3-backend-usergroups-your-clients-will-love

Step 3: Giving access to the page tree

The actions users and groups can perform on a given page are configured in the Access module. It allows you to disallow specific actions for specific pages and subpages:

1. Go to the **System ➤ Access** module, and in the page tree, select the "For members only" page (Figure 12-9).

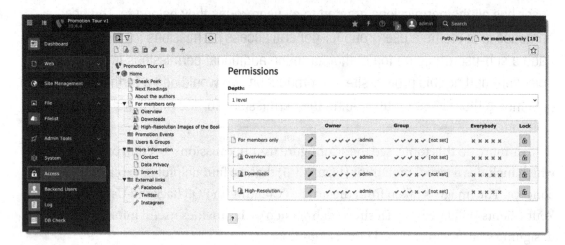

Figure 12-9. *The Access module and page tree*

2. Click the pencil **Change permissions** button next to the For members only page, so that we can add the newly created Group to this page and all subpages:

    ◦   In the **Group** list, select "Member Area Managers" (Figure 12-10).

    ◦   In the **Depth** list, select "Set recursively 1 level."

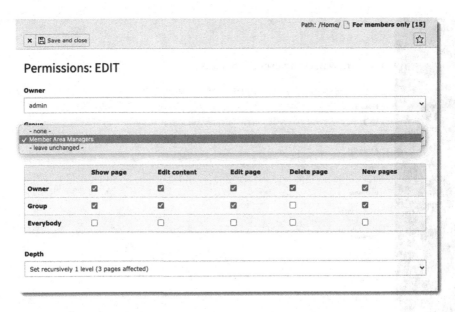

Figure 12-10. *The Permissions screen*

3. Save and close the record.

Expected outcome: You have given the Member Area Managers usergroup access to see, edit, and create pages in the "For members only" section of the page tree, as well as to edit content on those pages.

Step 4: Creating a user

Now that we've covered the steps to prepare our desired functionality, just like we would in a client project, we'll add a user, so we can make sure it all works:

1. Go to the **System ➤ Backend Users** module.

2. Click the "+" **Create new record** button.

3. Configure the user as follows:

   a. In the **Username** field, type "membereditor".

   b. In the **Password** field, type a password.

   c. In the **Group** section, select the newly created "Member Area Managers" group (Figure 12-11).

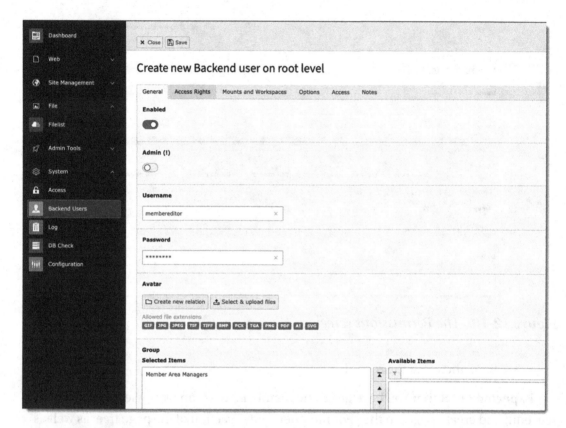

Figure 12-11. *The Create new user screen*

4. Toggle the "Enabled" switch to enable the user.

5. Save and close the record.

Expected outcome: You have added a user to the backend user group "Member Area Managers."

Step 5: Testing the permissions

In order to test this user, you could log out and log in again as the new user. A more convenient way is to use the "Switch User mode." This is a feature of TYPO3 that lets an administrator impersonate another user, without having to enter the password:

1. Click the **Switch to user** button at the far right end of the new editor user row (Figure 12-12).

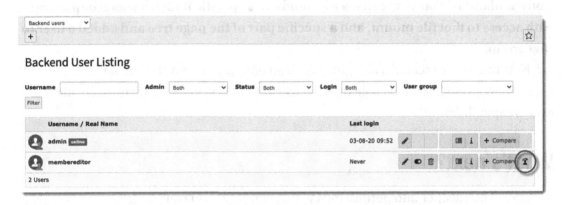

Figure 12-12. *The user listing with the Switch to user button circled*

2. Explore the page tree. You will see only the modules and pages that the "membereditor" user has access to (Figure 12-13).

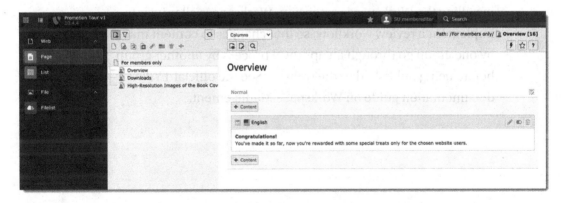

Figure 12-13. *The backend as seen by the "membereditor" user*

3. At the top of the screen, click the "SU membereditor" profile, and then click the Exit button to switch back to your original administrator login.

Expected outcome: You now have a backend user with access to edit and manage the restricted members' area content of the website, but not the rest of it. This is useful for removing visual noise for editors, so they can focus on their work and start editing content right away.

Summary

Congratulations! You've created a file mount to a specific folder, a usergroup access with access to that file mount, and a specific part of the page tree and added a user to that group.

Now that we've created a usergroup, and an editor, you know how to add more editors and groups. You'll be able to make use of TYPO3's powerful permission and access capabilities.

What's next?

- Dive deeper into permissions with subgroups. You can create sophisticated group structures that inherit permissions from others. Find out more on the Setting up User Permissions page[2] of the TYPO3 Getting Started tutorial.

- Further leverage the power of usergroups and permissions by installing the Workspaces extension. Workspaces allow you to implement a review workflow, so that changes to content made by one group go through an approval process by another group before being published to the website. See the official TYPO3 documentation guide on Workspace Management.[3]

---

[2]https://docs.typo3.org/m/typo3/tutorial-getting-started/master/en-us/
UserManagement/GroupPermissions/Index.html

[3]https://docs.typo3.org/c/typo3/cms-workspaces/master/en-us/Administration/
Versioning/Index.html

Resources: Learn more

- Consult the official TYPO3 documentation for comprehensive information about backend access control[4] and permissions.[5]

- Read the TSconfig Reference guide[6] for setting Page TSconfig and User TSconfig.

- The article "Creating TYPO3 Backend Usergroups Your Clients Will Love"[7] by Desirée Lochner at b13 provides useful information about designing well-organized backend usergroups.

---

[4]https://docs.typo3.org/m/typo3/reference-coreapi/master/en-us/ApiOverview/AccessControl/Index.html

[5]https://docs.typo3.org/m/typo3/reference-coreapi/master/en-us/ApiOverview/Fal/Administration/Permissions.html

[6]https://docs.typo3.org/m/typo3/reference-tsconfig/master/en-us/Index.html

[7]https://b13.com/blog/creating-typo3-backend-usergroups-your-clients-will-love

CHAPTER 13

Guide 9: Creating a Business Around TYPO3

TYPO3 is a professional-grade web publishing platform, and a perfect starting point to build—or expand—a professional web agency business.

This guide will be useful for you if you have (or would like to have) a web agency business built around TYPO3. It will help answer some important questions relating to running a business around TYPO3. It will show you how to use some of TYPO3's strengths to find a solid market segment to target and how to make your choice of CMS technology become a marketable unique selling point for your business. If TYPO3 is a technological step up for your business, you might find your sales conversations moving from securing quick wins to building long-term relationships.

This chapter contains ideas and suggested approaches that have worked for others and might work for you. Be creative and flexible when applying them to your own situation. Your particular expertise, knowledge of your local market, and business strengths are one of your unique advantages. Get started; try things out. Learning from your successes and your mistakes is the way to succeed over time.

At the end of this tutorial

You will know more about some areas in which other businesses have succeeded by creating value for clients with TYPO3. You will also understand that

- Certain TYPO3 core features are especially interesting for certain types of clients.

- Internalizing the TYPO3 community's professional approach to website building might change the way you talk with clients.

© Felicity Brand, Heather McNamee, and Jeffrey A. McGuire 2021
F. Brand et al., *The TYPO3 Guidebook*, https://doi.org/10.1007/978-1-4842-6525-3_13

- Certain ways of talking about open source, TYPO3, and your business will leave you with more friends and allies in the business.

- Working with TYPO3, your business philosophy itself might become an inbound marketing channel.

Prerequisites

- Some knowledge of sales and marketing will help you out, but don't let a lack of experience stop you; all of us had to start somewhere.

- The first four chapters of this book contain background information about TYPO3 CMS that will be useful for you in this chapter.

- It is a good idea to read up on TYPO3's features before you start: https://typo3.org/cms/features.

Step 1: Deciding the type of clients and projects to look for

This step will help you if you would like to build a new business or expand beyond your current customer base. If you already have a successful business, you might want to read step 2 first in order to gauge your current status:

1. **Map your current expertise** – This will tell you what type of projects you will be successful with. Do you and your team have knowledge and experience in particular fields or businesses? Any area that you understand well can be a fertile area for you to offer web-based solutions that deliver meaningful business results.

2. **Find out where TYPO3 and your expertise best overlap** – Too many unknowns increase risks; the overlapping area is a safe place to start looking for clients and projects. Even if they aren't the most exciting, they will allow you to build on existing knowledge and TYPO3's strengths and start to build your portfolio.

3. **Be aware of the maturity of potential clients.**

   o **Immature clients have little knowledge of what they need –**
   They might jump on any opportunity if you're a good
   salesperson, but they could easily become disappointed with
   what you deliver because they don't understand your (and their
   own) limitations. Be careful to clarify the goals explicitly, capture
   them in writing, and include definitions of "done" and success.

   o **Maturing clients are learning to know what they need –**
   They have experience from projects that may have failed or
   succeeded, but they understand that a website project is a mutual
   collaboration, in which both parties play a role in succeeding.
   At the same time, limited experience could still produce
   misconceptions about the real requirements.

   o **Mature clients know what they are looking for... and also
   that they don't know everything –** They might hire you as their
   website consultant or professional partner, but beware that an
   ingrown way of working might make introducing a new system
   harder. Changes in workflow can create frustration if it takes time
   to learn—even if it objectively is a better approach.

   Maturity often also varies and depends heavily on the people
   responsible for the various phases—procurement, project
   management, or execution. Even large corporations may turn out to
   be immature clients.

4. **Plan for building long-term relationships –** Whatever the
   maturity of your client, there is also another dimension to
   consider: thinking beyond the next project.

   o **Ask yourself how you can generate real value for the client –**
   Small SEO or user interface optimizations can add up and make
   a large difference quickly. A large project might be good for your
   bank account, but don't sell the project's size—sell the value and
   return on investment.

- **Include maintenance and updates in your planning** – Every website needs investment throughout its lifetime to retain its value as a sales and communication channel. The lifetime of a TYPO3 installation can be very long. As with any large investment, the client should be able to see the value increase year by year. On a $60,000 budget, for example, use only half and suggest the client plan to use the rest on maintenance and refinements over the next three to five years, until the next major revamp.

- **Include training and support in your offers** – All tools require training, and building good websites takes knowledge and experience. Training and support should be a part of your package and defined in a service-level agreement.

- **Stable client relationships are built on clearly defined roles** – If you are the technical service provider, the client should focus on marketing, for example. Think twice about clients who want to do everything themselves, or where their IT department doesn't let you get on with your job as a peer and expert partner.

5. **Define an ideal range of hours and effort you and your team should spend on a project** – How large is the optimal project for you and the client, and how long should it run for? Small projects can be easy to get, but provide small margins. Large projects have larger margins, but often require more experience, involve more risk (what would happen to your business if the project went wrong?), and are harder to estimate. Projects that never end can create fatigue on both sides and turn the client relationship sour.

6. **Write down clear criteria for why you should accept or reject a client and/or project** – Give a prospect a confident "no" if the project doesn't fit you. It can save everyone involved serious headaches. Many clients will value your honesty and still speak well about you, potentially creating valuable new leads elsewhere.

Tip   For all project phases, clients, and prospects, clarify goals explicitly, capture and share them in writing, and include definitions of "done" for your milestones to measure success.

Expected outcome: You have a clear set of decisions about what type of client maturity and project size you are looking for. You have clear criteria that help you choose which leads to pursue and which to drop. You have an understanding that the client relationship doesn't end with the project—it can and should continue for a long time into the future, delivering value to both sides. You know to set clear expectations and communicate them in writing.

Step 2: What features will my market be looking for?

TYPO3 has proven to be especially popular in these market segments:

- Medium and large businesses

- Government sector

- International organizations and NGOs

- Higher education

TYPO3's feature set is also excellent for businesses of these types:

- Franchises and resellers

- Multibrand and multimarket enterprises

- Those in need of integrations to many external systems

The reasons to choose TYPO3 as a website platform are dependent on many factors. For example, location and legal requirements can play a role. While multilingual support may be unnecessary for a business in Portugal, being able to reach German, French, and Italian readers is a frequent requirement in Switzerland. Some countries have stricter laws than others concerning accessibility and data protection.

Take a few minutes to consider the preceding points and then complete the following exercise to help you build a picture of your market:

1. Browse through the list of TYPO3 features[1] on the TYPO3 website.

2. For each market segment and business type, write down three to five TYPO3 features you consider the strongest selling points.

3. Consider which combination of customer needs and TYPO3 features you feel most comfortable with and highlight them. You should focus your attention on these categories in your "comfort zone."

4. Write down the names of real potential clients from your comfort zone categories.

Tip   You don't need to limit yourself to your local area. Distance doesn't matter much if you can offer the best combination of technology and experience.

---

5. Package your offering and highlight key features to simplify the sales process. Selling similar TYPO3 installs to multiple clients will increase your margins and improve your product. This means: don't spend all your energy being creative; it will affect your results.

6. Repeat the steps in this section as if you are one of your competitors looking for new opportunities and gaps in the market, where you fulfill a demand with reduced competition.

Repeat these steps regularly. If you get a client within one category, find similar clients. Understanding the needs of one type of client, knowing how they operate, having a grasp of how TYPO3 can benefit them, and having successful projects (and perhaps testimonials) under your belt can make new sales to similar clients easier.

Expected outcome: You now have a list of client-feature combinations that you would like to focus on. This list will let you focus your work where it makes the most sense, so you can confidently build a business on client insights, unique TYPO3 strong points, and your own expertise.

---

[1]https://typo3.org/cms/features

Step 3: Talking about TYPO3 with potential clients

Unless you are living in a country where TYPO3 has a large market share, name-dropping TYPO3 will have a very little effect. Luckily, it has a lot to offer, and you can build your business with the help of an active and enthusiastic professional open source community, great feature set, documentation, and proven case studies.

The following prompts will help you put together an introduction to TYPO3 as a viable solution for your potential clients:

- Look at your results from step 2, and find the strongest selling points based on your perception of client needs.

- If your client is looking for reliability or a professional partner, emphasize features that underscore TYPO3's predictability, scalability, etc.

- The case studies at typo3.com/case-studies may be a good source of success stories from similar businesses elsewhere. When available, read up on how problems were solved and how specific business needs were met. How could they apply to your client?

- The TYPO3 Project produces a wealth of materials: blogs, websites, documentation, videos, events, training, certification, books, presentations, and more. Immerse yourself in this material. Over time, you will feel a part of something larger and very valuable—the TYPO3 community.

- If your company has existed for a while, great! You have some proof that you are a reliable partner who will be there for your clients in the future.

- If your agency is new to the game, you still have TYPO3 and open source on your side. TYPO3 is built on proven, standard web technologies like PHP and SQL, and there are vibrant ecosystems all around you to prove that what you're offering is a solid choice.

- TYPO3's developer community has created some unique solutions to the CMS problem over the years. Concepts like the page tree, translation handling, the backend user experience, and more may be new to the client. You have the chance to introduce them to a well-planned UX that is a great fit for a wide variety of real-world business needs.

- Describing everything as "easy to use" is a slippery slope. Remember that what's easy for you might—at first—be difficult for the client. All tools require training, and building good websites takes knowledge and experience. Training and support should be a part of your package and defined in a service-level agreement.

- Be clear that no website is ever "perfect" or "done." A well-planned and well-built site is, however, the best-possible starting point from which to generate value online. It will give you the chance to improve it and get more out of it over time as you understand your business and clients better over time.

- All CMSs and technologies have their strengths and weaknesses. Study them, compare them honestly with TYPO3 and your offering, but never talk down other CMSs or agencies. It is certain to backfire. Your aim is to talk up the best of TYPO3 and what you do.

Expected outcome: You will know that talking to the client requires in-depth knowledge of the client, the competition, TYPO3, and yourself. Be honest and build your business persona on positive examples. This will help the client understand your strengths and choose you and TYPO3 as the best fit for their needs and for the right reasons.

Step 4: Using TYPO3 and open source as a door opener

Open source software, in general, has some advantages over the proprietary competition. TYPO3, specifically, has unique strengths and features to offer within the open source space. You can use this to your advantage to attract leads because you're an interesting source of information and fresh perspectives.

Being open is a strength that can set you apart, especially in a market where many competitors use closed source software, proprietary technologies, or keep their cards close to their chest.

Follow these tips to leverage some of the power of open source:

- Talk about what you do. Depending on the situation where you live, it may be TYPO3, contribution, or open source in general.

- Blog, not only about what's great about your business: tell stories about how you work, and share tips about open source technologies like TYPO3. Use topics from typo3.org, typo3.com, and the TYPO3 community as an inspiration to produce your own content.

- Build a network among local businesses and the technology community. You will learn what makes others tick and discover unsolved problems.

- Offer presentations and talks at user groups, meetups, and conferences about topics from the TYPO3 and open source world that might be interesting for others.

- Contribute to TYPO3 and other open source projects. Learn from others and share your knowledge. Build on friendship and collaboration. It is the core of the TYPO3 community and open source projects worldwide.

Expected outcome: You have the opportunity to start delivering value using TYPO3 and also to reach out and find strength in community and collaboration. It will help build your business and a valuable network of like-minded people and potential clients for whom you stand out in the crowd.

Summary

In the preceding steps, you have found a way to optimize your TYPO3 business based on client needs and market insights. You have an overview of what features may be especially useful for certain clients. TYPO3's strengths, combined with your expertise, can help you build a sustainable business through long-term customer relationships and value creation beyond the initial project. You have also learned how open source and TYPO3 can be a door opener and marketing topic highlighting your business's unique product offering.

What's next?

Make this guide the beginning of your new TYPO3-based business. Start taking steps to put the plan into action. Involve yourself in networking and learn more about TYPO3 by actively participating in the TYPO3 community.

Resources: Learn more

- The TYPO3 features[2] page gives a comprehensive description of the CMS's functionality.

- The TYPO3 company blog[3] is a good source of information for your sales and marketing.

- TYPO3 case studies[4] allow you to learn how others have solved their challenges with TYPO3.

- Join the TYPO3 marketing team[5] to help build TYPO3's marketing material. This means early access to information and joining a community of knowledgeable TYPO3 salespeople and marketers.

---

[2]https://typo3.org/cms/features
[3]https://typo3.com/blog
[4]https://typo3.com/case-studies
[5]https://typo3.org/community/teams/marketing

CHAPTER 14

Guide 10: Debugging and Troubleshooting TYPO3

As usual with software in general—and especially software where you yourself play a role in building and configuring it—you'll experience that something isn't working as it should, how you expected, or that it's not working at all.

It is best to optimize your workflow to reduce the risk of introducing bugs, but mistakes are a part of life, so debugging is inevitable. Often, figuring out where to look takes longer than the fix itself. In this guide, our aim is to show you the best places to look first to debug and troubleshoot problems with TYPO3.

There is a whole world of software testing and quality assurance tooling available for you to use and explore. There are many excellent resources available about debugging technologies like CSS, HTML, and PHP that are under the hood of TYPO3 that we're not covering here.

In this guide, we'll look at debugging TYPO3 quickly and efficiently, using some useful functionality built into TYPO3 itself.

Administrators can see the most important information about a TYPO3 instance's environment, health, and application context in the Application Information panel accessible from the System Information button at the top right of the screen (Figure 14-1).

© Felicity Brand, Heather McNamee, and Jeffrey A. McGuire 2021
F. Brand et al., *The TYPO3 Guidebook*, https://doi.org/10.1007/978-1-4842-6525-3_14

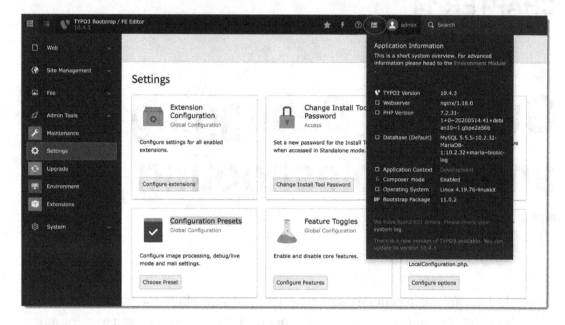

Figure 14-1. *The Application Information panel*

At the end of this tutorial...

You will have an overview of where to go looking when something isn't working as expected in

- Fluid templates

- TypoScript

- TYPO3-specific PHP code

    You will also know how to make TYPO3 tell you more about what's going on by outputting debugging information and how to reset an admin password using the Install tool.

Prerequisites

- You will need a modern computer, web browser, and an Internet connection.

- A TYPO3 site to test the methods suggested.

- A DDEV-Local development environment from the previous guides.

Considerations before you start

We recommend using unexpected behavior resulting from your work with the previous guides as a good reason to read this guide. As such, this guide can be used in parallel with the other guides.

Security considerations

- **Do not use development mode or debug configurations for a live or publicly accessible TYPO3 instance –** It will make TYPO3 slower, log files can eat up your storage quota, and the extensive error messages might disclose sensitive information.

- Never leave debug statements in production code.

- Disable the Install tool on live sites. If at all possible, do not reset your password as described below in step 6 on live production sites. You should perform the reset on a local copy of the site. In any case, be certain to follow all the steps, including deleting the temporary user and disabling the Install tool again at the end.

Step 1: Setting the application context to "Development"

The application context is the setting for whether your TYPO3 instance is in production (running live sites on a public server) or undergoing development. The environment variable "TYPO3_CONTEXT" is used to set TYPO3's application context.

The default context value is "Production," but we would like to set it to "Development" to do our troubleshooting. You can read more about how to set and use the application context in the TYPO3 documentation,[1] but here's how to set it for our example site in DDEV:

1. From the installation's root folder (where the composer.json file is located), create a new file in .ddev/docker-compose.typo3.yaml.

---

[1]https://docs.typo3.org/m/typo3/reference-coreapi/master/en-us/ApiOverview/
Bootstrapping/Index.html#application-context

2. Paste in the following content (this is a YAML file, so the indentations are important):

```
version: '3.6'
services:
  web:
    environment:
      - TYPO3_CONTEXT=Development
```

3. In the command line, run ddev `restart`.

Expected outcome: Your test site should now be running in development context, and "Development" should be displayed in the Application Information drop-down menu (see Figure 14-1). You'll be able to define different settings using conditions in the public/typo3conf/AdditionalConfiguration.php file and using conditions in TypoScript and Fluid.

Step 2: Enabling the debug configuration preset

By default, TYPO3's configuration is optimized for production settings. Production disables a number of useful debugging features and also hides PHP errors. In this step, we'll make sure your TYPO3 instance is running with the debug configuration preset enabled:

1. Log in to the TYPO3 backend as an admin user.

2. Go to the **Admin tools ➤ Settings** module.

3. In the Configuration Presets box, click the **Choose Preset** button. The Configuration Presets window displays.

4. In the Debug Settings section, select the **Debug** option.

5. Click the **Activate Preset** button.

You can also find information on how to fine-tune PHP error and exception logging in the TYPO3 documentation.[2]

---

[2]https://docs.typo3.org/m/typo3/reference-coreapi/master/en-us/ApiOverview/
 ErrorAndExceptionHandling/Configuration/Index.html

Expected outcome: TYPO3 is now configured for development. You will see more detailed exception messages and log output (Figure 14-2).

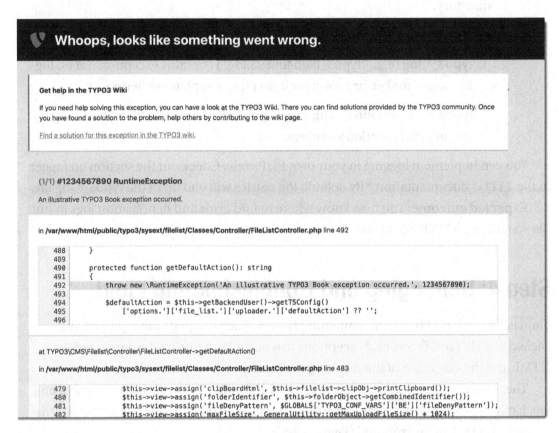

Figure 14-2. *TYPO3 can display information-rich exception information*

Step 3: Debugging and troubleshooting PHP in TYPO3

Enabling the debug configuration preset in step 2 will have enabled extensive and clean-formatted debugging output for any PHP exception thrown. You will also find that errors are logged to file and database:

1. Go to the **System ➤ Log** module (this module is part of the "belog" system extension).

2. In the **Action** drop-down list, select "Errors." The list of errors shows the backend user and workspace whose action generated the error.

3.   Now go to your file system. From the installation's root folder
     (where the composer.json file is located), go to the var/log/
     directory.

This directory contains two types of files:

    i.   **typo3_*.log** (e.g., "typo3_f80b4d6693.log") contains exception traces, log
     messages, and error messages from Fluid template rendering.

    ii. **typo3_deprecations_*.log** (e.g., "typo3_deprecations_f80b4d6693.log")
     contains deprecation warnings.

You can implement logging in your own PHP code. Check out the section on logger
in the TYPO3 documentation.[3] By default, log entries will end up in the typo3_*.log file.

Expected outcome: You now know where to find error and deprecation logs in the
file system and TYPO3 backend.

Step 4: Debugging and troubleshooting Fluid

Fluid is TYPO3's HTML-based templating system. Each template file is parsed and
cached as PHP files. Errors and exceptions can occur both during the parsing of the
HTML and the execution of the resulting PHP code.

The most common way of debugging a Fluid template is to use the built-in f:debug
tag. It can be inserted anywhere in the template file and will output data you supply as
formatted HTML in the frontend (Figure 14-3).

---

[3]https://docs.typo3.org/m/typo3/reference-coreapi/master/en-us/ApiOverview/Logging/
Quickstart/Index.html

```
Extbase Variable Dump

array (102 items)
   uid => 30 (integer)
   rowDescription => '' (0 chars)
   pid => 65 (integer)
   tstamp => 1589464419 (integer)
   crdate => 1578402426 (integer)
   cruser_id => 1 (integer)
   deleted => 0 (integer)
   hidden => 0 (integer)
   starttime => 0 (integer)
   endtime => 0 (integer)
   fe_group => '' (0 chars)
   sorting => 512 (integer)
   editlock => 0 (integer)
   sys_language_uid => 0 (integer)
   l18n_parent => 0 (integer)
   l10n_source => 0 (integer)
   l10n_state => NULL
   t3_origuid => 0 (integer)
   l18n_diffsource => 'a:26:{s:5:"CType";N;s:6:"colPos";N;s:6:"header";N;s:13:"header_layout";N;s:1
      5:"header_position";N;s:4:"date";N;s:11:"header_link";N;s:9:"subheader";N;s:
      8:"bodytext";N;s:6:"layout";N;s:11:"frame_class";N;s:18:"space_before_class"
      ;N;s:17:"space_after_class";N;s:22:"background_color_class";N;s:16:"backgrou
      nd_image";N;s:24:"background_image_options";N;s:12:"sectionIndex";N;s:9:"lin
      kToTop";N;s:16:"sys_language_uid";N;s:6:"hidden";N;s:9:"starttime";N;s:7:"en
      dtime";N;s:8:"fe_group";N;s:8:"editlock";N;s:10:"categories";N;s:14:"rowDesc
      ription";N;}' (544 chars)
```

Figure 14-3. *Part of the output from the <f:debug> tag for a text content element's data*

The following is an example of how to insert the f:debug tag into the template for a text content element. You can find the original template in public/typo3/sysext/fluid_styled_content/Resources/Private/Templates/Text.html in your TYPO3 installation:

```
<html xmlns:f="http://typo3.org/ns/TYPO3/CMS/Fluid/ViewHelpers"
data-namespace-typo3-fluid="true">
<f:layout name="Default" />
<f:section name="Main">
    <f:debug>{data}</f:debug>
    <f:format.html>{data.bodytext}</f:format.html>

</f:section>
</html>
```

Security tip   Never leave debug statements in production code.

The Fluid template parser will throw an exception if it doesn't understand what you're trying to do (Figure 14-4). In this case it can't find a way to parse the f:typo3book viewHelper.

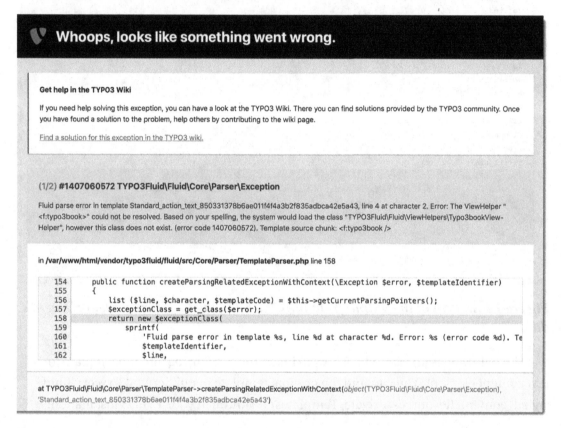

Figure 14-4. We tried to use the f:typo3book viewHelper in a Fluid template, but it doesn't exist

In the preceding screenshot, you can see how a Fluid parser exception will look when you have enabled the debug configuration preset in step 2.

There are a few things to note:

- The exception message tells you that it is trying to find a class called TYPO3Fluid\Fluid\ViewHelpers\Typo3bookViewHelper. This is because the tag has the "f" XML namespace, which is assigned to the TYPO3Fluid\Fluid\ViewHelpers class namespace. If you have created a custom Typo3bookViewHelper class, it is somewhere else than within the Fluid extension.

- The parser doesn't display the original file name and calls it "Standard_action_text_850331378b6ae011f4f4a3b2f835adbca42e 5a43". You'll find somewhat more information about the template-include-paths by scrolling down in the exception message. The best approach is to test your templates often to avoid spending time looking for your mistake.

- Fluid templates are cached. This means you should disable caching or clear the cache (through the TYPO3 backend) to see your changes. Otherwise, you might not see your own mistake until it's too late. Another way is to append "?no_cache=1" to the URL. This will disable caching and will often be all you need to do (as in "example.ddev.site/contact?no_cache=1"). This trick can be a nonintrusive help during debugging, but it should be disabled on production sites by setting $GLOBALS['TYPO3_CONF_VARS']['FE']['disableNoCacheParameter'] = true in LocalConfiguration.php or AdditionalConfiguration.php.

Expected outcome: You now know how to debug data within the Fluid templates and know a little bit about the exceptions that the Fluid parser will throw and how to read them.

Step 5: Debugging and troubleshooting TypoScript

TypoScript is unique to TYPO3, so it can only be debugged within the CMS. TypoScript has not always been easy to debug, but new core features, such as code highlighting and autocompletion, have made it easier to edit TypoScript in the backend. TypoScript is designed to "fail gracefully," without displaying an error message on your public website.

When working with TypoScript in files, check if your IDE has support for TypoScript. In the IDEs PhpStorm, WebStorm, and IntelliJ from JetBrains, purchasing sgalinski's TypoScript plugin[4] will give you code highlighting, autocompletion, type hinting, and a long list of other helpful, powerful features.

Here are three ways to debug your TypoScript code within TYPO3.

Method 1: Template module

The Template module will give you access to all the TypoScript code on your site:

1. In the TYPO3 backend, navigate to the **Web ➤ Template** module.

2. Select your site's root page in the page tree. The template module will load.

3. Click the root page in the list of pages on the Template tools screen.

4. From the drop-down list at the top of the screen, choose "TypoScript Object Browser" (Figure 14-5). This view allows you to navigate and search the TypoScript object hierarchy and see the parsed TypoScript properties. Using the **Browse** list, you can see both "Constants" and "Setup" (see Guide 2: Creating your first TYPO3 site to learn more). You can even simulate TypoScript conditions using check boxes at the bottom of the listing. Errors are highlighted and include a **Show details** link bringing you to the "Template Analyzer."

---

[4]https://www.sgalinski.de/en/typo3-products-web-development/
typoscript-phpstorm-webstorm-intellij/

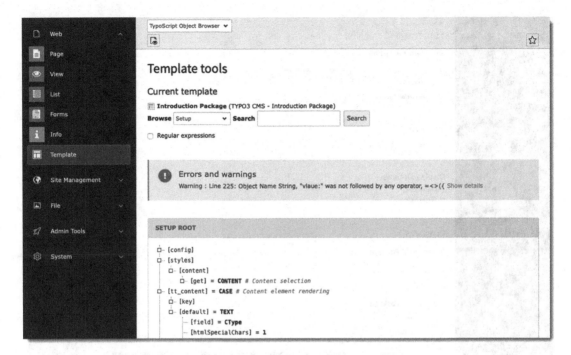

Figure 14-5. *The TypoScript Object Browser*

5. You can also reach the Template Analyzer from the drop-down list at the top of the screen, by choosing "Template Analyzer." Scroll down to see the template hierarchy in their actual load order, a button to display the complete TypoScript, and check boxes for display options.

6. Click a TypoScript template in the Template hierarchy, or click the **View the complete TS listing** to see the full TypoScript code with any parser errors highlighted (Figure 14-6). A single TYPO3 website might include tens of thousands of lines of TypoScript code, so the web browser's text search ("Find") feature will come in handy.

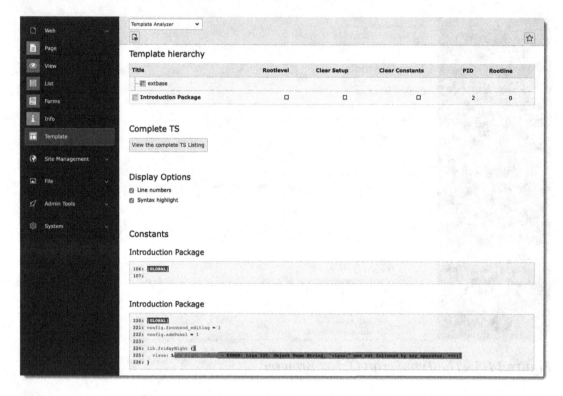

Figure 14-6. *The Template Analyzer showing a parser error highlighted in the Introduction Package*

Method 2: Isolate the TypoScript

If you have written TypoScript, and it doesn't work as expected, you might want to isolate it from the influence of other TypoScript code. As long as the code doesn't depend on any previous code, you can insert it on its own page type.

You can test any TypoScript code you like using this method, without it appearing on your live site—although the output is still public for those who guess the URL:

1. In the TYPO3 backend, navigate to the **Web ➤ Template** module.

2. Select your site's root page in the page tree. The template module will load.

3. Click the root page in the list of pages on the Template tools screen.

4. From the drop-down list at the top of the screen, choose "Info/Modify."

5. Click the **edit** (pen) button on the "Setup" row.

6. On a blank line below any other code, paste the following code and adapt it to your needs. See Table 14-1 for more information:

```
testPage = PAGE
testPage {
  typeNum = 999

  10 = TEXT
  10 {
    data = date : d-m-y
    wrap = <p>|</p>
  }

  20 < lib.typo3Book
}
```

Table 14-1. *Code analysis*

Item	Description
testPage = PAGE	Creates a new page object.
typeNum = 999	Sets the page's type number to "999", meaning you can access it at example.ddev.site/?type=999.
10 = TEXT and the following four lines	Outputs the current date based on hardcoded TypoScript.
20 < lib.typo3Book	Inserts TypoScript from lib.typo3Book onto the page. Maybe we have created TypoScript here to insert somewhere else.

Method 3: Use the stdWrap function

Many TypoScript objects implement the stdWrap function, such as the "TEXT" object used earlier. It includes useful properties to enable debug output, especially "debug," "debugFunc," and "debugData," explained in detail in the official TYPO3 documentation's TypoScript reference.[5]

The following snippet will output the value of the field "title" as well as debug information listing all the possible field names you can specify in the "field" property. The "field" property accesses a PHP array that can be populated with record data. It's often the current page or content element record's field data, but setting debugData = 1 will give you a definite answer to what data you are accessing:

```
10 = TEXT
10 {
  field = title
  wrap = <p>|</p>
  debugData = 1
}
```

If you expect to work a lot with TypoScript, we recommend a deep dive into the TypoScript Template Reference[6] (also dubbed "TSRef"). (Tip: If you are using continuous integration or deployment (CI/CD), you could find the TypoScript linter by Martin Helmich[7] helpful.)

Expected outcome: You will now know three ways to debug TypoScript code from within TYPO3. You'll be better equipped to find out where and what is wrong in a site when your TypoScript code isn't working as you expect.

Step 6: Resetting your backend admin password

It has happened to everyone. You set up a new local development environment, but forget your "easy-to-remember" admin password. How do you get back into your TYPO3 installation? TYPO3 doesn't store your password in plain text; it hashes it using

---

[5]https://docs.typo3.org/m/typo3/reference-typoscript/master/en-us/Functions/
 Stdwrap.html#debug
[6]https://docs.typo3.org/m/typo3/reference-typoscript/master/en-us/Index.html
[7]https://github.com/martin-helmich/typo3-typoscript-lint

a complex salt plus algorithm combination, so you can't just change the database field. Instead, we are going to show you how to use the Installer tool and a temporary user to reset your admin password.

Security tip   Avoid doing this on a live production site. These steps are much safer to carry out on a local development environment. Do not reset your password as described below in step 6 on live production sites, if you can avoid it. Perform the reset on a local copy of the site, if possible, and be certain to follow all the steps, including deleting the temporary user and disabling the Install tool again at the end.

---

1. In a web browser, visit your website's Install tool. The URL will be similar to example.ddev.site/typo3/install.php, though the domain will probably be different; "/typo3/install.php" is always a part of it.

2. In your terminal, move into the typo3conf folder by running `cd public/typo3conf`.

3. Create the file that enables the Install tool by running `touch ENABLE_INSTALL_TOOL`.

4. Reload example.ddev.site/typo3/install.php in the browser.

5. Enter a password of your choice, and click **Login**. The Install tool will tell you the password doesn't work, but will also output a hash.

6. Copy the hash.

7. Open public/typo3conf/LocalConfiguration.php in a plain text editor or IDE.

8. On line six (where it says ""), paste in the new hash to replace the old hash:

    ```
    'installToolPassword' => 'PASTE HASH HERE',
    ```

9. Save and close the LocalConfiguration.php file.

10. Return to your browser, and click the login button again. (Your password should still be in the field; otherwise, retype it.) You should be able to log in successfully.

11. Click the **Create administrative user** button, and follow the instructions to set a new username and password.

12. **Remove the ENABLE_INSTALL_TOOL file** you created in step 3 to disable the Install tool. This file should never be present on a live system.

13. **Reset your original admin user's password** in the backend.

14. **Delete the temporary user** you created.

Expected outcome: You should have access to TYPO3's backend again with your original admin user.

Summary

In this guide, you have learned how to enable debugging output, how to debug different aspects of your TYPO3 installation, and how to reset your admin user password.

What's next?

Debugging is a skill that develops with experience. Everyone was a beginning once, and the TYPO3 community will be happy to help if you have problems. We recommend visiting Stack Overflow[8] or using the TYPO3 Slack.[9] You should also not be afraid to ask your questions at meetups, camps, or conferences, too.

If you know an answer, give back by helping and answering others. Even those times when you might be wrong, you'll probably learn useful ways to improve your own code, too!

---

[8]https://stackoverflow.com/questions/tagged/typo3
[9]https://typo3.org/community/meet/how-to-use-slack-in-the-typo3-community

Resources: Learn more

- Dive into the TYPO3 documentation.[10]

- TYPO3 has many helpful core APIs that can help you avoid bugs. Check out the official API.[11]

- Watch videos on the official TYPO3 YouTube channel.[12] Some conference videos include presentations on improving security, performance, and code quality—and avoiding bugs.

---

[10]https://docs.typo3.org/Home/References.html
[11]https://api.typo3.org
[12]https://www.youtube.com/typo3

CHAPTER 15

A Guidebook to Your New TYPO3 Home

We called this a "guidebook" because we imagined an intrepid explorer discovering and settling down to use this new platform. We wanted to save you hours of research and unwanted detours along the way. You see where you can go, how to plan the journey, how to use the equipment, and the skills you need to get you there successfully.

Take your first steps: Try it yourself!

TYPO3 is amazingly powerful. In this book, we narrow down the potentially overwhelming possibilities it offers to the most essential concepts and shows you how and where to find further information that you'll find helpful sooner or later.

An advantage of a feature-rich system like TYPO3 is that you rely less on third-party code to get the most important things done.

We are excited to see how you will use what you have learned. Our advice is to keep it simple and start small. Feel free to come back again and again. Dip into sections of the book to follow a guide and learn something new.

No one in the TYPO3 community masters absolutely every relevant topic. Most projects involve multiple people and roles. Some people focus on the content and page building, some on configuration and features, while others work on testing and performance. Yet it's good for everyone to understand how the system works as a whole.

Even if you are not a developer or editor, running through the guides will enhance your understanding.

© Felicity Brand, Heather McNamee, and Jeffrey A. McGuire 2021
F. Brand et al., *The TYPO3 Guidebook*, https://doi.org/10.1007/978-1-4842-6525-3_15

Bridging knowledge gaps

Be kind to yourself. How "easy" it is to learn something depends on what prior knowledge you have. If you are familiar with another CMS, you may have started out confused by TYPO3's different approach to menu management or the concept of content elements, for example.

We hope that reading this book helps you find your way into TYPO3. Keep in mind that if you find something particularly confusing, it could be something that you can help address! One of the beauties of open source software like TYPO3 CMS is that you can help make it easier or better for the next person. You can improve the documentation, file or fix bug reports, teach someone else, and so much more. Anything you make better will be better for everyone out there using TYPO3 and the Internet.

Get connected through contribution

You might be surprised to see how welcoming TYPO3's community is. In this book, you can learn how the community is organized and how you can get in contact with other TYPO3 users and professionals.

On the official TYPO3 Project home, typo3.org, you'll see regular opportunities to participate in sprints, surveys, and other community events. The more you participate, the more you can get out of this (or any) open source project. And we're not just talking about coding:

- You can also share your time and expertise in one or more community teams,[1] such as marketing, design, localization, etc.

- The "Strategic Development Initiatives[2]" work on long-term improvements in specific areas within TYPO3 Core. You can share your expertise in areas like UX design, accessibility, or programming.

---

[1]https://typo3.org/community/teams
[2]https://typo3.org/community/teams/typo3-development

Share your fresh perspective

As a newcomer, you bring fresh perspectives to TYPO3. Contribution makes you a part of it all. We find it incredibly motivating knowing that part of the project is ours that we made a positive difference around the software we use. We invite you to join us in this community of shared practice, ideals, and goals—and this feeling!

Always assume that whatever has blocked you might be frustrating to someone else, too. With TYPO3, you can improve it yourself. Take notes about what you discover and report back. A bug report is a significant contribution, too!

Improving documentation is a helpful way for newcomers to make a difference. Every official documentation page[3] has an "Edit on GitHub" link ready for what your fresh eyes have picked up and know how to improve.

The community is constantly working to improve TYPO3. Your insight and feedback help TYPO3 evolve. Learn how to report issues and test patches for improvements.[4]

Your improvement might help thousands of users. Seeing the results of your contributions in the software you use every day is a truly gratifying experience.

Having your UI change, commit message, or meetup presentation shared in the community is a motivating reminder that you're not alone. There's help out there and a friendly community of web development professionals to learn and grow with.

We hope that you will feel welcome and be a part of it with us. Welcome!

---

[3]https://docs.typo3.org/
[4]https://typo3.com/blog/tutorial-report-typo3-issues-and-test-patches

APPENDIX A

Glossary

Extbase

Extbase is an object-oriented framework written in PHP, developed especially for TYPO3 CMS.

The model-view-controller framework ensures a clear separation of concerns. The combination of Extbase and the fluid templating engine provides a holistic solution for creating TYPO3 extensions, controlling everything from data persistence to frontend output.

Extbase helps you make your source code easier to read and extend by following the "convention over configuration" paradigm. Once a developer becomes familiar with the conventions, they will know how to name classes, methods, and properties and where to locate files and directories.

For more information about Extbase, see "Building custom extensions" in Chapter 3.

File Abstraction Layer (FAL)

The file abstraction layer (FAL) is the part of TYPO3's internal digital asset management (DAM) system used to store, classify, and manage files across platforms and file systems.

Files are stored where you specify, and information about them is stored in the database. FAL creates a virtual representation of a given file in TYPO3.

By default, TYPO3 is the file system on the server, but you can configure drivers for remote storage technologies like SFTP, Amazon S3, and others.

333

F. Brand et al., *The TYPO3 Guidebook*, https://doi.org/10.1007/978-1-4842-6525-3

Find out more about FAL in the "Reusing content" section in Chapter 2 and the "File storage" section of Chapter 3.

Fluid template engine

The Fluid template engine evolved over time together with Extbase as a part of the TYPO3 universe, but it is now published as a stand-alone, open source PHP library. It is a secure and extensible way to customize the output of any PHP project, most commonly, but not limited to, HTML.

Its encapsulation means no PHP code is ever mixed with HTML code.

Fluid enables you to add conditional statements, variables, and loops into a normal HTML file. Behind the scenes, the Fluid engine reads your template files, processes and compiles them, and then caches them as PHP code.

For more information, see the "Visual design and theming" section in Chapter 2 and the "Configuring TYPO3" section in Chapter 3.

Form framework

The form system extension lets you build forms for the frontend.

For more information, see "Guide 6: Creating a password-protected members' area" and the "Form Framework guide[1]" in the TYPO3 documentation.

Flexform

Flexforms let you store data within an XML structure in a single database column and edit the data in the backend. Flexforms have all the features of the TCA, so it is possible to configure input fields, drop-down menus, conditional options, and more.

For more information, see Flexforms[2] in the TYPO3 documentation.

---

[1] https://docs.typo3.org/c/typo3/cms-form/master/en-us/Introduction/Index.html
[2] https://docs.typo3.org/m/typo3/reference-coreapi/master/en-us/ApiOverview/ FlexForms/Index.html

Integrator

A TYPO3 integrator is a person who is responsible for the website template, installing and configuring extensions, and setting up user permissions.

This role has administrator access and requires good knowledge of the general architecture of TYPO3 (frontend, backend, extensions, TypoScript, TSconfig, etc.).

The TYPO3 integrator role can often overlap with that of a system administrator, and one person can fulfill both roles.

For more information, see "Guidelines for TYPO3 Integrators[3]" in the TYPO3 documentation.

Layout

This is a Fluid term.

Layouts are used for global styling, for example, displaying a logo across the entire site.

For more information, see "Creating a Consistent Look and Feel with Layouts[4]" in the TYPO3 documentation.

Partial

This is a Fluid term.

Partials are reusable elements of a Fluid template. They are stored in a separate file and can be included in multiple templates.

For more information, see "Moving Repeating Snippets to Partials[5]" in the TYPO3 documentation.

---

[3]https://docs.typo3.org/m/typo3/reference-coreapi/master/en-us/Security/GuidelinesIntegrators/Index.html

[4]https://docs.typo3.org/m/typo3/book-extbasefluid/master/en-us/8-Fluid/4-creating-a-consistent-look-and-feel-with-layouts.html

[5]https://docs.typo3.org/m/typo3/book-extbasefluid/master/en-us/8-Fluid/3-moving-repeating-snippets-to-partials.html

Sitepackage

> A sitepackage is a way to bundle everything your site needs—
> including the theme and configuration—into an extension.

> It gives you a storage location for your site's static files and
> configurations that you can put under version control and include
> as a composer dependency. You can either download a third-
> party sitepackage extension or create your own.

> For more information about sitepackages, see the "Configuring
> and customizing" section in Chapter 3.

Table Configuration Array (TCA)

> The TCA is a global PHP array and a central element of TYPO3's
> architecture. It defines how fields are displayed and validated in
> the backend and how fields are used in the frontend by Extbase
> extensions.

> It extends the definition of database tables beyond what can be
> done with SQL and defines which tables and fields are visible and
> editable.

> For more information about the TCA, see the "Configuring and
> customizing" section in Chapter 3, and "Guide 4: Planning,
> Building, and Using Content Elements."

Template

> Templates for content and pages let you create websites that
> provide the exact customer experience you need for any given
> project.

> The TYPO3 Core and most TYPO3 websites today rely on the
> Fluid template engine. "Template" can also refer to TypoScript
> configurations.

> For more information, see the "Visual design and theming"
> section in Chapter 2.

TSconfig

TSconfig uses the same syntax as TypoScript and allows you to configure the backend without the need to write PHP code.

TSconfig has two variants: configuration for pages (Page TSconfig) and configuration for users and groups (User TSconfig). Its power lies in its hierarchical structure.

For more information, see the "Configuring and customizing" section in Chapter 3.

TypoScript

TypoScript is a declarative configuration language. It is used to build a PHP array, so it is a language for configuration, rather than a programming language, although it supports conditions and can define limited control structures.

It is used in TypoScript templates to configure plugins and frontend rendering, often in combination with the Fluid template engine. TypoScript can be looked at as the glue between the content in the database and output rendering.

For more information, see the "Configuring and customizing" section in Chapter 3.

ViewHelper

ViewHelpers are PHP classes used in Fluid templates. They extend the standard set of Fluid features to meet the specific needs of your project. You can use them to render data in your HTML with logic such as if-then-else comparisons, counting, formatting, and debugging.

For more information, see the "Building custom extensions" section in Chapter 3.

References

Chapter 1

"Case Study of an Online Publisher - Texere" n.d. https://b13.com/case-studies/the-science-of-compelling-content-texere

"Coding Standards in TYPO3." SkillDisplay. https://www.skilldisplay.eu/skillsets/cms-certified-developer-10-lts/skill/coding-standards-in-typo3/

"Core Development." April 06, 2020. https://typo3.org/community/teams/typo3-development/

"Getting Started Tutorial." TYPO3 Documentation. February 27, 2020. https://docs.typo3.org/typo3cms/GettingStartedTutorial/

"Introduction." TYPO3 Documentation. April 01, 2019. https://docs.typo3.org/m/typo3/reference-coreapi/master/en-us/ExtensionArchitecture/Introduction/Index.html

"Knowledge to Go with TYPO3." TYPO3. https://typo3.com/case-studies/universitaet-wien

"Official TYPO3 Partner Finder: TYPO3 GmbH." TYPO3. https://typo3.com/services/find-a-typo3-partner

"Open Source Definition." https://typo3.org/project/association/partnerships/open-source-definition/

"OSS Watch." OSS Watch. http://oss-watch.ac.uk/resources/governancemodels

"Program." TYPO3 Conference 2015 Amsterdam. https://t3con15eu.typo3.org/program-detail/talk/detail/reorganisation-of-the-blsv.html

Schams, Michael. "TYPO3 CMS Certified Developer (English)." TYPO3 CMS Certified... by Michael Schams [PDF/iPad/Kindle]. June 18, 2016. https://leanpub.com/typo3certifieddeveloper-en

Schams, Michael. "TYPO3 Extbase (English)." TYPO3 Extbase... by Michael Schams [Leanpub PDF/iPad/Kindle]. January 06, 2016. https://leanpub.com/typo3extbase-en

"Service Level Agreements for TYPO3 Extensions." Coders.care.
https://coders.care/blog/article/service-level-agreements-for-typo3-
extensions/

"Teams and Committees." November 13, 2019. https://typo3.org/community/
teams/

"The European Skill Verification Standard." SkillDisplay.
https://www.skilldisplay.eu/

"The TYPO3 Association." June 23, 2020. https://typo3.org/project/
association/

"TUI: TYPO3 GmbH," n.d. https://typo3.com/case-studies/tui

"Tutorials and Guides." TYPO3 Documentation. April 22, 2020.
https://docs.typo3.org/typo3cms/GuidesAndTutorials/Index.html

"TYPO3 Certification." https://typo3.org/certification/

"TYPO3 CMS Development Roadmap." Development Roadmap for TYPO3 CMS.
https://typo3.org/cms/roadmap/

"TYPO3 Contribution Guide - Core Development." TYPO3 Documentation. March
22, 2020. https://docs.typo3.org/m/typo3/guide-contributionworkflow/master/
en-us/Index.html

"TYPO3 Core Development - Strategic Initiatives." https://typo3.org/community/
teams/typo3-development/initiatives/

"TYPO3 Events." https://typo3.org/community/events/typo3-sprint/all/

"TYPO3 Extension Repository." https://extensions.typo3.org/

"TYPO3 - Recommended Resources!" Resources. https://www.typo3book.com/
resources

"TYPO3 User Groups." https://typo3.org/community/meet/user-groups/

"Universität Wien: TYPO3 GmbH," n.d. https://typo3.com/case-studies/
universitaet-wien

"Welcome to the Official TYPO3 Documentation." TYPO3 Documentation. July 03, 2020.
https://docs.typo3.org/

"What Is the Ninety-Ninety Rule? - Definition from Techopedia." Techopedia.com.
https://www.techopedia.com/definition/21014/ninety-ninety-rule

"Writing Documentation." TYPO3 Documentation. April 24, 2020. https://docs.
typo3.org/m/typo3/docs-how-to-document/master/en-us/

Chapter 2

"2.11 How to Create Categories." TYPO3manual.com. http://www.typo3manual.com/extension-manuals/news-module-typo3-version-7/2-create-new-news-article/211-how-to-create-categories/

"2.2 Page Properties." TYPO3manual.com. https://www.typo3manual.com/typo3-version-8/2-create-and-edit-pages/22-page-properties/

"2.6 Settings for Different Page Types." TYPO3manual.com. http://www.typo3manual.com/typo3-version-8/2-create-and-edit-pages/26-settings-for-different-page-types/

"Achieving a State-of-the-art Backend Design for Neos." September 13, 2013. https://typo3.org/article/achieving-a-state-of-the-art-backend-design-for-neos

"Atomic Design Methodology." Atomic Design by Brad Frost. https://atomicdesign.bradfrost.com/chapter-2/

"Backend Interface." TYPO3 Documentation. April 09, 2019. https://docs.typo3.org/m/typo3/reference-coreapi/master/en-us/ApiOverview/BackendModules/Structure/Index.html

"Best Practices: Style Guide Driven Development With TYPO3." TYPO3. https://typo3.com/blog/best-practices-style-guide-driven-development-with-typo3

"Better Multilingual Support with Crowdin." September 23, 2019. https://typo3.org/article/better-multilingual-support-with-crowdin/

"CMS Certified Editor 9 LTS." SkillDisplay. https://www.skilldisplay.eu/skillsets/cms-certified-editor-9-lts/

"CMS Garden." TYPO3 | CMS Garden. January 01, 1970. https://www.cms-garden.org/en/cms/typo3-0

"Content Elements." TYPO3 Documentation. September 13, 2016. https://docs.typo3.org/m/typo3/tutorial-editors/master/en-us/ContentElements/Index.html

"Content Management, but Smart." https://typo3.org/cms/features/smart-content-management/

"Creating a Custom Workspace." TYPO3 Documentation. April 18, 2020. https://docs.typo3.org/c/typo3/cms-workspaces/master/en-us/Administration/CustomWorkspace/Index.html

"Deliver a Universal Frontend User Experience With TYPO3." https://typo3.org/cms/features/frontend-experience

"Discover Website Templates with Toujou TYPO3." Discover Website Templates with Toujou TYPO3. January 03, 2020. `https://www.toujou.de/en/templates/`

"Dummy News Article." Home: TYPO3 Template from Jweiland.net. April 16, 2020. `https://typo3muster.de/en/index.html`

"English Syllabus for TYPO3 CMS Certified Editors." `https://typo3.org/certification/editor/syllabus/syllabus-english/`

"EXT: L10nmgr." EXT: L10nmgr - L10nmgr 3.3.16 Documentation. March 20, 2018. `https://docs.typo3.org/typo3cms/extensions/l10nmgr/stable/Manual/Index.html#what-does-it-do`

"Fluid - A Fast and Secure Template Engine." Fluid Template Engine. `https://typo3.org/fluid`

"Fluid Guide." TYPO3 Documentation. May 11, 2018. `https://docs.typo3.org/m/typo3/guide-extbasefluid/master/en-us/Fluid/Index.html`

"Four Hidden Gems Every TYPO3 Editor Should Know." Your TYPO3 CMS Partner. January 22, 2019. `https://www.pixelant.net/blog/read/article/four-hidden-gems-every-typo3-editor-should-know/`

"Frequently Asked Questions (FAQ)." TYPO3 Documentation. May 07, 2020. `https://docs.typo3.org/m/typo3/reference-coreapi/master/en-us/ApiOverview/Internationalization/TranslationServer/Crowdin/Faq.html`

"General Backend Structure." TYPO3 Documentation. June 12, 2019. `https://docs.typo3.org/m/typo3/tutorial-getting-started/master/en-us/GeneralPrinciples/GeneralBackendStructure/Index.html`

"Home." T3kit. `http://www.t3kit.com/`

"How to Create Custom Content Elements in TYPO3." B13.com. `https://b13.com/blog/how-to-create-custom-content-elements-in-typo3`

"Internationalization and Localization." Internationalization and Localization - Inside TYPO3 CMS 8.7 Documentation. December 31, 2020. `https://docs.typo3.org/m/typo3/reference-inside/8.7/en-us/CoreArchitecture/Localization/Index.html`

"Introduction." Introduction - Inside TYPO3 CMS 8.7 Documentation. December 31, 2020. `https://docs.typo3.org/m/typo3/reference-inside/8.7/en-us/Introduction/Index.html#overview`

"Language Handling in TYPO3 - Part 1: Backend: TYPO3worx - "The" TYPO3 Blog." TYPO3worx. June 21, 2017. `https://typo3worx.eu/2017/04/language-handling-in-typo3-backend-configuration/`

"Localization with Crowdin Initiative." https://typo3.org/community/teams/typo3-development/initiatives/localization-with-crowdin/

"Main: TYPO3 Translation Server." Main | TYPO3 Translation Server. https://translation.typo3.org/

"Mod." TYPO3 Documentation. May 21, 2020. https://docs.typo3.org/m/typo3/reference-tsconfig/master/en-us/PageTsconfig/Mod.html

"Multidomain." Multidomain - TYPO3Wiki. https://wiki.typo3.org/Multidomain

"Multilingual and Multisite with TYPO3." https://typo3.org/cms/features/massively-multisite-multilingual

"Page Properties." TYPO3 Documentation. November 23, 2019. https://docs.typo3.org/m/typo3/tutorial-editors/master/en-us/Pages/PageProperties/Index.html

"Page Tree." TYPO3 Documentation. June 25, 2019. https://docs.typo3.org/m/typo3/tutorial-getting-started/master/en-us/GeneralPrinciples/PageTree/Index.html

"Responsive Images with TYPO3 8.7." Sitegeist · Digitalagentur Aus Hamburg. https://sitegeist.de/blog/typo3-blog/responsive-images-with-typo3-8-7.html

"Saving and Publishing Your WordPress Content." Easy WP Guide. December 23, 2019. https://easywpguide.com/wordpress-manual/adding-your-site-content/classic-editor/saving-and-publishing-content/

"Seiteninhalt Direkt Im Frontend Bearbeiten." TYPO3. https://www.typo3-hilfe.eu/online-hilfe/seiteninhalt/frontend-editing/

"SkillDisplay - Get Ready for the TYPO3 CMS Certified Editor Exam." TYPO3. https://typo3.com/blog/skilldisplay-get-ready-for-the-typo3-cms-certified-editor-exam

"Streamline Translation with the TYPO3 Connector." Streamline Translation with the TYPO3 Connector. https://www.languagewire.com/en/news/the-new-typo3-connector

"System Categories." TYPO3 Documentation. March 31, 2020. https://docs.typo3.org/m/typo3/reference-coreapi/master/en-us/ApiOverview/Categories/Index.html

"T3kit - A TYPO3 Template Package for Agencies." Pixelant. https://www.pixelant.net/typo3-cms/powerful-templates/

"The Basics: Templating with Backend Layouts." Use TYPO3. July 11, 2020. https://usetypo3.com/backend-layouts.html

"The Best Open Source Multisite CMS." TYPO3. https://typo3.com/blog/typo3-the-best-open-source-multisite-cms

"The Toujou Element Library." Building Blocks for Your Content. February 19, 2020. https://www.toujou.de/en/service/element-library/

"Translations." Translations - TYPO3Wiki. https://wiki.typo3.org/Translations

"TYPO3 CMS Certified Editor (TCCE)." https://typo3.org/certification/editor/

"TYPO3 CMS - Translation Project on Crowdin." Crowdin. https://crowdin.com/project/typo3-cms

"TYPO3 Core Development - Strategic Initiatives." https://typo3.org/community/teams/typo3-development/initiatives/

"TYPO3 Frontend Editor." Pixelant. https://www.pixelant.net/typo3-cms/extensions/frontend-editor/

"TYPO3 - Mandantenfähigkeit Für Domains." TYPO3 Agentur Stuttgart. August 09, 2018. https://www.typo3werk.com/typo3-mandantenfaehigkeit-fuer-domains/

"TYPO3 Multisite Mit Responsive Webdesign." Visual4. https://visual4.de/referenzen/typo3-multisite-mit-responsive-webdesign/

"TYPO3 Site Management and Routing: TYPO3worx - "The" TYPO3 Blog." TYPO3worx. October 13, 2018. https://typo3worx.eu/2018/10/typo3-site-management-and-routing/

"TYPO3 Version 10.3 - Almost There." February 25, 2020. https://typo3.org/article/typo3-version-103-almost-there

"Understanding Coupled, Decoupled and Headless CMS Platforms." Brightspot. June 10, 2020. https://www.brightspot.com/blog/decoupled-cms-and-headless-cms-platforms

"Workspaces." TYPO3 Documentation. October 28, 2018. https://docs.typo3.org/c/typo3/cms-workspaces/master/en-us/Administration/Workspaces/Index.html

Hasenau, Jo. "Localizer for TYPO3 (localizer)." February 06, 2020. https://extensions.typo3.org/extension/localizer/

House, Translate. "Multi-format Translation Tool." Virtaal. http://virtaal.translatehouse.org/index.html

Mack, Benni. "Workflows with TYPO3 Workspaces 4.5." LinkedIn SlideShare. October 12, 2011. https://www.slideshare.net/bennim/workflows-with-typo3-workspaces-45

Sitegeist. "Sitegeist/Sitegeist.Monocle." GitHub. https://github.com/sitegeist/
Sitegeist.Monocle

Skaarhoej, Kasper. "Localization Manager (l10nmgr)." January 13, 2020. https://
extensions.typo3.org/extension/l10nmgr/

Workflows and the Workbox. https://doc.sitecore.com/users/92/sitecore-
experience-platform/en/workflows-and-the-workbox.html

Chapter 3

Composer Helper. https://get.typo3.org/misc/composer/helper

Desirée Lochner. "Creating TYPO3 Backend Usergroups Your Clients Will Love." B13.
com. https://b13.com/blog/creating-typo3-backend-usergroups-your-clients-
will-love

"Backend User Management." TYPO3 Documentation. July 22, 2019. https://docs.
typo3.org/m/typo3/tutorial-getting-started/master/en-us/UserManagement/
Index.html

"Basic Concepts." TYPO3 Documentation. May 12, 2019. https://docs.typo3.
org/m/typo3/reference-coreapi/master/en-us/ApiOverview/Fal/Concepts/Index.
html#fal-concepts

"The Basics: Templating with Backend Layouts." Use TYPO3. July 11, 2020. https://
usetypo3.com/backend-layouts.html

"CLI with Symfony Console and TYPO3." Use TYPO3. July 11, 2020. https://
usetypo3.com/typo3-and-cli.html

"Coding Guidelines." TYPO3 Documentation. July 23, 2019. https://docs.typo3.
org/m/typo3/reference-coreapi/master/en-us/CodingGuidelines/Index.html

"Coding Guidelines." TYPO3 Documentation. December 02, 2019. https://docs.
typo3.org/m/typo3/book-extbasefluid/master/en-us/a-CodingGuidelines/Index.
html

"Configuration Methods List." TYPO3 Documentation. January 12, 2020. https://
docs.typo3.org/m/typo3/reference-coreapi/master/en-us/ApiOverview/
Configuration/ConfigurationMethods.html

"Customization Examples." TYPO3 Documentation. June 24, 2020. https://docs.
typo3.org/m/typo3/reference-coreapi/master/en-us/ExtensionArchitecture/
ExtendingTca/Examples/Index.html

"Developing TYPO3 Extensions with Extbase and Fluid." TYPO3 Documentation. April 21, 2020. https://docs.typo3.org/m/typo3/book-extbasefluid/master/en-us/ Index.html

"Extbase Guide." TYPO3 Documentation. June 28, 2019. https://docs.typo3. org/m/typo3/guide-extbasefluid/master/en-us/Extbase/Index.html

"Extbase Reference." TYPO3 Documentation. March 27, 2020. https://docs.typo3. org/m/typo3/book-extbasefluid/master/en-us/b-ExtbaseReference/Index.html

"Extension Development." TYPO3 Documentation. August 07, 2019. https://docs. typo3.org/m/typo3/reference-coreapi/master/en-us/ExtensionArchitecture/ Index.html

"Extensions Development Kickstarter." Events Site. August 01, 2019. https:// t3dd19.typo3.com/program/sessions/extensions-development-kickstarter-126

"Files and Locations." TYPO3 Documentation. March 25, 2020. https://docs. typo3.org/m/typo3/reference-coreapi/master/en-us/ExtensionArchitecture/ FilesAndLocations/Index.html

"Fluid - A Fast and Secure Template Engine." Fluid Template Engine. https:// typo3.org/fluid

"Fluid ViewHelper Documentation." TYPO3 Documentation. https://docs.typo3. org/other/typo3/view-helper-reference/master/en-us/Index.html

"For Integrators." TYPO3 Documentation. June 12, 2019. https://docs.typo3. org/m/typo3/tutorial-getting-started/master/en-us/NextSteps/Integrators/ Index.html

"Four Hidden Gems Every TYPO3 Editor Should Know." Your TYPO3 CMS Partner. January 22, 2019. https://www.pixelant.net/blog/read/article/four-hidden-gems- every-typo3-editor-should-know/

"General Principles." TYPO3 Documentation. July 21, 2019. https://docs.typo3. org/m/typo3/tutorial-getting-started/master/en-us/GeneralPrinciples/Index. html

"Gnu.org." [A GNU Head] . https://www.gnu.org/licenses/gpl-3.0.html

"Good Practices in Extensions." Use TYPO3. July 11, 2020. https://usetypo3.com/ good-practices-in-extensions.html

"Good Practices in TYPO3 Projects." Use TYPO3. July 11, 2020. https://usetypo3. com/good-practices-in-projects.html

Hacker News." Two More Quotes about This Subject: Jeff Atwood: "The Best Code Is No Code at All. | Hacker News. https://news.ycombinator.com/item?id=10979240

Haen, Nico De. "Extension Builder (extension_builder)." June 08, 2020. `https://extensions.typo3.org/extension/extension_builder`

"Installing Extensions." TYPO3 Documentation. June 17, 2017. `https://docs.typo3.org/m/typo3/reference-coreapi/8.7/en-us/ExtensionArchitecture/Installation/Index.html`

"Introduction." TYPO3 Documentation. January 28, 2020. `https://docs.typo3.org/m/typo3/reference-coreapi/master/en-us/Introduction/Index.html#system-overview`

"Introduction." TYPO3 Documentation. April 01, 2019. `https://docs.typo3.org/m/typo3/reference-coreapi/master/en-us/ExtensionArchitecture/Introduction/Index.html`

"Introduction." TYPO3 Documentation. July 21, 2019. `https://docs.typo3.org/m/typo3/tutorial-getting-started/master/en-us/Introduction/Index.html`

"Introduction." TYPO3 Documentation. July 13, 2020. `https://docs.typo3.org/c/typo3/cms-form/master/en-us/Introduction/Index.html`

Kott, Benjamin. "The Anatomy of TYPO3 Sitepackages." LinkedIn SlideShare. May 09, 2015. `https://www.slideshare.net/benjaminkott/typo3-the-anatomy-of-sitepackages`

"Mail API." TYPO3 Documentation. June 18, 2020. `https://docs.typo3.org/m/typo3/reference-coreapi/master/en-us/ApiOverview/Mail/Index.html`

Mailhog. "Mailhog/MailHog." GitHub. `https://github.com/mailhog/MailHog`

"More About File Mounts." TYPO3 Documentation. May 12, 2019. `https://docs.typo3.org/m/typo3/reference-coreapi/master/en-us/ApiOverview/AccessControl/MoreAboutFileMounts/Index.html`

"PSR-15: HTTP Server Request Handlers - PHP-FIG." PHP. `https://www.php-fig.org/psr/psr-15/`

"PSR-7: HTTP Message Interfaces - PHP-FIG." PHP. `https://www.php-fig.org/psr/psr-7/`

"The Package in Detail." TYPO3 Documentation. June 22, 2020. `https://docs.typo3.org/m/typo3/guide-installation/master/en-us/In-depth/ThePackageInDetail/Index.html`

"S/PKG/BLD." Kickstart Your TYPO3 Template Development - TYPO3 Sitepackage Builder. `https://www.sitepackagebuilder.com/`

Schulmeister, Gernot. "Architecture & TYPO3." LinkedIn SlideShare. September 11, 2016. `https://www.slideshare.net/GernotSchulmeister/architecture-typo3`

"Sitepackage Tutorial." TYPO3 Documentation. September 13, 2019. `https://docs.typo3.org/m/typo3/tutorial-sitepackage/master/en-us/`

"TCA Reference." TYPO3 Documentation. July 10, 2019. `https://docs.typo3.org/m/typo3/reference-tca/master/en-us/Index.html`

"TSconfig Reference." TYPO3 Documentation. May 20, 2019. `https://docs.typo3.org/m/typo3/reference-tsconfig/master/en-us/Index.html`

"TYPO3 Explained." TYPO3 Documentation. `https://docs.typo3.org/m/typo3/reference-coreapi/master/en-us/singlehtml/#system-overview`

"TYPO3 Explained." TYPO3 Documentation. July 11, 2020. `https://docs.typo3.org/m/typo3/reference-coreapi/master/en-us/Index.html`

"The TYPO3 Extbase Book-Interview with the Author." August 09, 2019. `https://typo3.org/article/the-typo3-extbase-book-interview-with-the-author/`

TYPO3. "TYPO3/Fluid." GitHub. `https://github.com/TYPO3/Fluid`

"Templating Manual · Introduction." Fluid Powered TYPO3: Introduction. `https://fluidtypo3.org/documentation/templating-manual/introduction.html`

"TypoScript Template Reference." TYPO3 Documentation. January 26, 2020. `https://docs.typo3.org/m/typo3/reference-typoscript/master/en-us/Index.html`

"Using FAL." TYPO3 Documentation. May 12, 2019. `https://docs.typo3.org/m/typo3/reference-coreapi/master/en-us/ApiOverview/Fal/UsingFal/Index.html`

Chapter 4

"7 Reasons for an Independent TYPO3 Project Review." TYPO3. `https://typo3.com/blog/7-reasons-for-an-independent-project-review/`

"A High Performance Open Source MySQL Proxy." ProxySQL. July 08, 2020. `https://www.proxysql.com/`

"A New Structure for the TYPO3 Core Team." July 25, 2018. `https://typo3.org/article/a-new-structure-for-the-typo3-core-team/`

"APC User Cache." Php. `https://www.php.net/manual/en/book.apcu.php`

"Backup Strategy." TYPO3 Documentation. May 12, 2019. `https://docs.typo3.org/m/typo3/reference-coreapi/master/en-us/Security/Backups/Index.html`

"Basics." TYPO3 Documentation. June 27, 2020. `https://docs.typo3.org/m/typo3/reference-coreapi/master/en-us/ApiOverview/SiteHandling/Basics.html`

"Beech.it - Pragmatic Value and Partnership - TYPO3 GmbH." TYPO3. `https://typo3.com/blog/beechit-pragmatic-value-and-partnership-typo3-gmbh`

"Build Blazingly Fast, Flexible Websites." Download TYPO3 - Get.typo3.org. `http://typo3.org/download/`

"Build Your Own Upgrade Wizard." Events Site. August 02, 2019. `https://t3dd19.typo3.com/program/sessions/build-your-own-upgrade-wizard-27`

"Caching Framework." TYPO3 Documentation. May 12, 2019. `https://docs.typo3.org/m/typo3/reference-coreapi/master/en-us/ApiOverview/CachingFramework/Index.html`

"Ceph File System." Ceph File System - Ceph Documentation. `https://docs.ceph.com/docs/master/cephfs/`

"Content Delivery Network." Wikipedia. June 24, 2020. `https://en.wikipedia.org/wiki/Content_delivery_network`

"Contribution, Flexibility, Sustainability in TYPO3 - Meet Helmut Hummel." TYPO3. `https://typo3.com/blog/contribution-flexibility-sustainability-in-typo3-meet-helmut-hummel`

"Cybercraft Media Manufactory - an Agency Supporting Other Agencies." TYPO3. `https://typo3.com/blog/cybercraft-media-manufactory-an-agency-supporting-other-agencies/`.

"Detect, Analyze and Repair a Hacked Site." TYPO3 Documentation. October 12, 2018. `https://docs.typo3.org/m/typo3/reference-coreapi/master/en-us/Security/HackedSite/Index.html`

"Detect a Hacked Website." TYPO3 Documentation. June 21, 2016. `https://docs.typo3.org/m/typo3/guide-security/8.7/en-us/HackedSite/Detect/Index.html`

"Development Environments for Drupal with DDEV." Development Environments for Drupal with DDEV. `https://davidjguru.github.io/blog/creating-development-environments-for-drupal-with-ddev`

"Did You Know ... ?" Use TYPO3. July 11, 2020. `https://usetypo3.com/did-you-know.html`

"Do You Know the Technical Condition of Your TYPO3 Website?" TYPO3. `https://typo3.com/blog/do-you-know-the-technical-condition-of-your-typo3-website`

"Embrace and Innovate - TYPO3 CMS 7." November 02, 2014. `https://typo3.org/article/embrace-and-innovate-typo3-cms-7/`

"Enhanced and Secure Content Management." `https://typo3.org/cms/features/secure-performant-scalable/`

"Essential Solutions for TYPO3 Productivity [Part 1]." Events Site. August 02, 2019.
https://t3dd19.typo3.com/program/sessions/t3dd19-talk-part-1-essential-
solutions-for-typo3-productivity-18

"Frontend Localization Guide." TYPO3 Documentation. April 20, 2020. https://
docs.typo3.org/m/typo3/guide-frontendlocalization/master/en-us/Index.html

"GDPR Initiative." https://typo3.org/community/teams/typo3-development/
initiatives/gdpr/

"GDPR - What You Need to Know." TYPO3. https://typo3.com/blog/gdpr-what-
you-need-to-know

"General Information." TYPO3 Documentation. October 12, 2018. https://
docs.typo3.org/m/typo3/reference-coreapi/master/en-us/Security/
GeneralInformation/Index.html

"Guidelines for System Administrators." TYPO3 Documentation. May 11, 2020.
https://docs.typo3.org/m/typo3/reference-coreapi/master/en-us/Security/
GuidelinesAdministrators/Index.html

"How Do You Know When It's Time to Upgrade?" TYPO3. https://typo3.com/blog/
how-do-you-know-when-its-time-to-upgrade

"How to Make Your TYPO3 Application GDPR Compliant." TYPO3. https://typo3.
com/blog/how-to-make-your-typo3-application-gdpr-compliant

"Improving Performance with the Paint Timing API." SitePen. January 28, 2020.
https://www.sitepen.com/blog/improving-performance-with-the-paint-timing-
api/

"Incident Handling." https://typo3.org/community/teams/security/incident-
handling/

"In-Depth Project Review." TYPO3. https://typo3.com/services/project-
reviews/in-depth-project-review/

"Issues You Might Run Into When Upgrading TYPO3 Extensions." TYPO3. https://
typo3.com/blog/issues-you-might-run-into-when-upgrading-typo3-extensions/

"IT Security Laws in Europe Get Serious." TYPO3. https://typo3.com/blog/it-
security-laws-in-europe-get-serious/

"Kubernetes X TYPO3." Events Site. August 04, 2019. https://t3dd19.typo3.com/
program/sessions/kubernetes-x-typo3-10

"Language Handling in TYPO3 - Part 1: Backend: TYPO3worx - "The" TYPO3 Blog."
TYPO3worx. June 21, 2017. https://typo3worx.eu/2017/04/language-handling-in-
typo3-backend-configuration/

"Localization Modes." TYPO3 Documentation. August 11, 2019. `https://docs.typo3.org/m/typo3/guide-frontendlocalization/master/en-us/LocalizationModes/Index.html`

"Local to Live Deployment for a TYPO3 Beginner Public Copy." Google Slides. `https://docs.google.com/presentation/d/1znbgTSTOGh2W85vN1JUfWuOVDKss6H7qs5d4bzMtXCY/edit#slide=id.p1`

"Maintenance Releases." `https://typo3.org/cms/roadmap/maintenance-releases/`

"Master Challenging TYPO3 Upgrade Projects: TYPO3worx - "The" TYPO3 Blog." TYPO3worx. December 01, 2018. `https://typo3worx.eu/2018/12/master-challenging-typo3-upgrade-projects/`

"MaxServ Leverages the Roadmap with a TYPO3 GmbH Partnership: TYPO3 GmbH." TYPO3. `https://typo3.in/blog/maxserv-leverages-the-roadmap-with-a-typo3-gmbh-partnership`

"MaxServ Leverages the Roadmap with a TYPO3 GmbH Partnership." TYPO3. `https://typo3.com/blog/maxserv-leverages-the-roadmap-with-a-typo3-gmbh-partnership`

"More Breathing Space With ELTS." TYPO3. `https://typo3.com/products/extended-support`

"Multilingual and Multisite with TYPO3." `https://typo3.org/cms/features/massively-multisite-multilingual`

"Official TYPO3 Partner Finder: TYPO3 GmbH." TYPO3. `https://typo3.com/services/find-a-typo3-partner`

"Percona XtraDB Cluster – The MySQL Clustering Solution." Percona. `https://www.percona.com/software/mysql-database/percona-xtradb-cluster`

"Performance Tuning." Performance Tuning - TYPO3Wiki. `https://wiki.typo3.org/Performance_tuning`

"Prioritizing Your Resources with Link Rel='preload' | Web." Google. `https://developers.google.com/web/updates/2016/03/link-rel-preload`

"Privacy by Design." General Data Protection Regulation (GDPR). July 14, 2020. `https://gdpr-info.eu/issues/privacy-by-design/`

"Production-Grade Container Orchestration." Kubernetes. `https://kubernetes.io/`

"Project Reviews." TYPO3. `https://typo3.com/services/project-reviews/`

"Reasons to Invest in a TYPO3 Project Review." TYPO3. `https://typo3.com/blog/reasons-to-invest-in-a-typo3-project-review`

"Security Advisories." July 07, 2020. `https://typo3.org/help/security-advisories/`

"Security Guidelines." TYPO3 Documentation. October 12, 2018. `https://docs.typo3.org/m/typo3/reference-coreapi/master/en-us/Security/Index.html`

"Security Team Reboot." April 11, 2019. `https://typo3.org/article/security-team-reboot/`

"Service Level Agreements." TYPO3. `https://typo3.com/services/service-level-agreements`

"System Requirements." TYPO3 Documentation. March 21, 2020. `https://docs.typo3.org/m/typo3/guide-installation/master/en-us/In-depth/SystemRequirements/Index.html`

"T3DD19 Part 1 - Essential Solutions for TYPO3 Productivity: By Sanjay Chuahan (NITSAN)." Google Slides. `https://docs.google.com/presentation/d/1mxyJByjKuZ-Zr7bminJ7nflnGa8t-ytbtF8luM-765M/edit#slide=id.g5de5408a8b_0_244`

"The Best Open Source Multisite CMS." TYPO3. `https://typo3.com/blog/typo3-the-best-open-source-multisite-cms`

"The New Faces Behind TYPO3 Core Development." March 13, 2019. `https://typo3.org/article/the-new-faces-behind-typo3-core-development/`

"The Security Team." `https://typo3.org/community/teams/security/`

"The TYPO3 Association." June 23, 2020. `https://typo3.org/project/association/`

"The TYPO3 Extbase Book-Interview with the Author." August 09, 2019. `https://typo3.org/article/the-typo3-extbase-book-interview-with-the-author/`

"Things TYPO3 GmbH Does NOT Do." TYPO3. `https://typo3.com/company/what-we-dont-do`

TYPO3. 2019. "Essential Solutions for TYPO3 Productivity - Part 1 @ TYPO3 Developer Days 2019." YouTube Video. YouTube. `https://www.youtube.com/watch?v=EiIKz-wK6z8`

TYPO3. 2019. "Build Your Own Upgrade Wizard @ TYPO3 Developer Days 2019." YouTube Video. YouTube. `https://www.youtube.com/watch?v=gEVUfi5hfXQ`

"TYPO3 10 LTS (10.4.5)." Download TYPO3 10.4.5. `https://get.typo3.org/version/10#system-requirements`

"Typo3 CDN Integration - KeyCDN Support." KeyCDN. `https://www.keycdn.com/support/typo3-cdn-integration`

"TYPO3 CMS and Higher Educational Institutions - a Success Story." TYPO3. https://typo3.com/blog/typo3-cms-and-higher-educational-institutions-a-success-story

"TYPO3 CMS Development Roadmap." Development Roadmap for TYPO3 CMS. https://typo3.org/cms/roadmap/

"TYPO3 CMS Explained for the System Admin: TYPO3 GmbH." TYPO3. https://typo3.com/typo3-cms-explained-for-the-sysadmin

"TYPO3 Delivers Great Performance." TYPO3. https://typo3.com/blog/typo3-delivers-great-performance

"TYPO3 Extension Security Policy Version 1.0." https://typo3.org/community/teams/security/extension-security-policy/

"TYPO3 Open Source CMS and GDPR - Meet Georg Ringer." TYPO3. https://typo3.com/blog/typo3-open-source-cms-and-gdpr-meet-georg-ringer/

"TYPO3 Partner Program Registration." TYPO3. https://typo3.com/services/become-a-partner/typo3-partner-program-registration

"TYPO3 Performance :: Tools and Overview: TYPO3worx - "The" TYPO3 Blog." TYPO3worx. April 30, 2018. https://typo3worx.eu/2017/10/typo3-performance-introduction/

"TYPO3 Performance: Asset Delivery and Caching: TYPO3worx - "The" TYPO3 Blog." TYPO3worx. April 30, 2018. https://typo3worx.eu/2017/11/typo3-performance-asset-delivery-caching/

"TYPO3 Performance - Caching, TypoScript and More: TYPO3worx - "The" TYPO3 Blog." TYPO3worx. April 30, 2018. https://typo3worx.eu/2018/02/typo3-performance-caching-typoscript/

"TYPO3 Performance-Optimierung Durch CDN." Clickstorm. November 03, 2017. https://www.clickstorm.de/blog/typo3-performance-optimierung-mit-cs_cdn/

"TYPO3 Performance - TYPO3 CMS and Extensions: TYPO3worx - "The" TYPO3 Blog." TYPO3worx. August 09, 2018. https://typo3worx.eu/2018/08/typo3-performance-typo3-cms-extensions/

"TYPO3 Release Improvements & V8 Maintenance Release Schedule." June 30, 2017. https://typo3.org/article/typo3-release-improvements-v8-maintenance-release-schedule/

"TYPO3 V9's New Extension Scanner Makes Planning Upgrades Easier." TYPO3. https://typo3.com/blog/typo3-v9s-new-extension-scanner-makes-planning-upgrades-easier

"Updating TYPO3 Projects." Use TYPO3. July 11, 2020. https://usetypo3.com/upgrading-projects.html

"Upgrade." TYPO3 Documentation. April 08, 2020. https://docs.typo3.org/m/typo3/guide-installation/master/en-us/Upgrade/Index.html

"Use the Upgrade Wizard." TYPO3 Documentation. September 27, 2019. https://docs.typo3.org/m/typo3/guide-installation/master/en-us/Upgrade/UseTheUpgradeWizard/Index.html

"What Is MariaDB Galera Cluster?" MariaDB KnowledgeBase. https://mariadb.com/kb/en/library/what-is-mariadb-galera-cluster

"What Is Prefetching and Why Use It - KeyCDN Support." KeyCDN. https://www.keycdn.com/support/prefetching

"What Is Privacy by Design & Default?" Irish Computer Society 50th! https://www.ics.ie/news/what-is-privacy-by-design-a-default

"X Marks the Spot - TYPO3 V10.0 Is Here." July 23, 2019. https://typo3.org/article/x-marks-the-spot-typo3-v10-0-is-here

Alex Kellner. "TYPO3 Migration in Komplexen Upgrade- Und Relaunch-Projekten." LinkedIn SlideShare. September 15, 2018. https://www.slideshare.net/einpraegsam/typo3-migration-in-komplexen-upgrade-und-relaunchprojekten-114716116

Antoniou, Laura. "Marketplace." Amazon. 2015. https://aws.amazon.com/marketplace/pp/schamsnet-TYPO3-CMS-8x/B01D08DF2E

Blackfire. "Performance ." Blackfire.io. https://blackfire.io/

BlcknxBlcknx 1, and Rudy GnoddeRudy Gnodde 2. "What Is the TYPO3 Reference Index and Why Can It Contain Outdated Values?" Stack Overflow. June 01, 1968. https://stackoverflow.com/questions/53796965/what-is-the-typo3-reference-index-and-why-can-it-contain-outdated-values

Bslatkin. "Bslatkin/dpxdt." GitHub. https://github.com/bslatkin/dpxdt

Coders.care. "We Care for Coders, Our Coders Care for You." Coders.care. https://coders.care/

Daniel Siepmann. "TYPO3 Content Caching". https://daniel-siepmann.de/Posts/2019/2019-01-04-typo3-content-caching.html

DigitalOcean. "Using a CDN to Speed Up Static Content Delivery." DigitalOcean. August 06, 2018. https://www.digitalocean.com/community/tutorials/using-a-cdn-to-speed-up-static-content-delivery

Doc-Core-Insight. "TYPO3 Upgrades from Command Line." Doc_core_insight. June 26, 2017. `https://insight.helhum.io/post/162277469210/typo3-upgrades-from-command-line`

Dormando. "A Distributed Memory Object Caching System." Memcached. `https://memcached.org/`

Drud. "Drud/sig-cms." GitHub. `https://github.com/drud/sig-cms`

Eberhard, Moritz, and Moritz Eberhard. "AWS and Typo3: Hosting, Deployment and Cont. Integration." Meberhard. December 11, 2014. `http://meberhard.me/amazon-web-service-aws-typo3-hosting-deployment-methods-continuous-integration/`

Einpraegsam. "Einpraegsam/migration." GitHub. `https://github.com/einpraegsam/migration`

Elmar, and Elmar. "Elp's Blog." Elps Blog. January 16, 2015. `http://www.elp.co.at/2015/01/16/migration-from-typo3-4-5-4-6-4-7-to-typo3-6-2-lts-1/`

Hemert, Jigal Van. "Build Your Own Upgrade Wizard." LinkedIn SlideShare. August 05, 2019. `https://www.slideshare.net/JigalvanHemert/build-your-own-upgrade-wizard`

India, Spec. "Kubernetes in DevOps Space: Everything You Need To Know." Medium. July 16, 2019. `https://medium.com/faun/kubernetes-in-devops-space-everything-you-need-to-know-6ac3c94f12df`

Hasenau, Jo. "Service Level Agreements for TYPO3 Extensions." Coders.care. `https://coders.care/blog/article/service-level-agreements-for-typo3-extensions/`

Kott, Benjamin. "Reliable Open Industry." `https://drive.google.com/file/d/1ujHLObONKHuXJt3_aqNYnNV_CdxFmDVc/view`

Mack, Benni. "Cache Me If You Can-Insights into Frontend Caches in TYPO3." B13.com. `https://b13.com/blog/caching-in-typo3-part-1-frontend-caches`

Moog, Susanne. "Download TYPO3 Partner Program Information and Subscribe to the Partner Newsletter: TYPO3 GmbH." TYPO3. `https://typo3.com/download-typo3-partner-program-information-and-subscribe-to-the-partner-newsletter`

Nitsan. "How To Secure Your TYPO3 Sites From Hack Attempts?" TYPO3 Agency. May 01, 2019. `https://www.nitsan.in/blog/how-to-secure-your-typo3-sites-from-hack-attempts/`

Nitsan. "The Ultimate Guide to TYPO3 Update/Upgrade." TYPO3 Update/Upgrade: The Ultimate Guide for TYPO3 Developers. February 14, 2019. `https://www.nitsan.in/blog/typo3-update-upgrade/`

Pandya, T3:Keval. "[NITSAN] TYPO3 Extensions Compatibility Report (ns_ext_compatibility)." April 16, 2020. `https://extensions.typo3.org/extension/ns_ext_compatibility/`

Redis. `https://redis.io/`

Ringer, Georg. "Georgringer/gdpr." GitHub. `https://github.com/georgringer/gdpr`

Rviscomi, Eva2000, TeamUpDevelopment, Dawnieando, Riking, RKomen2609, Senormunoz, and J0udini. "CMS Performance." HTTP Archive. September 11, 2018. `https://discuss.httparchive.org/t/cms-performance/1468`

Steiner, Andri. "Varnish Connector (varnish)." February 20, 2020. `https://extensions.typo3.org/extension/varnish/`

Typo3tutorials.net. "Home." TYPO3tutorials.net. `https://typo3tutorials.net/system/requirements/`

Well Contained: Running TYPO3 in Docker. `https://www.martin-helmich.de/en/blog/typo3-cms-docker.html`

Index

Printed in the United States
By Bookmasters